ON BECOMING A SCHOLAR

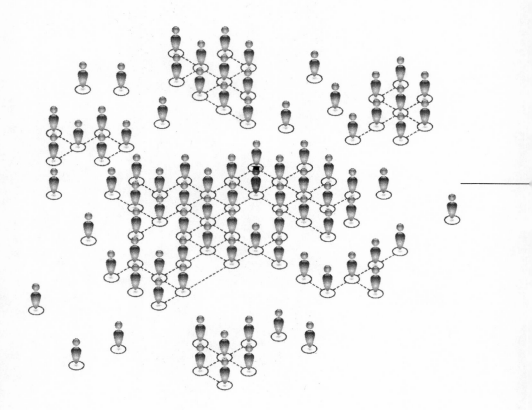

ON BECOMING
A SCHOLAR

Socialization and Development
in Doctoral Education

*Edited by Susan K. Gardner
and Pilar Mendoza*

Foreword by Ann E. Austin

STERLING, VIRGINIA

COPYRIGHT © 2010 BY
STYLUS PUBLISHING, LLC.

Published by Stylus Publishing, LLC
22883 Quicksilver Drive
Sterling, Virginia 20166-2102

Library of Congress Cataloging-in-Publication-Data
On becoming a scholar : socialization and development in
doctoral education / edited by Susan K. Gardner and Pilar
Mendoza ; foreword by Ann E. Austin. – 1st ed.
    p.   cm.
Includes index.
ISBN 978-1-57922-444-8 (cloth : alk. paper)
ISBN 978-1-57922-445-5 (pbk. : alk. paper)
1. Doctor of philosophy degree–United States.
2. Doctoral students–United States–Social conditions.
3. Scholars–United States–Social conditions.
4. Professional socialization–United States.   I. Gardner,
Susan K. (Susan Kristina), 1974-   II. Mendoza, Pilar, 1974-
LB2386.O5   2010
378.2′4—dc22

                                      2009047565

13-digit ISBN: 978-1-57922-444-8 (cloth)
13-digit ISBN: 978-1-57922-445-5 (paper)

Printed in the United States of America

All first editions printed on acid free paper
that meets the American National Standards Institute
Z39-48 Standard.

> Bulk Purchases
>
> Quantity discounts are available for use in workshops
> and for staff development.
> Call 1-800-232-0223

First Edition, 2010

10 9 8 7 6 5 4 3 2 1

We wish to dedicate this book to the amazing scholars, students,
and colleagues who have helped us form our own development and socialization as
scholars, especially to those whose writing appears in this book.
And, to Hazel Sofía, from her mother Pilar.

CONTENTS

ACKNOWLEDGMENTS

The editors wish to express gratitude to John von Knorring of Stylus Publishing, who took a chance on two emerging scholars.

Scholarship on the doctoral experience has expanded and deepened considerably over the past two decades. Early in that period, several higher education researchers (some recently finishing their own doctoral experiences and some seeing research on the socialization of doctoral students as the next logical step in their study of the faculty career), along with some faculty developers and teaching assistant directors, began to ask questions and conduct research about the doctoral experience. By the mid-1990s, interest in studying doctoral education was increasing, with more scholars entering the field and many graduate deans, employers, and funding agency leaders encouraging research as well as innovations to enhance the quality of the doctoral experience, strengthen the pipeline through graduate education, and ensure that those who complete the Ph.D. are well prepared for their professional responsibilities. This book signals the continuing expansion of the field. It brings together the work of an impressive and sizable group of scholars, a number of whom are themselves early in their careers, to highlight, synthesize, and reflect on key research and findings concerning the process through which doctoral students become scholars. Synthesizing and focusing on the socialization processes that occur in doctoral education, the volume also opens the door for new theoretical perspectives to explain and guide the process as well as creative strategies for enhancing the effectiveness of doctoral education.

The timing of this book is important for various reasons. Higher education institutions face a number of significant expectations and challenges, including the needs and interests of diverse student bodies, expectations that universities and colleges will produce doctoral graduates who can relate research to practical needs within society, the press to conduct cutting-edge research, and fiscal constraints that require wisdom and creativity as well as efficiency and productivity. Other sectors of work also need well-prepared, competent, and creative employees who can handle the pressures for high-quality work. Doctoral programs must prepare graduates who can meet these expectations and excel. At the same time, as the population of graduate students is becoming more diverse (a development to applaud), socialization processes should recognize and reflect the diversity in age, race and ethnicity, and gender of doctoral students. Concerns about attrition among doctoral students, widely noted in recent years, also invite analysis of the doctoral experience. At the same time that challenges motivate research on the doctoral experience, the innovative strategies that have been implemented at many universities in recent years—often in response to both the expanding body of research and various national projects and programs to improve doctoral education—also invite reflection and celebration. Thus, this book makes a significant contribution in this context in which interest in the quality of doctoral education is high.

The authors in this book describe a number of studies and offer many conclusions as well as recommendations and strategies, addressed to various audiences, to enhance the processes of socialization and development through which doctoral students learn to be scholars. Some of the findings in the studies described in this book echo lessons consistently reported in earlier research, a repetition that is not a shortcoming but rather a useful emphasis on issues that graduate faculty and institutional leaders should take very seriously. Other findings shed new light on the doctoral experience. Here, I highlight several of the most important themes that weave through many of the chapters in this book and that invite the attention, as the book chapters argue, of faculty members, departments, universities, external agencies, and—of equal importance—doctoral student themselves.

Theme 1: The doctoral process has the responsibility to prepare prospective scholars for a wide array of responsibilities.

While historically doctoral education may have focused primarily on research training, graduate programs today should ensure that students are prepared for the full array of responsibilities that they may assume. Such preparation requires recognition that graduates may take positions within academe or in other professional areas. The chapter by McDaniels discusses the role of doctoral education in preparing students for their teaching roles, building on earlier work by Austin and McDaniels (2006) to outline an extensive array of competencies that should be explicitly addressed. Other chapters address the importance of attention to research (Weidman), to the service role (Ward), and to preparing students for the entrepreneurial context they are likely to enter (Mendoza).

Taken as a whole, the book reminds those who work in graduate education that students have a wide array of aspirations—including positions within academe, where they may take positions in institutions of different types with varying missions and cultures, as well as options outside the academic world. How to prepare doctoral students for the variety of contexts and appointment types in which they may work as well as for the array of skills and abilities they will need requires faculty members to think about graduate study in a comprehensive way. This responsibility requires more explicit attention than may have been typical in the past to assessing workplace expectations, ensuring explicit attention to the full spectrum of work responsibilities that a graduate may face, and developing strategies for helping students identify and reflect on their career aspirations and their plans for systematic development to move toward those aspirations.

Theme 2: Socialization and development processes are not the same for all doctoral students. Practical strategies and interventions should be based on recognition of the different variables and factors that affect how individuals experience doctoral education.

The early years of research on the doctoral experience tended to look at doctoral students as an overall group, an understandable approach in the absence of much existing work at the time to explain the graduate experience. However, as this book shows, the field of study has advanced to the point where the most useful new work recognizes the diversity within the graduate student body. One major factor that frames the doctoral experience is the discipline. As Golde's chapter reminds us, the department is the primary context for socialization and the department is situated within disciplinary norms. Disciplines vary in many dimensions that are critically relevant to the doctoral experience, including in the way work is done, the structure of the dissertation, and the relationships that are customary between the advisor and the student. Thus, the processes of socialization and development experienced as graduate students learn to be scholars must take into account specific disciplinary contexts.

Students' experiences also cannot be separated from several other variables. Processes of socialization are highly gendered, as Sallee's chapter explains. While she notes that women now comprise more than half of the doctoral student population, she also explains that the experiences of men and women can be very different. Disciplines and departments vary greatly in regard to the ways in which gender has played a role in their histories, structures, and norms. For example, males and females can experience advising relationships, financial opportunities, and informal relationships in very different ways, resulting in varying perceptions regarding competition, isolation versus inclusion, and discrimination versus opportunity. Race and ethnicity also play a role in socialization and development. Students of color are increasing overall in graduate education, but the nature of their experiences can be very different from that of their White colleagues, as discussed by Winkle-Wagner, Johnson, Morelon-Quainoo, and Santiague. Students who find themselves in a minority may feel isolated, alienated, and marginalized. Similarly, age is a factor that is relevant to the socialization process, as discussed by Kasworm and Bowles. In addition, such personal factors as marital/partner status, as Millett and Nettles explore, can be relevant to the way in which individuals experience the process of doctoral study.

Through the research reported in this book and the vignettes describing the lives of students diverse in their disciplines, gender, race and ethnicity, age, and partner status, this book advances our understanding of the complex and diverse ways in which individuals experience doctoral education. Strategies to enhance the experience and more effectively prepare scholars must be conceptualized and implemented with consideration of the different people they will affect, and the varying ways in which variables such as gender, race/ethnicity, and age interact with the interventions. The vignettes that punctuate the chapters, describing the lives of specific (fictional, but very realistic) students, remind readers that the findings about the socialization process—and the strategies developed to enhance this experience—must be understood in the context of the lives of each of the individuals who enter our graduate programs.

Theme 3: Opportunities for both challenge and support are essential ingredients of doctoral education. Students need to experience community and interaction with both faculty members and peers.

A consistent finding since the early years of research on the doctoral experience, and reinforced in the findings of many of the studies in this book, is the importance of both challenge and support in doctoral study. By definition, the doctoral experience is a demanding new experience during which students move from being readers and "consumers" of research (as Shinew and Moore point out in their chapter) to being producers of knowledge. To develop into independent scholars, however, students need the support of both faculty members. In fact, research findings repeatedly point out that regular interaction with faculty advisors and mentors is a key variable in regard to student persistence, productivity, and satisfaction. Students need to feel that they belong, they need opportunities to interact both formally and informally with faculty members, and they need environments characterized by trust such that they can seek assistance for weaknesses and experience shared celebration for their progress and successes. The accessibility and interest of faculty members are essential—and such faculty accessibility is a specific strategy that graduate advisors and departments can address to support doctoral student development.

At the same time, interaction with peers can be an important component of doctoral study. Advanced students can help socialize newcomers to the norms of the department. Students who find a strong peer group can experience both challenge (such as when friends remind them to stay focused) and support (when difficulties inevitably arise). Creating and nurturing environments that intertwine challenge and support through an array of formal and informal means is a key ingredient in ensuring effective socialization and development.

Theme 4: The responsibility for excellent doctoral education is shared by multiple stakeholders. Furthermore, socialization involves more than a "one-way process." Students themselves contribute to the process and affect the contexts in which they are learning.

In our work, several years ago, synthesizing and advancing the literature on graduate socialization for faculty careers (Austin & McDaniels, 2006), my colleague Melissa McDaniels and I cited the work of several other scholars (Antony, 2002; Staton, 1990; Tierney, 1997; Tierney & Rhoads, 1994) and, like them, argued that socialization processes should not be conceptualized as a "one-way" process; instead, it should be seen as a dialectical, two-way process in which experienced scholars influence the newcomers, while, simultaneously, the newcomers affect the organization. Gardner and Mendoza's volume is also based on the premise that the socialization of doctoral students involves more than simply faculty members informing students of what they should become. Rather, throughout each chapter, the book's chapter authors recognize the role of multiple stakeholders in the socialization process. They offer extensive, detailed, and strategically focused recommendations for faculty members, departments, universities, external agencies, and students themselves. My point here is that they emphasize through practical recommendations that the effectiveness, relevance, inclusiveness, and impact of the process through which doctoral students learn to be scholars is indeed shared by many people. And of particular importance, I believe, is that students themselves have the opportunity and responsibility to do much to shape their experiences. In doing so, these aspiring scholars make their own mark on the academy, contributing to the dialectical process through which the socialization process affects not only doctoral students but also the organization itself.

Readers will undoubtedly reflect on additional themes in this well-constructed book, but the ones I have identified are, I think, particularly important for researchers, institutional leaders, and doctoral students themselves. Finally, I note that this book moves the field forward not only by synthesizing what we know but also by identifying important directions for future research. I mention here three areas in which I see the opportunity and need for much more research.

Much more remains to be learned about how factors such as gender, race/ethnicity, and age relate to the process through which doctoral students learn to be scholars. As the body of students entering doctoral programs becomes more diverse, the stakeholders concerned about doctoral education should strive to learn more about an array of strategies to support students and how different strategies relate to different students' circumstances and needs. Exploring other theoretical approaches for explaining development, in addition to socialization theory, is another promising direction for future research. Gardner's chapter on doctoral student development highlights psychosocial theory, social identity theory, and cognitive structure theory, and, in their chapter, Kasworm and Bowles discuss the relevance of theories regarding adult learning, transformational learning, and communities of practice. Each of these theories offers new windows through which to study how doctoral students learn to be scholars. Interdisciplinarity in relation to doctoral education is a third issue to be explored in future research. As the boundaries between disciplines blur, universities will need to consider how best to prepare new scholars for work in emerging fields that cross or link multiple disciplines. Holley raises a number of the important issues that invite study, and Shinew and Moore reflect on the kind of research preparation that enables developing scholars to gain an appreciation of the diverse epistemological perspectives that they may use or encounter.

The need is great for doctoral education that effectively prepares scholars for the many responsibilities they will be asked to fulfill. As this book emphasizes, both research and strategic actions are needed to ensure high-quality doctoral education. Furthermore, those who care about doctoral education—faculty members, department and university administrators, leaders of external agencies and associations, and graduate students themselves—each have the responsibility to learn from the research, implement practices informed by research findings, and pursue the questions still unanswered about effective learning in doctoral education.

References

Antony, J. S. (2002). Reexamining doctoral student socialization and professional development: Moving beyond the congruence and assimilation orientation. In J. C. Smart (Ed.), *Higher education: Handbook of theory and research* (Vol. XVII, pp. 349–380). New York: Agathon Press.

Austin, A. E., & McDaniels, M. (2006). Preparing the professoriate of the future: Graduate student socialization for faculty roles. In J. C. Smart (Ed.), *Higher education: Handbook of theory and research* (Vol. XXI, pp. 397–456). Netherlands: Springer.

Staton, A. Q. (1990). *Communication and student socialization.* Norwood, NJ: Ablex.

Tierney, W. G. (1997). Organizational socialization in higher education. Journal of Higher Education, *68*(1): 1–16.

Tierney, W. G., & Rhoads, R. A. (1994). Enhancing promotion, tenure and beyond: Faculty socialization as a cultural process. *ASHE-ERIC Higher Education Report*, *6*. Washington, DC: The George Washington University, School of Education and Human Development.

Ann E. Austin
East Lansing, Michigan
October, 2009

PART ONE

SETTING THE CONTEXT

INTRODUCTION

Susan K. Gardner and Pilar Mendoza

Ling is 22 years old and is beginning her doctoral journey in a polymer science program at Flagship University, a large, public research institution. Ling is the third in her family to get a graduate degree. She looks forward to her experience but feels a bit of trepidation about it as well. Not only is she uncertain about what awaits her in graduate school but she is also concerned that she will have a difficult time finding friends, as she is moving far away from her family in China to attend school in the Midwest. Beyond these challenges, Ling is uncertain of how many other Asians she will find in this largely White region and how many other women she will meet in her department. Ling at least feels security in the fact that she has been provided funding through her research assistantship, something that she believes will prepare her well for her anticipated career in academia.

Scott is a 29-year-old in the midst of coursework for his doctorate in child psychology at Ivy League U, a prestigious, private institution on the East Coast. While brought to the institution by the nationally renowned reputation of his new advisor, he is nevertheless disconcerted by the lack of peer and faculty support he has found, particularly given that he is one of the few men in the program, but also that he is African American and the first in his family to go to college and beyond. Given that he has been granted a prestigious fellowship, he feels he has much to prove to himself, his wife, his funders, and his family as well. At this point, he is undecided about his future career goals. He really enjoys teaching; however, he is not sure that he is willing to put up with the drama that seems to plague academia.

Nate is a 27-year-old chemistry student at Prestige University, a large, private institution on the West Coast, in the midst of completing his research through

3

an assistantship in his advisor's lab. After graduating from college, he worked in industry for two years and then decided to return to school to obtain his Ph.D. As a single, White male without children, Nate fits in well with the rest of his department but he does feel stymied by his future choices. Torn between a faculty position in academia or further work in industry, he is currently uncertain about the steps he will take upon completion in the next year.

Eva is 42 years old and is about to embark upon what she considers one of the most frightening experiences of her life—a part-time doctoral program in educational leadership at Comprehensive University, a regional institution in the South. Having spent the majority of her life as a teacher in the public school system, Eva has always been the expert in the classroom. She now faces the reality that she will be a student once again, balancing her studies with a large family and a full-time job. Being the first in her Latino family to go to graduate school, she realizes she has little understanding of what awaits her. Her partner is quite supportive of this endeavor but she still has doubts about her abilities in the classroom. She just hopes she can manage it all successfully.

Jennifer is 27 years old, completing her English Ph.D. and, like Nate, a student at Prestige University on the West Coast. Waist deep in her dissertation, Jennifer is now eyeing the tenuous academic job market with apprehension. As others in her family have received doctorates in the humanities, Jennifer feels she knows the obstacles that await her as a single, White female, but is nevertheless uncertain about her teaching skills: the currency she knows will make or break her on the job market. She tries to dutifully balance her teaching assistantship with her dissertation research, hoping that she'll be able to finish within the next year.

Although representing different backgrounds, institutions, disciplines, and career aspirations, Ling, Scott, Nate, Eva, and Jennifer nevertheless share the common goal of obtaining their doctorate. The United States now confers over 60,000 doctorate degrees each year (Snyder, Dillow, & Hoffman, 2009), with graduates going on to become the world's scholars, educators, innovators, and leaders (Walker, Golde, Jones, Conklin Bueschel, & Hutchings, 2008). Underscoring the importance of graduate education in today's society, a report by the Council of Graduate Schools (2007), *Graduate education: The backbone of American competitiveness and innovation*, stated, "We can no longer take for granted America's continued leadership in innovation and competitiveness. We face the risk of losing the highly trained workforce that is essential to maintain our economic leadership" (p. 1). Given the global importance of doctoral programs in this light, it is disconcerting that only 57% of all doctoral students will complete their programs (Council of Graduate Schools, 2008). Concerned about these high rates of attrition, a plethora of scholars, foundations, and institutions have risen to the occasion. Through programs such as the Carnegie Initiative on the Doctorate, the Ph.D. Completion Project, the Responsive Ph.D., Preparing Future Faculty, and others, we are beginning to understand the challenges that exist in doctoral education. Moreover, the scholarship on doctoral education and doctoral students has grown exponentially in the past several decades, allowing us to view the multifaceted nature of the experience.

A reoccurring topic of study in doctoral education focuses on the student experience overall. Through understanding the pathways to, through, and from the doctoral experience, scholars have hoped to assist in the recruitment, retention, and graduation of doctoral students. In the quest to describe the doctoral student experience, scholars have utilized many different approaches and frameworks; however, more than any other, socialization has become the common theoretical lens through which to better understand the complexity of the doctoral student experience (e.g., Antony, 2002; Austin, 2002; Clark & Corcoran, 1986; Egan, 1989; Ellis, 2001; Gardner, 2007; Gonzalez, 2006; Gottlieb, 1960; Kirk & Todd-Mancillas, 1991; Weidman, Twale, & Stein, 2001). In particular, theories of socialization have been connected to the issue of attrition in doctoral education, with researchers often attributing poor or inappropriate socialization to a student's decision to depart the graduate program (e.g., Clark & Corcoran, 1986; Ellis, 2001; Gardner, 2010; Golde, 1998; Lovitts, 2001). However, while socialization in the context of doctoral education has been widely studied, it is generally viewed monolithically in that graduate students' experiences, in general, are viewed as a whole without any consideration to specific individual, disciplinary, or institutional differences. Indeed, the often cited monograph by Weidman, Twale, and Stein (2001) is the only existing contemporary text on the subject of graduate student socialization and does not differentiate by disciplinary or institutional contexts or by individual characteristics of the student. Moreover, recent studies indicate that other experiences beyond socialization are also influential on doctoral students' decision to persist (Walker et al., 2008).

Since the publication of Weidman, Twale, and Stein's text in 2001, multiple perspectives of the socialization process in graduate school have arisen in the literature including the experiences of graduate students of color and women (Antony & Taylor, 2004; Ellis, 2001; Gonzalez, 2006; Jackson, 2004), socialization through disciplinary lenses (Gardner, 2007; Herzig, 2004; MacLachlan, 2006), socialization to particular professional fields (Austin, 2002; Haviland et al., 2004; Wulff & Austin, 2004), and the effect of market forces on doctoral students' experiences and socialization (Mendoza, 2007; Slaughter, Campbell, Hollernan, & Morgan, 2002). However, no existing text comprehensively addresses these topics and other views of socialization and the graduate student experience. As we know, higher education is a con-glomerate of academic tribes with unique cultures, standards, rewards, and tasks (Becher, 1989). This academic tapestry intersects with the individual characteristics of doctoral students, which result in an array of contextual experiences and socialization processes. A deeper understanding of the variety of experiences and socialization process affecting doctoral students is essential in order to implement programmatic and institutional policies and practices aimed at closing the persistent and pervasive attainment gap throughout the entire postsecondary system.

Based on the contributors' own scholarship, the purpose of this book is to comprehensively expand, discuss, analyze, and critique existing mod-els and views of doctoral student socialization as well as provide alternative views of the doctoral student experience that exist beyond the traditionally viewed socialization model, specifically that of the developmental processes that also occur during graduate school. Taken together, this book addresses past and existing views of the socialization process in a comprehensive liter-ature review, speaks to the different kinds of socialization that occur based on disciplinary differences as well as the different professional components of the process, and forwards more detailed understandings of the socializa-tion process as experienced by particular demographic groups. Culminating chapters in the text also posit new ways of thinking about the graduate student experience that go beyond these traditional models of socialization, including the concepts of identity development, adult learning, and episte-mological development. Within these chapters, the authors include practical recommendations to doctoral students, faculty, departments, universities, and external agencies meant to facilitate doctoral student success. Each chapter provides these constituencies with a deeper understanding of doctoral edu-cation, its challenges, and very specific ways to overcome these challenges. In order to contextualize these challenges, we will revisit our five students,

Ling, Scott, Nate, Eva, and Jennifer, as they progress through their doctoral programs.

We have divided the book into five parts. The book begins by setting the context with an overview of the Ph.D., including its roots, structure, constituencies, and outcomes. The second part of the text begins by viewing the doctoral experience as one in which the student is socialized to a profession. As we know that about half of all Ph.D.s will obtain positions in academic institutions after graduation (Walker et al., 2008), the first three chapters in the text focus on the three main elements of faculty work: teaching, service, and research. In chapter 1, Melissa McDaniels describes how students are prepared to teach through the framework of socialization, John Weidman discusses how doctoral students are prepared to do research in chapter 2, while Kelly Ward details the socialization to the service piece of faculty work in chapter 3.

Part three of the book contextualizes the doctoral experience. In chapter 4, Chris Golde provides an overview of disciplinary socialization, followed by Karri Holley, who speaks to the challenges of interdisciplinary socialization in chapter 5. Part three culminates with chapter 6 by Pilar Mendoza, who focuses on the socialization of doctoral students in light of academic capitalism.

Part four is structured around the experience of different populations in doctoral education. In chapter 7, Margaret Sallee presents an overview of gender and doctoral education, focusing specifically on how disciplinary cultures can affect the socialization of men and women. Chapter 8, by Catherine Millett and Michael Nettles, deals with the interconnection of the doctoral experience and marital status. Chapter 9, by Rachelle Winkle-Wagner, Carla Morelon-Quainoo, Susan Johnson, and Lilia Santiague, then speaks to the doctoral experience in regard to race.

Part five goes beyond socialization, seeing the doctoral experience as one that also changes students in very personal ways. Chapter 10, by Susan K. Gardner, speaks to psychosocial, identity, and cognitive development in doctoral education. Carol Kasworm and Tuere Bowles in chapter 11 then discuss adult learning and its connections to doctoral education. Finally, in chapter 12, Dawn Shinew and Tami Moore discuss how students in one doctoral program experienced epistemological development.

We conclude the text with an overview of the complexity of the doctoral experience and the recommendations by our authors, then again revisit our five students and how they can resolve their challenges.

References

Antony, J. S. (2002). Reexamining doctoral student socialization and professional development: Moving beyond the congruence and assimilation orientation. In John C. Smart (Ed.), *Higher education: Handbook of theory and research* (Vol. XVII, pp. 349–380). New York, NY: Agathon Press.

Antony, J. S., & Taylor, E. (2004). Theories and strategies of academic career socialization: Improving paths to the professoriate for black graduate students. In D. H. Wulff & A. E. Austin (Eds.), *Paths to the professoriate: Strategies for enriching the preparation of future faculty* (pp. 92–114). San Francisco: Jossey-Bass.

Austin, A. E. (2002). Preparing the next generation of faculty: Graduate school as socialization to the academic career. *The Journal of Higher Education, 73,* 94–121.

Becher, T. (1989). *Academic tribes and territories: Intellectual enquiry and the culture of disciplines.* Bristol, PA: SRHE and Open University Press.

Clark, S. M., & Corcoran, M. (1986). Perspectives on the professional socialization of women faculty: A case of accumulative disadvantage? *The Journal of Higher Education, 57,* 20–43.

Council of Graduate Schools. (2007). *Graduate education: The backbone of American competitiveness and innovation.* Washington, DC: Author.

Council of Graduate Schools. (2008). *Ph.D. completion and attrition: Analysis of baseline program data from the Ph.D. completion project.* Washington, DC: Author

Egan, J. M. (1989). Graduate school and the self: A theoretical view of some negative effects of professional socialization. *Teaching Sociology, 17,* 200–208.

Ellis, E. M. (2001). The impact of race and gender on graduate school socialization, satisfaction with doctoral study, and commitment to degree completion. *The Western Journal of Black Studies, 25,* 30–45.

Gardner, S. K. (2007). "I heard it through the grapevine": Doctoral student socialization in chemistry and history. *Higher Education, 54,* 723–740.

Gardner, S. K. (2010). Contrasting the socialization experiences of doctoral students in high- and low-completing departments: A qualitative analysis of disciplinary and institutional context. *Journal of Higher Education, 81,* 61–81.

Golde, C. M. (1998). Beginning graduate school: Explaining first-year doctoral attrition. In M. S. Anderson (Ed.), *The experience of being in graduate school: An exploration* (pp. 55–64). San Francisco: Jossey-Bass.

Gonzalez, J. C. (2006). Academic socialization experiences of Latina doctoral students: A qualitative understanding of support systems that aid and challenges that hinder the process. *Journal of Hispanic Higher Education, 5*(4), 347–365.

Gottlieb, D. (1960). *Process of socialization in the American graduate school.* Unpublished doctoral dissertation, University of Chicago.

Haviland, D., Goldsmith, S. S., & Dailey, K. D. (2004). *Socializing tomorrow's professors: The value-added of PFF programs.* San Diego, CA: Paper presented at the American Educational Research Association.

Herzig, A. H. (2004). Becoming mathematicians: Women and students of color choosing and leaving doctoral mathematics. *Review of Educational Research, 74*(2), 171–214.

Jackson, J. (2004). The story is not in the numbers: Academic socialization and diversifying the faculty. *NWSA Journal, 16*(1), 172–185.

Kirk, D., & Todd-Mancillas, W. R. (1991). Turning points in graduate student socialization: Implications for recruiting future faculty. *The Review of Higher Education, 14*(3), 407–422.

Lovitts, B. E. (2001). *Leaving the ivory tower: The causes and consequences of departure from doctoral study.* Lanham, MD: Rowman and Littlefield.

MacLachlan, A. J. (2006). *Developing graduate students of color for the professoriate in science, technology, engineering and mathematics.* Berkeley, CA: Center for Studies in Higher Education.

Mendoza, P. (2007). Academic capitalism and doctoral student socialization: A case study. *Journal of Higher Education, 78*(1), 71–96.

Slaughter, S., Campbell, T., Hollernan, M., & Morgan, E. (2002). The "traffic" in graduate students: Graduate students as tokens of exchange between academe and industry. *Science, Technology, and Human Values, 27*(2), 282–313.

Snyder, T. D., Dillow, S. A., & Hoffman, C. M. (2009). *Digest of Education Statistics, 2008.* Washington, DC: National Center for Education Statistics.

Walker, G. E., Golde, C. M., Jones, L., Conklin Bueschel, A., & Hutchings, P. (2008). *The formation of scholars: Rethinking doctoral education for the twenty-first century.* San Francisco: Jossey-Bass.

Weidman, J. C., Twale, D. J., & Stein, E. L. (2001). *Socialization of graduate and professional students in higher education: A perilous passage?* San Francisco: Jossey-Bass.

Wulff, D. H., & Austin, A. E. (2004). *Paths to the professoriate: Strategies for enriching the preparation of future faculty.* San Francisco: Jossey-Bass.

THE Ph.D. IN THE
UNITED STATES

Pilar Mendoza and Susan K. Gardner

As with any subject, doctoral education, and the Ph.D. in particular, is best understood when viewed through its historical roots. A brief historical account of the doctorate and the Ph.D.'s place in this history is followed by commentary on the purposes of the Ph.D. Given the interdependence between the Ph.D. and research, such a historical overview inevitably includes an account of the research enterprise in this country. We culminate this chapter with different ways to understand the experience of doctoral students.

A Brief History of the Ph.D. and Research Enterprise in the United States

The first doctorate was awarded by Yale in 1861. Then, Johns Hopkins University opened in 1876 pioneering research-oriented Ph.D. degrees in the arts and sciences, supporting students with fellowships (Rudolph, 1962). At the end of the century, other undergraduate universities started their graduate programs as well, such as the University of Chicago, Stanford University, Harvard University, and Columbia University. By 1900, a total of about 3,500 doctorates had been granted. Funding for graduate schools and research normally came from undergraduate teaching and philanthropic donations and, in some cases, from the government through scientific bureaus promoting research mainly in agriculture and engineering according to identified national needs (Geiger, 1986). Many of the faculty in these early doctoral programs obtained their doctorates in Europe, mainly in Germany. By one estimate, some 10,000 U.S. citizens took German degrees during the nineteenth century (Berelson, 1960). Not surprisingly, most of the characteristics of the Ph.D. program in the United States resembled the German model whereas undergraduate education was based on the British model. In the twenty-first century, these features are still the cornerstone of Ph.D. programs in the United States. (Gumport, 2005).

The German model of graduate education emphasizes scientific inquiry and the expectation of faculty members' engagement in active research. In the early years of the Ph.D., research became a prestigious endeavor sought by the best minds. Upon graduation from undergraduate programs, doctoral students entered a community of scholars devoted to research and scholarship through graduate seminars and one-on-one teaching with faculty. Another program requisite included passing language and comprehensive examinations. The few that passed the comprehensive examination had to submit a thesis, which was subjected to the scrutiny of a faculty committee. The normal length of the Ph.D. program was two years. Upon graduation, Ph.D. graduates embarked in a professional career working closely with faculty in mentor-like relationships until achieving the status of faculty (Walker, Golde, Jones, Conklin Bueschel, & Hutchings, 2008).

Between the late 1800s and 1930s, specialization in science proliferated mainly in the social and natural sciences, which led to the formation of disciplines and departments. As such, doctoral education programs were homed within disciplines and within departments. As disciplines matured, national associations around these disciplines emerged and became the most important referent for faculty scholars. These associations delineated standardized guidelines for doctoral programs and scholarship, facilitating the proliferation of Ph.D. programs and research. Also, the disciplinary specialization and corresponding consolidation of national associations gave faculty greater authority and autonomy over academic matters and scholarship. Resources for research at this time normally came from benefactors such as the Rockefeller Foundation and the Carnegie Corporation. This philanthropic sponsorship helped universities to institutionalize graduate education and research as interdependent endeavors (Geiger, 1986; Gumport, 2005).

Those universities that had the resources to support promising Ph.D. programs became leaders and pioneers to which other universities aspired. In

1900, 14 presidents, representing a selective group of successful universities with doctoral programs, came together to form the Association of American Universities (AAU) to address issues of quality and prestige, especially in relation to their European peers. Since then, AAU institutions have been a prestigious set of elite research universities not only nationally, but across the globe. Today, AAU members include 60 private and public American universities and two Canadian institutions (Gumport, 2005; Walker et al., 2008).

At the end of World War I, the National Research Council (NRC) was created to coordinate the scientific organizations that emerged during the war. It represented the merging of basic and applied research as well as the acting research force after the war, setting the new landscape of the American science for the decades to come. Philanthropic foundations were still major stakeholders in the American scientific endeavor between the two wars and in the expansion of university research. These foundations also fostered the formation of units within universities and facilitated research through postdoctoral fellowships and direct support (Geiger, 1986).

During the second decade of the twentieth century, the need for research became an important aspect of universities' missions, and so, universities responded by implementing mechanisms such as lowering teaching loads, instituting sabbatical leaves, revolving research funds, and the creation of graduate assistant positions. Philanthropic support to graduate students grew, both in public and in private institutions. As a result, graduate education enrollments soared, allowing considerable flexibility in the handling of teaching loads of faculty, and therefore, improving their research opportunities. Industrial research also grew substantially during the 1920s, and doctoral graduates from universities were actively recruited by these industrial laboratories. Some industries promoted fellowships to increase scientific manpower in areas that were important to them. In addition, some professors consulted with corporations in exchange for contracted funds for their departments (Geiger, 1986).

Federal investment in applied research rose during the 1930s, leaving almost nonexistent the involvement of the federal government with basic research. However, during this decade, despite the hardships brought by the Great Depression, the top research universities made substantial commitments to sustain the research enterprise with "hard" budgetary allocations. Thanks to these efforts, American research reached parity with that of the leading scientific nations of Europe. By the 1940s, a different kind of relationship emerged as the central paradigm of research created ties between universities and industry. This new relationship was based on the large and successful firms in technology-based industries like chemistry, pharmaceuticals, and telecommunications looking to university research for theoretical knowledge that would supplement and enrich their own internal investigations (Geiger, 1986).

Federal grants became more significant during World War II as the government contracted massive amounts of university research, starting with the Manhattan Project. After the war, there was a general dissatisfaction with the concentration of war research in a handful of firms and universities. President Roosevelt directed the Office of Scientific Research and Development (OSRD) in 1944 to advise him on how the wartime government experience in sponsoring scientific research could be applied after the cessation of hostilities. The recommendations by Vannevar Bush, the director of OSRD, were crystallized with the creation in 1950 of The National Science Foundation (NSF), whose main mission was to support basic research and graduate education and to appraise the impact of research upon industrial development and general welfare (Geiger, 1993; Thelin, 2004). Despite the efforts of Vannevar Bush to protect basic research, the Cold War called for a U.S. commitment to develop the hydrogen bomb and to plan for a vast rearmament plan. This pressing national interest mobilized a network of scientists engaged in defense-related research. In the meantime, foundation support to universities in the 1950s was mainly directed at the medical and health sciences, a variety of activities to strengthen universities (such as graduate and postdoctoral fellowships, physical plant endowments, and libraries), and support for the social and behavioral sciences (Geiger, 1993).

When the Soviet Union launched Sputnik I on the October 4, 1957, the U.S. government realized that they were in a race for space against the Soviets. As a result, the government founded the National Aeronautics and Space Administration (NASA) a year after. NASA quickly became another federal agency with significant involvement in university research. In 1950, there were six federal agencies sponsoring academic research: The Department of Health Education and Welfare, the Department of Defense, the Atomic Energy Commission, the Department of Education, NSF, and NASA. By 1968, federal support increased even more, with more emphasis on basic research, marking the golden age of research universities (Geiger, 1993; Thelin, 2004). Support for graduate education also increased significantly, mainly to train scientists in science and engineering. This support for graduate students came in the form of direct financial aid, fellowships, and assistantships through research grants (Gumport, 2005). At this time, almost every field in higher education experienced a shortage of teachers and researchers. Those with doctorates found employment easily, and universities reduced teaching loads in order to retain faculty members. University budgets also grew substantially; access to research funds increased significantly in all fields; some professors founded institutes and research centers; the federal government fueled research in technical fields to keep up with the demands of the Cold War; and top universities became national leaders in science and technology (Kerr, 2002). During this time, the main features of doctoral education as we know them today were consolidated, such as the interdependence of research sponsorship, faculty research agendas, and doctoral education; reduced teaching loads to allow faculty to develop their research; and increased responsibilities to doctoral students as research and teaching assistants (Thelin, 2004). In the 1960s, there were more than 550 fields in doctoral education. By 1965, doctorates in engineering, the physical sciences, and life sciences accounted for half of the doctorates granted. About 20% of doctorates were granted in the social sciences and psychology, about 20% in the humanities and about 15% in education (Gumport, 2005).

By the 1970s, the golden age of American higher education began to end due to population shifts, inflation, and government fiscal deficits. As a result, funding for academic research started to decrease as global markets began to emerge (Altbach, Berdhal, & Gumport, 2005; Slaughter & Leslie, 1997). Additionally, the ideology in support of basic research started to vanish as access to higher education became the main concern in the baby-boom age (Geiger, 1993). The student movements of the 1970s demanded universities to account for their responsibility to society, including research useful for the public well-being. Therefore, research universities in the 1970s faced a decline of support for graduate students, with questions raised about the quality of graduate education, and the market for junior faculty members became stagnant. However, given the massive expansion of undergraduate enrollments during the decade, teaching assistantships proliferated among doctoral students (Gumport, 2005). Many faculty members no longer received research support, and equipment was aging to the point of inadequacy. As a survival strategy, departments started to specialize in order to show their relative strength and to compete for increasingly shrinking research support. Departments also admitted to be moving toward applied research as a way to attract sponsors. This marked the beginning of an unprecedented relationship with industry and a drift away from the paradigm that flourished in the 1960s based on faith in basic research (Geiger, 1993).

At the height of the biotechnology boom of the 1980s, universities found themselves in a global economical context where American industry was losing competitive ground. Federal support for research and graduate education decreased significantly. Stipends for assistantships declined when they became reconfigured as taxable pay for work instead of tax-exempt educational subsides in the Tax Reform Act of 1986. Consequently, since that time, doctoral students have been graduating with increasingly larger amounts of debt. In addition, as national support for research and graduate education declined and the number of doctoral graduates increased, the labor market for recent doctoral graduates shrunk, especially in those fields with fewer career opportunities outside academia, such as in the humanities and social sciences (Gumport, 2005). As a result, more and more graduates landed in postdoctoral, nontenure track, and nonacademic positions. The faces of doctoral students also changed considerably during the 1980s and 1990s, especially in terms of gender. Forty percent of doctorates awarded to women in the twentieth century were awarded in the last decade; and about half of the doctorates in science and engineering in the 1990s were awarded to international students. However, less than 10% of American minorities obtained doctorates in this period (Walker et al., 2008).

Since universities needed funds and industry was losing competitive ground in the global market in the 1980s and 1990s, both sectors were in need of each other. Economic competitiveness and technology transfer became the cornerstones of an emerging consensus on university research at the end of the twentieth century. This imperative toward the commercialization of research induced a drift in the direction of more practical work (Geiger, 1993). Thus, faculty members and universities moved toward greater participation in the market (Slaughter & Leslie, 1997). Throughout the 1980s and 1990s, science and engineering fields became more entrepreneurial and involved with technology. Leaders of large corporations, heads of universities, and political leaders developed policies and organizations to promote the growth of centers and institutes that involved partnerships between academia and industry around new technologies (Gumport, 2005; Slaughter & Rhoades, 2004). Under this scenario, higher education became an important source of national wealth-development through applied research rather than primarily a means for liberal education of undergraduates and warfare research. Subsequently, state leaders have stimulated programs around innovation through industry–government–academia partnerships led by industry, held together by government, and serviced by universities (Slaughter & Leslie, 1997).

At the start of the twentieth century, about 500 Ph.Ds were awarded each year; by 1960, annual production exceeded 10,000. Now, as the twenty-first century begins, more than 60,000 doctoral degrees are awarded each year (Snyder, Dillow, & Hoffman, 2009), adding to the more than 1.36 million doctorates granted by U.S. universities during the twentieth century (Walker et al., 2008). Universities have become key agents in the global economy as research centers for the development of competitive products and as training institutions of skilled labor for the global economy (Slaughter & Leslie, 1997). Today, society expects higher education to prepare the workforce of today's corporations, which has to be more highly trained and educated than in the industrial society. Moreover, product innovation depends heavily on university-educated personnel, and persons with doctoral degrees almost always fill managerial positions (Campbell & Slaughter, 1999). Despite the significant role of higher education in the global economy, federal and state funding have been steadily decreasing in the last years, pushing higher education institutions to seek other sources of revenue in order to survive, thus giving rise to interdisciplinarity and academic capitalism. As discussed in the chapters by Holley and Mendoza in this book, doctoral education has been affected in mixed ways by these trends (Holley, 2009; Mendoza, 2007; Slaughter, Campbell, Hollernan, & Morgan, 2002).

Graduate education in the United States has clearly undergone significant changes since its inception in 1876; however, the old adage still pertains: *Plus ça change, plus c'est la même chose.* Berelson (1960) commented, "The graduate school has always been accused of abnormal resistance to change by those who had a reform to introduce" (p. 40). Graduate education has changed its structure insofar as eliminating certain program requirements and the changing demographics of its students, but it still remains an institution focused on producing knowledge and research (Council of Graduate Schools, 2005). The Ph.D., however, has also become the focus of much of this strife as it has struggled to define itself in the midst of changing societal shifts and demands. It is often through trying to define the purpose of the Ph.D. that the controversy begins.

The Purpose of the Ph.D.

The doctoral degree is considered the terminal degree in many fields. The Survey of Earned Doctorates lists over 50 doctoral degree designations (Hoffer, Hess, Welch, & Williams, 2007), including the M.D., J.D., Ed.D., and the Ph.D. And, while many doctoral degrees exist, about 90% of all doctorates produced annually in the United States are those from the Ph.D. designation (Thurgood, Golladay, & Hill, 2006). It is the Ph.D., or the Doctor of Philosophy, that is the primary focus of this book.

The discussion of what purpose doctoral education serves has persisted since the inception of graduate education in the United States. While many posit the purpose of doctoral education to be the preparation to conduct original research (e.g., Council of Graduate Schools, 1990), others forward that the purposes of doctoral education should be further reaching, including training to teach (Adams & Association of American Colleges and Universities, 2002; Gaff, 2002), and instilling skills necessary for participation in the labor market outside of academia (Atwell, 1996; Jones, 2003). On one side of the discussion is the market-driven argument: to prepare the product directly for its subsequent use (Berelson, 1960). As the doctoral student may become faculty, researcher, or something altogether different, this "use" depends widely on the individual student's career choice and the job market. On the other side of this argument, however, is the degree's purpose existing as producing knowledge for "knowledge sake" (Berelson, 1960).

As previously stated, this debate over the purpose of doctoral education was particularly intense during the retrenchment period in the 1970s, where federal funding for research and development (R&D) diminished considerably and the job market for doctoral graduates shrunk. In fact, the National Board on Graduate Education was formed in 1971 to address issues of purpose and structure in graduate education nationwide. Interestingly, this board lasted three short years only, but issued six reports urging change in graduate education tailored toward national needs such as serving nontraditional students and the use of applied fields to solve national problems (Walker et al., 2008). Similarly, since the 1990s, several initiatives emerged to improve graduate education such as the Preparing Future Faculty Initiative, with the goal of exposing students to the various faculty roles in different types of institutions (Walker et al., 2008).

The Carnegie Initiative on the Doctorate was another major project aimed at improving doctoral education. It was designed as an action research program involving 88 departments in 44 universities across the country meant to evaluate, reflect, and restructure current doctoral programs across disciplines aligned with the present needs of society. These initiatives suggested that no clear directive on doctoral education or its mission exists, owing to a history of succumbing to societal demands, shifting emphases, and fiscal imperatives (Walker et al., 2008).

With no clear consensus on the purpose of doctoral education, we forward the definition given by the Council of Graduate Schools (1990): The Ph.D. "is designed to prepare a student to become a scholar, that is, to discover, integrate, and apply knowledge, as well as communicate and disseminate it" (p. 10). In other words, the purpose of the Ph.D. program is to prepare students to become scholars. Part of this preparation for the student generally includes mastery of content in the chosen field of study and, given the research focus of the Ph.D., the demonstration of independent scholarship. With this definition in mind, the Ph.D. is paramount to higher education and society, as it influences not only the students who enroll within its programs, but also the faculty they work with, the students they teach, the larger disciplinary context to which they contribute, and the society in which they will practice their skills and disseminate their knowledge. How and when these elements occur, however, can vary greatly depending on the field and the institution; it is here where doctoral education begins to show its complexity. Added to this complexity is the diversity of the students who pursue the degree. Much like Ling, Scott, Nate, Eva, and Jennifer, students bring myriad backgrounds and concerns with them, further complicating the study of the doctoral experience.

Ways to View the Doctoral Experience   *Socialization defined*

A central component to understanding the life and experiences of the doctoral student is socialization. Socialization, generally defined, is the process through which an individual learns to adopt the values, skills, attitudes, norms, and knowledge needed for membership in a given society, group, or organization (Bragg, 1976; Golde, 1998; Merton, 1957; Tierney, 1997; Van Maanen, 1978). The concept of socialization as it relates to doctoral education and the students' role in it is best understood through the lens of organizational

of PhD + purpose

socialization. Van Maanen and Schein (1979) described organizational social-ization as "the process by which an individual acquires the social knowledge and skills necessary to assume an organizational role" (p. 211). Organizational socialization typically occurs through two major stages. The initial phase is generally referred to as anticipatory socialization, and often begins before the individual makes the decision to join the organization as he or she learns about the organization through the recruitment and selection process (Tierney & Rhoads, 1994). After successfully gaining entrance to the organization, the individual enters the role continuance stage of socialization, which consists of the time when the individual experiences the socialization processes that will ultimately influence the decision to remain in the organization, and allowing the individual to adopt the values, attitudes, and beliefs of its culture (Tierney & Rhoads, 1994). Socialization of an individual occurs through experiences with various processes, traditions, relationships, and rules that govern the culture of the particular organization, be they formal or informal (Sherlock & Morris, 1967; Tierney, 1997; Van Maanen, 1978). In regard to professional so-cialization, or preparation for a particular professional role, an individual will learn through observation of others and through his or her own experience over time with policies, procedures, and traditions (Sherlock & Morris, 1967).

The Stages of Graduate School Socialization

Golde (1998) described the process of graduate school socialization as one "in which a newcomer is made a member of a community – in the case of graduate students, the community of an academic department in a particular discipline." She continued, "The socialization of graduate students is an un-usual double socialization. New students are simultaneously directly socialized into the role of graduate student and are given preparatory socialization into graduate student life and the future career" (p. 56). Tierney and Bensimon (1996) further elaborated on how the socialization process functions for all newcomers in academe: "The beliefs one holds about the academy inevitably frame how one acts in a postsecondary institution" (p. 5). It is this under-standing of how to act, what role is to be played, and how that role relates to others that is an inherent part of the socialization process for graduate stu-dents. Taken together, socialization is integral to the success of the doctoral student and to his or her progression through the degree process (Turner & Thompson, 1993).

Golde (1998) ₹ Weidman et all (2001)
models of socialization
THE Ph.D. IN THE UNITED STATES   *21*

The socialization of graduate students tends to occur in stages or developmental phases. Lovitts (2001) offered a four-stage model of graduate student development, beginning with Stage Zero, or anticipatory socialization into the degree program, to the first stage, occurring simultaneously with the first year, as the period of Entry and Adjustment. In the Entry and Adjustment Stage, the transition is made as the student moves from the feeling of being an outsider to that of an insider in the system. Stage Two, the Development of Competence, also corresponds to the second year of the student's program, and persists through the completion of all course and examination requirements, or candidacy. Finally, the Research Stage constitutes Stage Three, and encompasses the time period from the beginning to the completion of the dissertation, where the student decides upon a dissertation topic, organizes a doctoral committee, completes the research work, and finally writes and defends the dissertation.

Lovitts' (2001) model parallels that of Weidman, Twale, and Stein (2001) and their theory of graduate student socialization. Weidman et al. (2001) described graduate student socialization as "the processes through which individuals gain the knowledge, skills, and values necessary for successful entry into a professional career requiring an advanced level of specialized knowledge and skills" (p. iii). According to Weidman et al. (2001), socialization for graduate students occurs in four developmental stages: Anticipatory, Formal, Informal, and Personal Stages.

The Anticipatory Stage occurs primarily as students enter the program, and need to learn new roles, procedures, and agendas to be followed. These students will tend to seek information and listen carefully to directions. This stage can be described as the student becoming "aware of the behavioral, attitudinal, and cognitive expectations held for a role incumbent" (Weidman et al., 2001, p. 12). In other words, in this stage the student comes to understand the roles and expectations that are expected of other graduate students. The Formal Stage is characterized by the graduate student observing roles of incumbents and advanced students, while learning about role expectations and how they are carried out. Students in this stage are primarily concerned about task issues, and communication at this stage is informative through course material, regulative through embracing normative expectations, and integrative through faculty and student interactions. The Informal Stage is described as the stage in which "the novice learns of the informal role expectations transmitted by interactions with others who are current role incumbents"

(p. 14). At this stage, the graduate student receives behavioral cues, observes acceptable behavior, thereby responding and reacting accordingly. Accordingly, the students' cohorts are those with whom most interaction occurs. The student will begin feeling less student-like and more professional at the Informal Stage. The final stage, the Personal Stage, is characterized as the time when the students' "individual and social roles, personalities and social structures become fused and the role is internalized" (p. 14). During this final stage, the graduate student accepts a value orientation and adjusts his or her behavior to meet the expectations that exist. The conflict that exists between the former graduate student identity and the new professional identity is resolved, and the graduate student will be able to separate from the department in search of his or her own identity.

Finally, Tinto (1993), while known primarily for his work on undergraduate student persistence, also developed a working theory of doctoral persistence, which aligns with existing models of graduate student socialization. His theory is implicitly linked with socialization, implying that successful socialization results in persistence on the part of the graduate student. Tinto's theory of graduate persistence includes three stages. The first stage, Transition, typically covers the first year of study. During this stage the "individual seeks to establish membership in the academic and social communities of the university" (p. 235). This stage is shaped by social and academic interactions, especially those interactions within the graduate department. Persistence at this stage is marked by the student making a personal commitment to the goal of completion, which will depend upon the desirability of membership and the likely costs and benefits of further involvement. The second stage, Candidacy, "entails the acquisition of knowledge and the development of competencies deemed necessary for doctoral research" (p. 236). This stage will depend greatly upon the success in the individual's abilities and skills as well as the interactions with faculty. The final stage, Doctoral Completion, "covers that period of time from the gaining of candidacy, through the completion of a doctoral research proposal, to the successful completion of the research project and defense of the dissertation" (p. 237). At this stage, the nature of the interaction with faculty shifts from interacting with many faculty to interacting with few; as in the case of the dissertation advisor. Tinto asserted, "The character of the candidate's commitments to those communities, such as families and work, and the support they provide for continued study may spell the difference between success and failure at this stage" (p. 237).

As presented in the following chapters, many have begun to question these modernist and positivist views of the socialization process (e.g., Tierney, 1997), seeing prevailing models as only one-directional. New ways of viewing the socialization process include consideration of how the individual, or in this case, the student, can also influence and change the organization (see McDaniels, chapter 1 for further discussion). More research has yet to be conducted on how socially-constructed and postmodern views of socialization can characterize the graduate student experience.

Conclusion

While all of these models assist us in understanding how doctoral students experience their induction into graduate school and their future professions, there is still much to learn. As we position ourselves in the twenty-first century, a host of recent empirical evidence indicates that we must rethink how we structure doctoral education. Growing evidence demonstrates that as other nations continue to strengthen their graduate programs, the United States is still struggling with unacceptable attrition rates in graduate school, where about half of students enrolled in doctoral programs leave without a degree. In addition, stakeholders continue to question the currency of doctoral programs for the needs of today's society (Council of Graduate Schools, 2004; Nettles & Millett, 2006; Walker et al., 2008). The purpose of this edited book is to provide both empirical evidence and specific recommendations to enhance doctoral education in the United States based on the needs of our present students and society at large.

References

Adams, K. A., & Association of American Colleges and Universities (2002). *What colleges and universities want in new faculty. Preparing future faculty occasional paper series.* Washington, DC: Association of American Colleges and Universities.

Altbach, P. G., Berdhal, R. O., & Gumport, P. J. (Eds.)(2005). *American higher education in the twenty-first century: Social, political, and economic challenges* (2nd ed.). Baltimore: The Johns Hopkins University Press.

Atwell, R. H. (1996). Doctoral education must match the nation's needs and the realities of the marketplace. *The Chronicle of Higher Education, 43*(14), B4–B6.

Berelson, B. (1960). *Graduate education in the United States.* New York: McGraw-Hill.

Bragg, A. K. (1976). *The socialization process in higher education.* Washington, DC: The George Washington University.

Campbell, T., & Slaughter S. (1999). Faculty and administrators' attitudes towards potential conflicts of interests, commitment, and equity in university-industry relationships. *Journal of Higher Education, 70*(3), 309–352.

Council of Graduate Schools (2004). *Organization and administration of graduate education.* Washington, DC: Author.

Council of Graduate Schools (1990). *The doctor of philosophy degree: A policy statement.* Washington, DC: Author.

Council of Graduate Schools (2005). *The doctor of philosophy degree: A policy statement.* Washington, DC: Author.

Gaff, J. G. (2002). The disconnect between graduate education and faculty realities. *Liberal Education, 88*(3), 6–14.

Geiger, R. L. (1986). *To advance knowledge: The growth of research universities, 1900–1940.* New York: Oxford University Press.

Geiger, R. L. (1993). *Research and relevant knowledge: American research universities since World War II.* New York: Oxford University Press.

Golde, C. M. (1998). Beginning graduate school: Explaining first-year doctoral attrition. In M. S. Anderson (Ed.), *The experience of being in graduate school: An exploration* (pp. 55–64). San Francisco: Jossey-Bass.

Gumport, P. J. (2005). Graduate education and research: Interdependence and strain. In P. G. Altbach, R. O. Berdahl., & P. J Gumport (Eds.), *American higher education in the twenty-first century: Social, political, and economic challenges* (2nd ed, pp. 425–461). Baltimore: The Johns Hopkins University Press.

Hoffer, T. B., Hess, M., Welch, V., & Williams, K. (2007). *Doctorate recipients from United States universities: Summary report 2006.* Chicago: National Opinion Research Center.

Holley, K. (2009). The challenge of an interdisciplinary curriculum: A cultural analysis of a doctoral degree program in neuroscience. *Higher Education, 58*(2), 241–255.

Jones, E. (2003). Beyond supply and demand: Assessing the Ph.D. job market. *Occupational Outlook Quarterly, 46*(4), 22–33.

Kerr, C. (2002). Shock wave II: An introduction to the twenty-first century. In S. Brint (Ed.), *The future of the city of intellect: The changing American university.* Stanford, CA: Stanford University Press.

Lovitts, B. (2001). *Leaving the ivory Tower: The causes and consequences of departure from doctoral study.* Lanham, MD: Rowman & Littlefield.

Mendoza, P. (2007). Academic capitalism and doctoral student socialization: A case study. *Journal of Higher Education, 78*(1), 71–96.

Merton, R. K. (1957). *Social theory and social structure.* New York: The Free Press.

Nettles, M. T., & Millett, C. M. (2006). *Three magic letters: Getting to Ph.D.* Baltimore: The Johns Hopkins University Press.

Rudolph, F. (1962). *The American college and university: A history.* New York: Knopf.

Sherlock, B. J., & Morris, R. T. (1967). The evolution of the professional: A paradigm. *Sociological Inquiry, 37,* 27–46.

Slaughter, S., Campbell, T., Hollernan, M., & Morgan, E. (2002). The "traffic" in graduate students: Graduate students as tokens of exchange between academe and industry. *Science, Technology, and Human Values, 27*(2), 282–313.

Slaughter, S., & Leslie, L. (1997). *Academic capitalism: Politics, policies, and the entrepreneurial university.* Baltimore: The Johns Hopkins University Press.

Slaughter, S., & Rhoades, G. (2004). *Academic capitalism and the new economy: Markets, state, and higher education.* Baltimore: The Johns Hopkins University Press.

Snyder, T. D., Dillow, S. A., & Hoffman, C. M. (2009). *Digest of Education Statistics, 2008.* Washington, DC: National Center for Education Statistics.

Thelin, J. R. (2004). *A history of American higher education.* Baltimore: The Johns Hopkins University Press.

Thurgood, L., Golladay, M. J., & Hill, S. T. (2006). *U.S. doctorates in the 20th century.* Arlington, VA: National Science Foundation.

Tierney, W. G. (1997). Organizational socialization in higher education. *The Journal of Higher Education, 68,* 1–16.

Tierney, W. G., & Bensimon, E. M. (1996). *Promotion and tenure: Community and socialization in academe.* Albany, NY: State University of New York Press.

Tierney, W. G., & Rhoads, R. A. (1994). *Enhancing promotion, tenure and beyond: Faculty socialization as a cultural process.* Washington, DC: George Washington University.

Tinto, V. (1993). *Leaving college: Rethinking the causes and cures of student attrition* (2nd ed.). Chicago: The University of Chicago Press.

Turner, C. S. V., & Thompson, J. R. (1993). Socializing women doctoral students: Minority and majority experiences. *The Review of Higher Education, 16,* 355–370.

Van Maanen, J. (1978). People processing: Strategies of organizational socialization. *Organizational Dynamics, 7,* 19–36.

Van Maanen, J., & Schein, E. H. (1979). Toward a theory of organizational socialization. *Research in Organizational Behavior, 1,* 209–264.

Walker, G. E., Golde, C. M., Jones, L., Conklin Bueschel, A., & Hutchings, P. (2008). *The formation of scholars: Rethinking doctoral education for the twenty-first century.* San Francisco: Jossey-Bass.

Weidman, J. C., Twale, D. J., & Stein, E. L. (2001). *Socialization of graduate and professional students in higher education: A perilous passage?* San Francisco: Jossey-Bass.

PART TWO

SOCIALIZATION FOR THE PROFESSION

I

DOCTORAL STUDENT SOCIALIZATION FOR TEACHING ROLES

Melissa McDaniels

Scott is just beginning his coursework in child psychology and is very thankful for the prestigious and generous fellowship he won because he can now fully concentrate on his studies. Nevertheless, Scott regrets not being able to find a teaching assistantship. He really feels teaching is his passion but is dismayed that there is no formal training in the program. He is wondering if he can find a way to get some experience in the classroom. He will raise this issue during his next meeting with his advisor.

Jennifer is starting her doctoral program in English. Like her peers, she has been funded through a teaching assistantship in the department. One day in her shared office space, a more advanced peer talks about a recent job interview she had at a private, liberal arts college. According to this student, the interview didn't go well. The committee expected a higher caliber of teaching and less focus on research, something that she and Jennifer agree that they haven't had. The reality is that their program has never formally exposed students to teaching pedagogies. Filled with dread about her own future job prospects, Jennifer considers contacting a faculty member in the College of Education to help her think through these issues.

T he purpose of this chapter is to review what is known about how doctoral students are socialized for the professoriate, with a particular goal of understanding how they are prepared for teaching roles. As is evident from the collection of chapters in this book, teaching is just one of many important responsibilities that doctoral students may have in their role as faculty members. In addition to teaching, other faculty responsibilities often include research (see Weidman, chapter 2), service (institutional and disciplinary), and community outreach (see Ward, chapter 3). The multiple possible roles of faculty members are necessarily interconnected. However, the balance of these roles and the related performance expectations will vary depending upon the institutional and appointment types that aspiring faculty members may pursue. This chapter attempts to isolate what scholars, policymakers, and administrators have learned about the key components of the socialization process for teaching in postsecondary education institutions.

The term *teaching* includes a broad range of pedagogical activities. Too often, *teaching* is narrowly defined (Wulff, Austin, Nyquist, & Sprague, 2004) as interacting directly with students in face-to-face or online classrooms. However, other types of pedagogical activity exist, including advising; curriculum and program development; and classroom research and assessment at the individual, course, and programmatic levels (Gibson, 1992). In addition, many "micro-activities" of course instruction (grading, syllabus development, small group facilitation, lesson development) (McKeachie, 1994) require a different set of skills on the part of faculty members. In this chapter, I use this broader definition of pedagogical activity when describing the socialization of doctoral students for teaching roles.

In 1966, Brim defined *socialization* as "the process by which persons acquire the knowledge, skills, and dispositions that make them more or less effective members of society" (p. 3). This definition served as a starting point for scholars engaged in empirical research on graduate student socialization (Weidman, Twale, & Stein, 2001). Underlying this definition, and others like it, are the modernist assumptions (Tierney, 1997) that socialization is both a one-way process and a process by which a newcomer is molded by one monolithic professional and/or institutional culture. Other scholars have suggested, alternatively, that socialization is a dialectical process "through which newcomers bring perspectives, values, and ideas that interact with expectations within the organization" (Austin & McDaniels, 2006, p. 401). More postmodern perspectives on socialization thus embrace socialization as a two-way process by which a newcomer molds and is molded by an organizational or professional culture that is less monolithic and more complex. These theoretical variations allowed scholars of graduate education to recognize that socialization processes do not just "happen" to a graduate student.

Graduate students themselves are instrumental to ensuring the success of the socialization processes that will prepare them for their early careers in the college classroom. Graduate students also have the potential to impact the other members in the organizations (programs, universities) of which they are a part.

This chapter aims to do several things:

1. Provide a brief overview of how writing on this topic, by both academics and policymakers, has evolved over the past several decades;
2. Identify what socialization outcomes have been suggested as important for doctoral students aspiring to teaching roles;
3. Recognize the role that interested stakeholders have in the successful socialization of doctoral students for teaching, and suggestions for what role these parties might play in remedying gaps that still exist in doctoral student preparation for teaching roles.

Evolution of Scholarship on Doctoral Student Socialization for Teaching

The early conceptual and empirical work on the processes and outcomes of doctoral student preparation for teaching began in the mid- to late-1980s, and continued into the early 1990s, just as energetic policy debates were taking place about the growing use of teaching assistants (TAs) in the undergraduate classroom (Chism, 1998). Concerns about exploitation of teaching assistants, as well as the quality of undergraduate education, dominated this discourse. Leading scholars from the field of speech communication began to undertake research that led to the development of the first conceptual models depicting the stages of teaching assistant development (Sprague & Nyquist, 1989), as well as a framework that individual faculty members could use to reflect upon how they might support their graduate students in their development as teachers (Sprague & Nyquist, 1991).

In the mid-1990s, a team of scholars from communication and higher education undertook a four-year longitudinal study in which they followed approximately 70 Ph.D. and master's students who aspired to become faculty members. The team wanted to learn more about how these graduate teaching assistants interested in pursuing careers as teaching scholars (Nyquist et al.,

1999) experienced their graduate programs. After amassing data from twice-yearly interviews, questionnaires, and pictures drawn by participants, this research team concluded that

1. much of a graduate student's socialization occurs through observing, listening to, and interacting with faculty members;
2. graduate students are not given developmental and systematic preparation for their future roles as faculty members;
3. graduate students receive insufficient mentoring and feedback on their developmental progress; and
4. few opportunities exist for guided reflection.

Thus, the early empirical work on teaching assistant development was built upon by scholars who hoped to explore, more generally, how doctoral students are prepared for the range of roles and responsibilities as future faculty members. While study results indicated that doctoral students needed to be better prepared for the wide array of roles that faculty members are expected to undertake, other research indicated that a love of teaching was still the primary reason provided by graduate students for desiring employment as faculty members (Golde & Dore, 2001). These results suggest that positive socialization experiences for teaching roles have the capacity to influence the decisions of many talented young scholars to pursue academic careers or to leave the academy to pursue other careers. In addition to these empirical studies and conceptual projects, several nationwide policy initiatives (e.g., Carnegie Initiative on the Doctorate, Preparing Future Faculty) were introduced in the late 1990s and in the early years of this century to provide recommendations for large-scale changes to doctoral education. I share many of these findings, and how they specifically apply to how doctoral students are socialized for teaching roles, throughout this chapter.

Socialization for Teaching Roles: Outcomes

Literature on doctoral student socialization suggests that aspiring faculty members should develop a set of core competencies while in their doctoral programs to assist them in making the transition to successful careers as faculty members in 21st-century postsecondary institutions. In 2006, Austin and

McDaniels presented a framework in *Higher Education: Handbook of Theory and Research* that summarizes what the literature suggests are the desired outcomes of doctoral student socialization. After an extensive review of the theoretical and empirical literature on graduate student socialization, the authors concluded that graduate students aspiring to faculty roles would be well served if they developed sets of (a) conceptual understandings; (b) knowledge and skills in the core areas of faculty work; (c) interpersonal skills; and (d) professional attitudes and habits. I use this four-part framework as a guide to highlight what is known about the desired socialization outcomes related specifically to the teaching and instruction role.

Conceptual Understandings

A review of the doctoral student socialization literature reveals agreement that doctoral students, as a part of their socialization processes, would be well served to develop an understanding of (a) their professional identity as a teaching faculty member; (b) the discipline; (c) the wide array of institutional types in which they might find themselves working; and (d) the purposes and history of higher education (Austin & McDaniels, 2006).

Understanding themselves: development of a professional identity. One of the developmental milestones of a doctoral student's graduate school career is to begin to develop an identity as a future member of the professoriate. Optimally, students will be given a series of increasingly more demanding teaching experiences that will help them "try on" the identity of a teaching faculty member. Hopefully, such experiences will encourage students to contemplate answers to such questions as

1. To what degree do I want teaching to be a part of my academic career?
2. At what elements of teaching do I excel?
3. What are my developmental needs as a teacher?

Doctoral students can then begin to visualize what being a teaching faculty member will entail. Thus, if successful, socialization processes can result in a doctoral student embracing his or her professional identity as a faculty member with teaching responsibilities.

Understanding the discipline. In order for prospective faculty members to maximize their chances of being successful in their teaching roles, they must first develop a foundation of knowledge in their disciplinary content area

(Chism, 1998; Ronkowski, 1998). This disciplinary knowledge must include the theoretical underpinnings of the discipline; the paradigms, traditions; criteria for excellence in the field; and methodological approaches accepted by disciplinary members. In sum, good teachers are experts in their fields of study.

Understanding institutional types. Prior to accepting a position upon graduation from a doctoral program, all students will be well served if they have developed an awareness of the impact of institutional mission, student population (size, degree level, preparation), and fiscal control on the amount and type of teaching expected by an institution's teaching faculty. Ideally, aspiring faculty should be able to make informed decisions about what academic jobs to apply for and accept if they understand how institutional type can impact

1. a teaching and advising load;
2. the instructional level of students (e.g., undergraduate or graduate);
3. the variety of courses (content/level) a faculty member will teach;
4. forms of instruction a faculty member will be asked to provide (e.g., lecture, lab); and
5. the reward system vis-à-vis teaching.

Understanding the purposes and history of higher education. Finally, a fourth conceptual understanding that the literature suggests doctoral students develop while in graduate school is an understanding of and appreciation for the purposes and history of higher education. As was noted earlier, in order to be successful at one's role as a teacher, a faculty member needs to be an expert in his or her discipline. However, that disciplinary expertise is not enough. A faculty member also needs to understand the role that colleges and universities play in the development of individuals who are critical thinkers and full participants (as professionals and citizens). Understanding this history will enable future teaching faculty to think about how they contextualize the disciplinary content knowledge they deliver in the classroom, and how to encourage higher-order thinking among students they teach and advise.

Knowledge and Skills in the Core Areas of Faculty Work

As mentioned at the beginning of this chapter, pedagogical activity is one of four areas of faculty work, each of which demands the development of knowledge and skills to carry out responsibilities in each of these domains. Thus, a second outcome of doctoral student socialization for teaching roles can be a thorough understanding of teaching and learning processes (Austin & McDaniels, 2006). The literature suggests that prospective faculty should understand

1. the different ways students learn;
2. the usefulness of different teaching strategies to facilitate learning in a discipline;
3. how disciplinary differences impact methods and modes of inquiry, criteria for determining validity, as well as how problems are identified and solved in the field (Donald, 2002); and
4. the conceptual roadblocks that novices face in learning disciplinary topics.

There is also a growing need for teaching faculty to understand how instructional technologies can be integrated into a faculty member's disciplinarily informed pedagogical approaches (Mishra & Koehler, 2006).

Interpersonal Skills

A third desired outcome (or category of outcomes) of doctoral student socialization for teaching roles is the development of a set of interpersonal abilities that will allow them to use a variety of channels to communicate with a diverse set of students and colleagues (Austin & McDaniels, 2006). These interpersonal abilities include (a) written and oral communication; (b) collaboration; and (c) the ability to interact successfully with diverse students and colleagues.

Written and oral communication. Successful teaching faculty will need to be able to successfully communicate with students and faculty colleagues in both written and oral form. Good oral and written communication skills will enable teaching faculty to not just deliver content but to also differentiate important concepts from the less important, as well as frame topics for students in such a way that they start to make sense of the subject matter for themselves. The increasing number of online courses—and increased use of technology by students and colleagues—will require that aspiring teaching faculty learn how to most effectively use written and oral communication strategies in an online context, recognizing the influence that online tools (e.g., wikis, video, podcasts, blogs) will have on how, and to what extent, they make use of oral and written communication strategies.

Collaboration. In order to excel in the multiple dimensions of teaching practice, aspiring teaching faculty will need to cultivate their ability to collaborate with others. The increasingly interdisciplinary nature of knowledge has demanded more collaboration among faculty members in instruction, curriculum design, and assessment. In addition, future faculty who are interested in working at an institution with graduate programs will need to be able to collaborate with graduate students who work with them via teaching assistantships. Furthermore, faculty often find themselves working with colleagues on pedagogical projects such as curriculum redesign and program development.

Ability to interact successfully with diverse students and faculty colleagues. The college student population continues to grow increasingly socially diverse, as is evident in the following trends:

- An increase in the number of students ages 25 and older;
- An increase in the number of first-generation college attendees;
- An increase in the racial/ethnic diversity of student populations; and
- A change in educational expectations on the part of students and parents, including an increasing consumer orientation (Gappa, Austin, & Trice, 2007; Schuster & Finkelstein, 2006)

Doctoral students interested in pursuing teaching opportunities need to understand the impact of an increasingly diverse student population on both curricular and instructional implications activity. In addition, the professoriate in the 21st century is also becoming more diverse, as more women, racial and ethnic minorities, and foreign-born faculty (Schuster & Finkelstein, 2006) join the faculty ranks. The trend toward an increasingly diverse faculty population suggests that an important goal of doctoral student socialization should be to make prospective faculty aware of the impact of gender and cultural diversity on faculty collaboration in instruction and/or curriculum design (see Sallee, chapter 7, and Winkle-Wagner, Johnson, Morelon-Quanoo, & Santiague, chapter 9, for more discussion on gender and race among graduate students).

Professional Attitudes and Habits

Finally, emerging from the literature is a fourth category of desired outcomes for doctoral student socialization. Austin and McDaniels (2006) found that students would be well served if they started to develop a set of attitudes and habits, while in graduate school, that will provide a foundation for ethical conduct in all faculty roles, an appreciation for life-long learning, and an awareness of the importance of balancing one's passions and one's own life outside of work. In the next several paragraphs I will focus on those attitudes and habits as they relate to the faculty teaching role.

Ethics and integrity. A key component of the socialization of doctoral students for teaching roles needs to include at least an introductory understanding of the ethical issues related to teaching such as appropriate student–faculty relationships and academic honesty. Of course, each institution has its own set of codes of student conduct, and new faculty members will be well served to familiarize themselves with these guidelines upon arrival in their new campuses. In addition to teaching students about the content of the discipline, aspiring faculty will most likely have the opportunity to introduce students of all levels to research and scholarship in the discipline. In order to have the ability to teach students how to become ethical researchers, doctoral students will have to have a comprehensive grasp of issues related to the ethical conduct of research in their discipline, including the protection of human subjects and animal rights, and strategies for avoiding conflicts of interest vis-à-vis research projects (see Weidman, chapter 2, for more discussion on research socialization).

Ongoing professional development and cultivation of teaching network. The one thing that is certain about faculty careers in the 21st century is *change*! The existence of rapidly changing institutional and disciplinary environments almost guarantees that the roles and activities of teaching faculty will not remain the same throughout their professorial careers. Therefore, it will be imperative for aspiring faculty to understand and commit to ongoing professional development in support of their teaching roles.

Nurture teaching passion while maintaining life balance. Research has shown that doctoral students name a love of teaching as one of the primary reasons for pursing faculty careers (Golde & Dore, 2001). Therefore, doctoral students who teach are often deeply committed to the quality of their teaching and to their students. What doctoral students (and faculty at all career stages) need to learn is how to nurture their teaching passion (and other professional responsibilities), while maintaining balance in their lives. The challenge of setting boundaries between one's teaching (e.g., students) and one's life and other responsibilities has become increasingly more challenging in an era of instant messaging and 24-hour-a-day "access" that students have to their faculty members. Doctoral students will be well served by learning to set clear expectations with students about how quickly messages and assignments will be responded to or returned.

Socialization for Teaching Roles: Roles of Different Stakeholders

The literature on the socialization of doctoral students for teaching roles identifies five stakeholders who have an important role to play in supporting the preparation of aspiring faculty for their future teaching duties. These individuals, groups, and institutional stakeholders are (a) doctoral students; (b) individual faculty members; (c) academic departments (and their leaders); (d) postsecondary institutions (and their leaders); and (e) external agencies (and their representatives). In the remainder of this chapter I discuss the potential contributions that each of these parties can make to a doctoral student's preparation for teaching.

Doctoral Students

Doctoral students have a significant role to play in their own successful socialization for teaching roles. They are not merely "actors" in a larger sociocultural process; they have agency and can have a significant influence on the socialization processes they experience in graduate school. Doctoral students can

1. get direct teaching experience by taking advantage of teaching opportunities offered by faculty members, departments, or institutions, or create their own opportunities if none are formally offered to them.
2. gather information by determining what resources can provide them with information about both how to teach and what a teaching career entails. Resources may include
   ○ curricular or cocurricular opportunities (e.g., courses/workshops on teaching),
   ○ campus-based teaching centers (e.g., workshops, consulting, literature),

○ online teaching resources, and

○ informal conversations with others, including peers, faculty, and other professional mentors (Austin, 2002; Nyquist, Woodford, & Rogers, 2004).

3. observe others by seeking out models (Austin & McDaniels, 2007) of excellent teaching and watching other doctoral students and faculty members run class sessions.

4. engage in planning with an advisor to create a development plan for his or her own teaching improvement.

5. attend meetings of associations committed to the development of teaching and learning in specific disciplines (e.g., American Association of Physics Teachers) and read journals published by these associations (e.g., *Journal of College Biology Teaching*).

6. reflect upon one's own development as a teacher by

○ requesting feedback from students, peers, and faculty mentors, engaging in systematic reflection upon one's development as a teacher (Allen, 1991; Nyquist et al., 1999);

○ creating and maintaining a teaching portfolio to document one's development as a teacher.

7. provide feedback to trusted faculty or administrators about improving the way a department/institution prepares doctoral students for teaching roles.

Faculty Members

Not surprisingly, individual faculty members have the potential to have a tremendous impact on doctoral students as they prepare for roles as teaching faculty. They can

1. provide students with teaching experiences by

○ inviting doctoral students to be formally or informally involved in their own teaching and

○ offering students teaching experiences that gradually require more responsibility over time.

2. provide students with information about how to develop their teaching skills by

- letting students know about formal teaching opportunities currently available to doctoral students in their degree program. If formal opportunities are not available, individual faculty members may talk to interested students about what opportunities (e.g., teaching postdocs) they might take advantage of, prior to pursuing full-time positions as faculty members;
- letting students know about departmental and institutional resources available to help them learn more about teaching at a postsecondary level (e.g., course- or department-based orientation programs);
- engaging in impromptu or informal conversations with students about teaching; and
- communicating to doctoral students the value that he or she places on teaching.

3. recognize that one way doctoral students learn is by *observation*, and therefore recognize that students will play close attention to what faculty say (and actions they take) about their teaching responsibilities (McDaniels & Austin, 2006). As a result, doctoral student observations about the value their programs place on teaching can negatively or positively impact the processes and outcomes of their socialization for teaching roles.

4. provide opportunities for students to *reflect* upon their own teaching by
   - listening carefully to what students say about the successes and challenges they encounter while teaching,
   - providing feedback to students on their teaching performance, and
   - providing feedback to students on the development of their teaching portfolios.

Departments

TA development was originally provided by departments, which is not surprising as the disciplinary context significantly impacts a doctoral student's socialization for teaching roles (see Golde, chapter 4). Some departments provide course-specific training, whereas others provide training that is department specific (Ronkowski, 1998). The most extensive department-based training occurs in programs where teaching assistants carry a large percentage of the teaching load (e.g., foreign languages, writing). Departments are served well when they collaborate with university-wide teaching development programs to develop programs with disciplinary relevance.

Departments can play a key role in the successful socialization of doctoral students for teaching roles. Specifically, they can provide

1. teaching experiences that are developmental in nature (Nyquist, Woodford, & Rogers, 2004; Pruitt-Logan & Gaff, 2004);
2. information on teaching by offering seminars on teaching in the disciplinary context (Golde & Dore, 2004);
3. opportunities for observation by soliciting volunteers on the part of faculty and more senior doctoral students to allow junior graduate students to observe class sessions; and
4. opportunities for reflection by
   ○ adding required teaching seminars to the doctoral student curriculum and
   ○ encouraging student participation in departmental and university-wide learning communities focusing on teaching.

Universities

Institutions can provide support to doctoral students through centralized structures such as TA development programs, teaching certification programs, teaching conferences, TA orientation sessions, courses and/or workshops on teaching, and English-language instruction for international students (Mintz, 1998). Each of these programmatic activities is a venue for doctoral students to gather information and reflect upon their own teaching practice.

Centralized teaching centers often collaborate with departments to supply discipline-specific training to teaching assistants. Finally, all of these programs that are supported centrally may be funded by units such as the graduate school or office of the provost.

External Agencies

Although government agencies and private foundations do not contribute directly to the socialization of individual doctoral students for teaching roles, they have served as advocates for improvement in the quality of graduate education, funding programs to develop strategies for enhancement of doctoral student preparation for the wide variety of roles that they may assume as faculty members. Disciplinary associations, such as the Modern Language Association (MLA) or the American Sociological Association (ASA), have written reports on the status of doctoral student preparation, and they present recommendations for policy change.

Conclusion

The literature on doctoral student socialization for teaching roles has increased dramatically since the 1980s and enhances the robust body of research on doctoral student socialization for all faculty roles. Desired outcomes of doctoral student preparation for teaching roles are quite clear. Student preparation for teaching faculty roles will be enhanced by more consistent efforts on the part of all stakeholders—students, faculty, departments, universities, and external agencies—to provide doctoral students with teaching experiences, information on teaching and teaching careers, and opportunities for observation and reflection about their development as teachers in a postsecondary context.

References

Allen, R. R. (1991). Encouraging reflection in teaching assistants. In J. D. Nyquist, R. D. Abbott, D. H. Wulff, & J. Sprague (Eds.), *Preparing the professoriate of tomorrow to teach: Selected readings in TA training* (pp. 313–318). Dubuque, IA: Kendall/Hunt.

Austin, A. E. (2002). Preparing the next generation of faculty: Graduate school as socialization to the academic career. *The Journal of Higher Education, 73*, 94–122.

Austin, A. E., & McDaniels, M. (2006). Preparing the professoriate of the future: Graduate student socialization for faculty roles. In J. C. Smart (Ed.), *Higher education: Handbook of theory and research* (Vol. XXI, pp. 397–486). New York: Agathon Press.

Austin, A. E., & McDaniels, M. (2007). Using doctoral education to prepare faculty to work within Boyer's four domains of scholarship. In J. Braxton (Ed.), *Delving further into Boyer's perspective on scholarship* (Vol. 129, pp. 51–65). San Francisco: New Directions for Institutional Research.

Brim, O. G., Jr. (1966). Socialization through the life cycle. In O. G. Brim, Jr., & S. Wheeler (Eds.), *Socialization after childhood: Two essays* (pp. 1–49). New York: Wiley.

Chism, N. (1998). Preparing graduate students to teach: Past, present, future. In M. Marincovich, J. Prostko, & F. Stout (Eds.), *The professional development of graduate teaching assistants* (pp. 1–17). Bolton, MA: Anker.

Donald, J. G. (2002). *Learning to think: Disciplinary perspectives.* San Francisco: Jossey-Bass.

Gappa, J. M., Austin, A. E., & Trice, A. G. (2007). *Rethinking faculty work: Higher education's strategic imperative.* San Francisco: Jossey-Bass.

Gibson, G. W. (1992). *Good start: A guidebook for new faculty in liberal arts colleges.* Bolton, MA: Anker.

Golde, C. M., & Dore, T. M. (2001). *At cross purposes: What the experiences of today's doctoral students reveal about doctoral education: A survey initiated by the Pew Charitable Trusts* (www.phd-survey.org). Philadelphia: A report prepared for The Pew Charitable Trusts.

Golde, C. M., & Dore, T. M. (2004). The survey of doctoral education and career preparation: The importance of disciplinary contexts. In D. H. Wulff & A. E. Austin (Eds.), *Paths to the professoriate: Strategies for enriching the preparation of future faculty* (pp. 19–45). San Francisco: Jossey-Bass.

McKeachie, W. J. (1994). *Teaching tips: Strategies, research, and theory for college and university teachers* (9th ed.). Lexington, MA: D.C. Heath.

Mintz, J. A. (1998). The role of centralized programs in preparing graduate students to teach. In M. Marincovich, J. Prostko, & F. Stout (Eds.), *The professional development of graduate teaching assistants* (pp. 19–39). Bolton, MA: Anker.

Mishra, P., & Koehler, M. J. (2006). Technological pedagogical content knowledge: A new framework for teacher knowledge. *Teachers College Record, 108,* 1017–1054.

Nyquist, J. D., Manning, L., Wulff, D. H., Austin, A. E., Sprague, J., Fraser, P. K., et al. (1999, May). On the road to becoming a professor: The graduate student experience. *Change, 31,* 18–27.

Nyquist, J. D., Woodford, B. J., & Rogers, D. L. (2004). Reenvisioning the Ph.D.: A challenge for the twenty-first century. In D. H. Wulff & A. E. Austin (Eds.), *Paths to the professoriate: Strategies for enriching the preparation of future faculty* (pp. 194–216). San Francisco: Jossey-Bass

Pruitt-Logan, A. S., & Gaff, J. G. (2004). Preparing future faculty: Changing the culture of doctoral education. In D. H. Wulff & A. E. Austin (Eds.), *Paths to the professoriate: Strategies for enriching the preparation of future faculty* (pp. 177–193). San Francisco: Jossey-Bass

Ronkowski, S. A. (1998). The disciplinary/departmental context of TA training. In M. Marincovich, J. Prostko, & F. Stout (Eds.), *The professional development of graduate teaching assistants* (pp. 41–60). Bolton, MA: Anker.

Schuster, J. H., & Finkelstein, M. J. (2006). *The American faculty: The restructuring of academic work and careers.* Baltimore, MD: Johns Hopkins University Press.

Sprague, J., & Nyquist, J. D. (1989). TA supervision. In J. D. Nyquist, R. D. Abbott, & D. H. Wulff (Eds.), *Teaching assistant training in the 1990s* (pp. 37–53). San Francisco: Jossey-Bass.

Sprague, J., & Nyquist, J. D. (1991). A developmental perspective on the TA role. In J. D. Nyquist, R. D. Abbott, D. H. Wulff, & J. Sprague (Eds.), *Preparing the professoriate of tomorrow to teach: Selected readings in TA training* (pp. 295–312). Dubuque, IA: Kendall/Hunt.

Tierney, W. G. (1997). Organizational socialization in higher education. *Journal of Higher Education, 68*, 1–16.

Weidman, J. C., Twale, D. J., & Stein, E. L. (2001). Socialization of graduate and professional students in higher education. *ASHE-ERIC Reader Report* (Vol. 28, No. 3). New York: John Wiley & Sons.

Wulff, D. H., Austin, A. E., Nyquist, J. D., & Sprague, J. (2004). The development of graduate students as teaching scholars: A four-year longitudinal study. In D. H. Wulff & A. E. Austin (Eds.), *Paths to the professoriate: Strategies for enriching the preparation of future faculty* (pp. 46–73). San Francisco: Jossey-Bass.

2

DOCTORAL STUDENT SOCIALIZATION FOR RESEARCH

John C. Weidman

Ling has been an extremely successful student her entire life. Very few have the opportunity to receive full funding to pursue a doctorate in the United States. She knows that success comes with great sacrifices and hard work, and so, when she started the program she knew that she had to continue working hard to succeed. Although she has all the energy and focus to spend long hours working in the lab, for the first time in her life she feels lost. She can't understand why her advisor is not giving her specific instructions on what she has to accomplish. Moreover, he is asking her to come up with her own research questions and follow her instincts. This is radically different from what she is used to doing. She even has problems questioning previous research, which according to her advisor, she needs to do. She fears she is going to fail this time. She desperately needs guidance and cannot find it.

Now beginning her coursework, Eva is struggling to balance work, family, and her academic duties. After returning home from 12 hours of work, she makes dinner for her family and then tries to settle into reading and homework. This course has been particularly difficult as she is expected to complete a small study by the end of the semester. Every Sunday evening she breaks down and cries, "Where does the time go?" She is aware that she is falling behind and that she needs to do something quickly before it's too late. She is considering taking an extended leave from work but wonders if her principal would support that.

T his chapter addresses the experiences of doctoral students as they develop the capacity to do research that is recognized within academic
fields and disciplines through publication. It looks at these experiences through the lens of socialization, namely, the processes through which
doctoral students develop the knowledge, skills, and values that will equip
them to be producers as well as consumers of research. Research productivity
is a key dimension of a successful academic career in terms of both salary
(Fairweather, 2005) and reputation/status as an academic. Although this has
long been the case for faculty in upper-echelon research universities, it has
begun to permeate the entire spectrum of graduate degree-awarding institutions as shown by a recent study documenting increasing pressure on faculty
in comprehensive institutions to provide evidence of research productivity in
order to gain tenure and advance in rank (Youn & Price, 2009).

The chapter begins with the general conceptual framework for socialization at the graduate level that frames the discussion, focusing on the
longitudinal process and the aspects of institutional context, especially de-
partment/program and broader institutional support structures, as well as
external disciplinary/academic communities that are key elements. Results
from several recent studies of doctoral students are used to illustrate the
nature of relevant socialization processes (Gardner, 2007, 2008; Gardner &
Barnes, 2007; Golde, 2005; Golde & Dore, 2004; Nettles & Millett, 2006;
Weidman & Stein, 2003). The concluding section suggests ways in which
universities might facilitate doctoral student socialization for research.

Processes and Contexts of Doctoral Socialization

The general conceptual framework underlying the discussion is drawn from
work with my former students on the socialization of graduate and professional
students (Weidman & Stein, 2003; Weidman, Twale, & Stein, 2001) as well as
the more general organizational socialization of students in higher education
(Weidman, 2006). According to this framework, a student (a) enters a graduate
program with a set of skills and predispositions about what is required to earn a
degree and pursue a successful career after graduation, (b) is socialized through
experiences occurring primarily within the normative context of the graduate
program, especially those dimensions related to developing research capacity,
and (c) completes the degree with the skills necessary for doing research that
is valued in the discipline/field of study.

At the doctoral level, the primary institutional contexts for socialization of students are academic departments/graduate programs representing disciplines and/or fields of study that have their own particular knowledge base and norms/expectations for research. Significant normative influences are also exerted by disciplines/fields of study, both within the graduate institution and external to it through professional associations and academic journals (Gardner, 2007; Golde, 2005; Golde & Dore, 2004; Weidman & Stein, 2003; Weidman et al., 2001).

The beginning doctoral student has knowledge and some level of research skills developed in the course of prior academic degree work at the bachelor's and/or master's level. It should be noted that selection into a particular doctoral program is also based on these prior experiences and qualifications. Many higher education institutions encourage undergraduates to learn to do research. Common approaches include honors programs in which students are required to produce theses and provision of dedicated funds to support either individual research by undergraduates or joint projects with faculty. Master's graduates who write theses also tend to have more advanced research skills than do those whose programs require less formal products or even none at all.

As prospective doctoral students develop expectations about the requirements they might encounter in coursework, exams, and research, the process of "anticipatory socialization" begins before they even arrive on campus to start their programs (Bess, 1978). Doctoral students' predispositions shape their expectations and experiences until they actually enroll in courses and begin engaging in the activities of the doctoral program. Socialization occurs through a variety of experiences that students have with faculty and peers within their academic programs as well as through their engagement in activities related to their particular disciplines/fields of study such as participation in conferences and professional associations.

It must also be noted, however, that academic disciplines are not monolithic entities. There is a great deal of variation within as well as between disciplines/fields of study, especially when they are differentiated by subspecialties (see Golde, chapter 4 of this book for more discussion). Institutional context, especially as reflected in the prevalence of research doctoral programs, is also very important. For instance, in a survey of 605 graduate students (including 357 doctoral students) in geography, Solem, Lee, and Schlemper (2009) found striking variations in climate by subfields within this particular discipline. Further, the type and status of the institution in which the programs/departments are housed also make a difference. Using the term "professional development" rather than "socialization," but basing it on the same general definition that is used in the present volume, these authors summarized the complex process as follows:

Professional development during graduate programs is a process influenced by an interlocking set of factors related to individual attitudes and abilities, the overall social and academic dynamics in the department environment, and the cultures of academic disciplines and institutions (Solem et al., 2009, p. 290).

Research activities also vary by academic disciplines and fields of study, again, both within and between disciplines. Natural sciences, such as chemistry, tend to be focused on laboratory research, whereas humanities disciplines, such as English and history, tend to focus on textual analysis and interpretation, each of which requires a different set of skills and techniques (Gardner, 2008; Golde, chapter 4 in this book; Golde & Dore, 2004). Approaches can also vary within disciplines. For instance, some social science departments emphasize quantitative approaches to research, whereas others emphasize more qualitative approaches, sometimes complementing each other and sometimes including one at the expense of the other. To the extent that particular orientations predominate in disciplines and are reflected in the host departments of leading universities, they are sometimes characterized as "schools" of thought and research practice.

The next section of this chapter looks more closely at some of the more important ways in which socialization for research occurs during the course of doctoral programs. It draws primarily from selected studies of the doctoral experience that include academic field of study/discipline as a major variable.

Encouraging Development of Research Skills in Doctoral Programs

Doctoral programs routinely include courses in research design and methodology, but developing and honing research skills requires much more than coursework. From a socialization perspective, this includes interpersonal interaction with faculty and peers, participation in professional activities related to the academic field of study, hands-on experience actually conducting research, and practice in writing the kinds of work that is appropriate for academic publication.

Studies of doctoral students that provide particularly cogent findings for understanding socialization for research include Gardner (2008), Nettles and Millett (2006), Millett and Nettles (chapter 8 in this book), Golde and Dore (2004), and Weidman and Stein (2003).

For their comprehensive study of the doctoral experience, Nettles and Millett (2006) obtained survey responses from 9,036 doctoral students attending 21 of the top 60 doctorate-granting universities in the United States, sampled by institution and field of study. For the data analysis, responses were weighted in order to represent the entire national population of doctoral students and collapsed into five fields of study: education; engineering; humanities (English and history); mathematics and sciences (physical sciences—chemistry and physics; biological sciences—biochemistry, biophysics, and molecular biology); and social sciences (economics, political science, psychology, and sociology).

With respect to operationalizing research productivity (other than writing a dissertation), a multi-dimensional definition was used to develop a set of 22 survey items for a composite index that included presentations at professional conferences; publishing books, book reviews, chapters, and articles; submitting articles for publication; writing grant proposals; submitting applications for copyrights or patents; and the like. Nettles and Millett also included indicators of interaction among faculty and students, both social and academic, as well as with faculty advisers and mentors.

Golde and Dore (2004) reported results from a survey of 4,114 doctoral students in 11 arts and sciences disciplines. Disciplinary comparisons were presented for students in English (506 of total) and chemistry (574 of total). Data on preparation for research were presented on those respondents indicating an interest in "ever becoming a faculty member" (2,505 of total; 391 in English and 200 in chemistry).

Weidman and Stein (2003) surveyed 26 doctoral students in sociology and 24 in educational foundations at a single, research-intensive, public university. Their research productivity variable (participation in scholarly activities) was a composite index of 11 items that included critiquing fellow students' work, attending a professional conference, making a presentation at conference, writing a grant proposal, submitting a paper for publication, having a paper accepted for publication, and more. Indicators of student–faculty and student–peer interaction as well as measures of departmental climate (supportive faculty environment; department collegiality; encouragement of student scholarly activities) were also included.

Participation in Research

Somewhat surprisingly, Nettles and Millett (2006) found that just 51% of doctoral students reported having done at least 1 of the 22 activities comprising their research productivity scale. Across all five fields, research productivity was positively related to degree completion, but students who spent more time in their doctoral programs were also more likely to report research productivity (pp. 165–166).

An even higher proportion of Golde and Dore's (2004) respondents reported research activities, with more than 80% having presented research findings at a conference. Among respondents indicating an interest in becoming a faculty member, 65% (56% in English, 71% in chemistry) reported they had been prepared for research and 43% (31% in English, 57% in chemistry) reported they had been prepared for publishing.

All of Weidman and Stein's (2003) respondents reported at least one scholarly activity, with the entire sample reporting an average of four. Interestingly, doctoral students in educational foundations reported substantially higher scholarly participation than did those in sociology. These findings across a range of studies provide additional evidence that doctoral student participation in research and research-related activities varies considerably by academic discipline/field of study.

Faculty and Peer Interaction

Neither Nettles and Millett (2006) nor Weidman and Stein (2003) found that either general student–faculty or student–peer interaction within the academic areas/departments was significantly related to research participation, but in the latter study, a departmental climate that encouraged scholarly work by students was significantly correlated with their scholarly research activities. In both studies, however, faculty and peer interaction was related to doctoral students' favorable perceptions of the general environment of their academic programs/departments.

Corroborating evidence is found in a qualitative study of 10 doctoral students in higher education by Gardner and Barnes (2007) that used Astin's (1984) conceptualization to explore aspects of doctoral students' involvement in local and national communities. This research pointed out that student involvement at the graduate level tends to be much more focused on career and professional development than at the undergraduate level.

Focusing on degree completion rather than explicitly on research, Gardner's (2007) qualitative study of 20 doctoral students in chemistry and history who were attending a land grant university also highlights faculty and student support in doctoral student socialization. She argued for the importance of providing a range of opportunities for interaction among students and faculty, including dedicated space if available.

Faculty Mentoring and Advising

A very important dimension of relationships with faculty related to student research productivity, mentoring, emerged in the Nettles and Millett's (2006) study. Faculty mentoring increased the likelihood of research productivity by 2.2 times in social science disciplines, 2.1 times in humanities, 1.7 times in engineering, and 1.4 times in education and science and mathematics. Fully 70% of respondents reported having a mentor, the large majority found within the first few months of entering a doctoral program (p. 157). Faculty mentoring is mentioned by Gardner and Barnes (2007), and Gardner (2007) discussed the importance of advising and faculty direction of doctoral students' progress throughout their entire graduate programs. Mentoring is also particularly important for students of color (Winkle-Wagner, Johnson, Morelon-Quainoo, & Santiague, chapter 9 in this book).

Financial Support

According to Nettles and Millett (2006), doctoral students holding research assistantships were more likely than their peers without support to report research productivity, by 2.0 times in education, by 2.7 times in science and mathematics, and by 1.8 times in engineering and social sciences. Gardner (2007) also highlighted the importance of financial support for doctoral student success. She pointed out that the chemistry doctoral students she interviewed tended to be funded, in the first year by teaching assistantships and then, subsequently, by research assistantships. In contrast, the history doctoral students she interviewed had less opportunity for receiving assistantships. Not only does overall student support vary widely by discipline and institution, but the type of support varies as well with research assistantships predominating in physical and biological sciences departments and teaching assistantships predominating in humanities departments. Although research assistantships tend to facilitate the development of research skills and productivity, other types of support (e.g., fellowships and teaching assistantships) are also important. Lack of funding may be reflected in lower probability of completion and/or longer time to degree (Golde, 2005).

Departmental Student Composition

With respect to gender and race, underrepresented groups in engineering, science, and mathematics departments were less likely to report research productivity than their peers: males in engineering were 2.3 times and 1.3 times as likely as females in science and mathematics and African American doctoral students in science and mathematics were 2.5 times less likely than Whites to report research productivity. African Americans in social sciences were also 1.7 times less likely than Whites to report research productivity (Nettles & Millett, 2006, pp. 165–166).

Marital status of doctoral students is also related to several doctoral student socialization outcomes (see Millett & Nettles, chapter 8 in this book). Gender of students and gendered orientation of academic disciplines may also influence socialization to research (see Sallee, chapter 7 in this book).

In sum, socialization of doctoral students to research reflects a complex set of processes involving faculty and peers in the context of an academic degree program as well as external professional associations that define the norms for research and publication. Doctoral students learn to negotiate the demands placed upon them in order to fulfill expectations, primarily by faculty, for building a portfolio of research accomplishments necessary for the type of careers graduates are seeking. Fundamentally, the doctorate is a research degree, so doctoral student socialization tends to include a heavy dose of research-related activities.

Recommendations

- Doctoral students
  - Because having a faculty mentor is so important for developing research skills, try to match personal interests with a specific faculty member either prior to or within the first semester of entering a doctoral program.
  - Try to land a research assistantship to gain hands-on experience.

- ○ Volunteer to help faculty members as an unpaid research intern. This may also be a way of earning graduate credits.
- ○ Find out about available resources for supporting research-related activities in addition to assistantships such as attendance at professional conferences, expenses for data collection and analysis, and discounted computers and software.
- Faculty members
  - ○ Be attentive to involving doctoral students in research activities not related to funded projects through unpaid research internships and other types of participation.
  - ○ Develop seminars focused on the mechanics of doing research, proposal writing, and preparation of articles for publication.
  - ○ Engage in activities that will improve capacity to serve as research mentors.
- Departments
  - ○ Provide opportunities for doctoral students to learn about faculty research activities across the department through periodic seminars, brown bag presentations, or other venues.
  - ○ Coordinate and/or provide information about research presentations and professional activities occurring at nearby universities.
  - ○ Because travel expenses often exceed personal resources of students, develop sources of supplemental funding for students' research presentations (e.g., pooling a portion of return money from research grants; renting a van for transportation to conferences within driving distance that generally costs much less than conventional commercial transportation; and organizing on-campus conferences). It is not essential that departments/schools cover full costs; rather, students and faculty can share at least a portion of expenses.
- Universities
  - ○ Provide competitive funding for student travel to professional conferences. Some universities use a portion of graduate students' activity fees for this purpose.
  - ○ Provide competitive funding for doctoral student research. (With respect to anticipatory socialization, note that many universities provide competitive funding for undergraduate student research as well, often requiring joint proposals with faculty.)

- ○ Encourage establishment of programs to provide doctoral students with university resources that support research (e.g., free or discounted software, electronic library databases, and resources for data collection such as survey research centers).
- ○ Assist departments and individual faculty with developing mentoring programs for doctoral students. There are a variety of models focusing on mentoring of junior faculty that are already in place and could be applied for doctoral students (Zellers et al., 2008).
- ○ Capital campaigns should put greater emphasis on seeking funds for endowed scholarships, fellowships, and assistantships to support doctoral students.
- • External agencies
  - ○ Support programs conducted by professional associations, often in conjunction with annual conferences, to mentor and strengthen research skills of doctoral students.
  - ○ Expand support of summer programs providing training in the use of national and international statistical databases.
  - ○ Expand funding to support doctoral student research by both federal (e.g., Fulbright, NSF, and NIH) and foundation (e.g., Lumina and Spencer) sources.

References

Astin, A. W. (1984). Student involvement: A developmental theory for higher education. *Journal of College Student Personnel*, *25*, 297–308.

Bess, J. L. (1978). Anticipatory socialization of graduate students. *Research in Higher Education*, *8*, 289–317.

Fairweather, J. S. (2005). Beyond the rhetoric: Trends in the relative value of teaching and research in faculty salaries. *Journal of Higher Education*, *76*, 401–422.

Gardner, S. K. (2007). "I heard it through the grapevine": Doctoral student socialization in chemistry and history. *Higher Education*, *54*, 723–740.

Gardner, S. K. (2008). "What's too much and what's too little?" The process of becoming an independent researcher in doctoral education. *Journal of Higher Education*, *79*, 326–350.

Gardner, S. K., & Barnes, B. J. (2007). Graduate student involvement: Socialization for the professional role. *Journal of College Student Development*, *48*, 369–387.

Golde, C. M. (2005). The role of the department and discipline in doctoral student attrition: Lessons from four departments. *Journal of Higher Education, 76,* 669–700.

Golde, C. M., & Dore, T. M. (2004). The survey of doctoral education and career preparation: The importance of disciplinary contexts. In D. H. Wulff & A. E. Austin (Eds.), *Paths to the professoriate: Strategies for enriching the preparation of future faculty* (pp. 19–45). San Francisco: Jossey-Bass.

Nettles, M. T., & Millett, C. M. (2006). *Three magic letters: Getting to the Ph.D.* Baltimore: Johns Hopkins University Press.

Solem, M., Lee, J., & Schlemper, B. (2009). Departmental climate and student experiences in graduate geography programs. *Research in Higher Education, 50,* 268–292.

Weidman, J. C. (2006). Student socialization in higher education: Organizational perspectives. In C. C. Conrad & R. C. Serlin (Eds.), *The Sage handbook for research in education: Engaging ideas and enriching inquiry* (pp. 253–262). Thousand Oaks, CA: Sage.

Weidman, J. C., & Stein, E. L. (2003). Socialization of graduate students to academic norms. *Research in Higher Education, 44,* 641–656.

Weidman, J. C., Twale, D. J., & Stein, E. L. (2001). Socialization of graduate and professional students in higher education: A perilous passage? *ASHE-ERIC Higher Education Report, 28*(3). San Francisco: Jossey-Bass.

Youn, T. I., & Price, T. M. (2009). Learning from the experience of others: The evolution of faculty tenure and promotion rules in comprehensive institutions. *Journal of Higher Education, 80,* 204–237.

Zellers, D. F., Howard, V. M., & Barcic, M. A. (2008). Faculty mentoring programs: Reenvisioning rather than reinventing the wheel. *Review of Educational Research, 78,* 552–588.

3

DOCTORAL STUDENT SOCIALIZATION FOR SERVICE

Kelly Ward

Jennifer has taken it upon herself to get involved with the university's faculty development center so that she can learn more about teaching and the faculty role. Today she is attending a workshop on service. Having heard a lot recently about service learning, Jennifer is excited to learn more. What she discovers at the workshop, however, is a conversation entirely focused on balancing service with teaching and research. She has never really heard anything before about service as it applies to a faculty position and feels a bit panicked. As she listens further to the faculty members in the workshop, she learns that there is whole lot more to the faculty role than she originally thought. She wonders to herself, "How could I have gotten this far in my program and never have heard anything about this?"

For Scott, working with communities comes naturally. In fact, the main motivation for pursuing his education in child psychology has been to ultimately give back to his African American community. As such, he has envisioned a dissertation that would contribute to the well-being of his people. He wants to make a difference and worries sometimes about being too detached from real applications in his academic work. He wishes his advisor understood better his desire to serve his community through concrete actions. Instead, Scott feels he spends too much time dealing with academic jargon far from the real world.

My first administrative job in higher education involved faculty development related to service learning (the connection of student learning and community needs). In this capacity I presented to many different faculty audiences about the service mission of higher education and about faculty work to support this mission. I often started these presentations by asking faculty to tell me what they thought of when I said the word *service*. Inevitably, the response was, "Committee work." The faculty with whom I worked generally saw their service work as bound to the campus and manifested in committee meetings. As a student of the study of higher education, including the history of higher education, as well as a faculty development administrator, I saw very clearly that faculty service went far beyond committee work. With this knowledge, I pursued my faculty development work mindful of a historically grounded and broad view of faculty service.

In the years since, my work has shifted from administration to teaching and research, but my focus on a fuller understanding of faculty work has remained constant. Even though campus rhetoric has shifted to talk about community engagement, campus outreach, and community service, faculty can still find themselves unclear about their service role, what it entails, and how it is rewarded. Furthermore, if faculty are uncertain about the service component of their jobs, to their graduate students it often remains a mystery. Effecting change in higher education calls for thinking about preparation and socialization of graduate students in new and different ways (Austin & McDaniels, 2006; Gaff, 2002; O'Meara, 2007). If graduate students learn about and adopt norms of faculty work as part of their doctoral student experience, they are likely to bring these norms and ideas to their faculty positions (e.g., Austin & McDaniels, 2006). This chapter proceeds from this idea.

Teaching, research, and service are common referents in campus mission statements and faculty handbooks, yet what each of these terms mean and how they are expressed on college campuses varies considerably. The teaching role tends to be viewed similarly by faculty, students, administrators, and other stakeholders. To profess is to teach. The teaching role conjures images of faculty members in the front of the classroom and interacting with students in an exchange and transfer of ideas and knowledge. Although the teaching role has evolved and changed in some ways with regard to how faculty teach and in what medium (see McDaniels, chapter 1), there is still common understanding about the teaching role of faculty (Fairweather, 1996; O'Meara, 1997). Teaching remains at the heart of what it means to be a faculty member in all types of institutions. Teaching is a "core function" of higher education that involves virtually all faculty directly or indirectly (Plater, 2008).

The research mission of colleges and universities differs from the teaching mission because it tends to be clearly understood on campus, but it is often less clear to those outside academe. Research activities are not always well understood by stakeholders beyond college campuses; yet among professors, especially those in familiar disciplines, there is some common understanding of the meaning of the research role. The research processes of inquiry, knowledge production, and dissemination are familiar to faculty and administrators and tend to be recognized and rewarded on all types of campuses (Fairweather, 1996; Weidman, chapter 2).

In contrast to teaching and research, the service role tends to be misunderstood, ill-defined, and often unrewarded (Neumann & LaPointe Terosky, 2007; Tierney & Bensimon, 1996; Ward, 2003). Although service is often equated with committee work, this is only part of the role; "service as committee work" tends to devalue the contributions faculty make to support their institutions and their disciplines. Service can include roles and responsibilities to the institution, the discipline, and/or communities beyond the campus. In spite of recent attention to service (e.g., Checkoway, 2001; Kezar, Chambers, & Burkhardt, 2005), and, in particular, external service as a means to fulfill community service and outreach initiatives, the service role of faculty and of graduate preparation continues to be overlooked.

If graduate students are to be socialized to the complexities of the academic role, this socialization needs to include all aspects of faculty work (Austin & McDaniels, 2006; Colbeck, O'Meara, & Austin, 2008; Gaff, 2002; Golde & Dore, 2001; Walker, Golde, Jones, Conklin Bueschel, & Hutchings, 2008). The goal of this chapter is to provide an overview of the intricacies of the service role, including an overview of the service mission of college campuses and service as part of the faculty role. The chapter addresses how service roles vary by institutional type and demographics and concludes with recommendations to faculty members and graduate students wanting to be cognizant of the service aspect of faculty work.

The Complexities of Service

Prior to addressing graduate student socialization to service it is important to first provide an overview of the service role of faculty and the service mission of higher education. Service is a concept that is bantered about with a fair amount of frequency in higher education and among its faculty, but what the term means needs to be deciphered. Service to whom? For what? In what context? There are three areas of service I present here: service as part of the mission of higher education, faculty service within higher education, and faculty service beyond the campus.

The Service Mission of Higher Education

The majority of colleges and universities mention service in their mission statements (Lynton, 1999). Service is an outgrowth of colleges and universities being "in service" to their local, state, regional, and national communities, an extension of the covenant between universities and the various communities that sponsor and support them. Teaching, service, and research missions are interrelated in that campuses serve their communities through their teaching and research missions. At the campus level, service is not a stand-alone mission but rather a vehicle used to connect research and teaching to needs beyond the campus and to the improvement of society.

The teaching mission of higher education is part of the historical core of higher education (Fairweather, 1996; Plater, 2008). Teaching manifests in the classroom and beyond with the intent of developing the expertise of students in particular areas and fostering an educated citizenry. The student with a major in biology, for example, is not necessarily studying biology as an end unto itself but may be preparing for additional education to support a medical or research career. This career choice, in turn, contributes to society. The campus where this student was educated serves the community by preparing students who, in turn, become members of an educated citizenry (Fairweather, 1996).

The research role on the college campus is carried out through faculty, staff, and students working to create knowledge as a means to address societal needs. The history professor conducting research related to the Civil Rights Movement is not just conducting this research to satisfy individual curiosity (although that can play a part), she is also helping to identify the connections between that time and this, and helping to shed greater understanding on civil rights in society today. The same is true for the nursing professor studying palliative care. The professor is not just conducting this research out of personal interest or as an outgrowth of his clinical work with students, he is also conducting this research so that a general understanding of palliative care can improve nursing care for patients at the end of life, not just in his clinical setting, but in other settings as well.

The dissemination element of research plays an important role in communicating research findings beyond a particular campus setting. Faculty members carry out their research in laboratory, library, and office or other settings on- and off-campus, but it is through the process of writing and disseminating findings that the researcher is poised to contribute to the service role of a campus. As research results are shared with larger communities, the research and service missions of the campus are addressed.

The extension mission of higher education is often associated with land grant colleges and universities, which have a specific mission to "extend" the resources of the campus to communities beyond, as formalized in the passage of the Morrill Act of 1862 (Veysey, 1965). Land grant colleges and universities played a key role in establishing the service extension idea of higher education, and other campuses have used this model as well (Kerr, 1963). Leaders at the University of Wisconsin were some of the first to pledge campus resources to meet the needs of the state through research, teaching, and service (Veysey, 1965). This idea migrated to other land grant institutions and other types of campuses, public, private, large, and small. Through the land grant university promise to meet the needs of their states, the campuses received support from state and federal governments. Land grant universities continue to fulfill their mission of service through extension and have played a leadership role as other campuses strive to extend campus resources to multiple publics.

The service mission can also be enacted in other ways. The location of a campus within a particular community has an element of service. The presence of students, faculty, and staff contribute to a community economically, socially, and culturally (Fairweather, 1996). Economically, campuses serve their communities in many aspects. Historically, communities competed vigorously to host campuses, given the economic benefit of having a college or university and its faculty, students, and staff within a particular community (Potts, 1977). Campuses can be hubs of social and cultural activity as well. The infrastructure of a campus is well suited to host community events that benefit the campus and the community. For example, a community health fair hosted by Salish Kootenai College (a tribal college in Pablo, MT) certainly has benefits to the campus and may also have links to the campus through student and faculty participation, but the fair is created for a community purpose. The fair brings people together socially with the intent of sharing community health information. The multiple classrooms and common areas on campus are the ideal space for people to congregate. Campuses also often meet the cultural needs of a community. The Andy Warhol art exhibit or the musical at a campus theater are sure to benefit student, staff, and faculty in a myriad of areas, but just as importantly they bring cultural enrichment opportunities to members of the community. As colleges and universities are called upon to be more accountable to their constituents and to make clear their utility to the public, it is particularly important for campus leaders to be mindful of the individual elements of teaching, research, and service as well as the integration and connection of these three missions and how they shape faculty life (Colbeck et al., 2008).

Faculty Service Internal to Campus and to the Discipline

There are two distinct elements to the faculty service role in higher education: the service faculty perform on campus to support the internal functioning of the campus and their discipline, discussed in this section, and the external service roles faculty engage in to extend faculty expertise beyond the campus and the profession, discussed in the next section.[1]

I use "internal service" to refer to the service faculty provide to support their campuses and also the work faculty do to support their disciplinary associations (e.g., conference work). I group these together under the rubric of internal service because activities associated with supporting the campus and supporting disciplines are focused on internal audiences familiar with faculty work and faculty roles. Although it is often overlooked as vital to success as a faculty member, internal service is important to help familiarize new faculty members with the dynamics of their campus and their discipline. Given the importance of internal service to success as a faculty member, graduate students need to understand the nuances of internal service activities. Unfortunately, this part of the faculty role is not one for which graduate students are very well-prepared (Golde & Dore, 2001).

Faculty involvement in service on campus contributes to the shared governance approach to decision making that exists on most campuses (Burgan, 1998; Plater, 2008). Shared governance involves faculty, staff, administrators, and sometimes students in contributing to management of campus processes. Faculty share responsibility for the success of the institution, and they enact this responsibility through their work on committees that range from hiring fellow faculty and administrators, to setting parking fees, to establishing general education requirements for the campus.

Finsen (2002) identified three areas of faculty service on campus: academic oversight (e.g., curriculum, faculty evaluation), institutional governance (e.g., strategic planning, administrator hiring), and institutional support (e.g., parking, alumni relationships). Faculty service to campus is also referred to as institutional or academic citizenship (Burgan, 1998; Fear & Sandmann, 1995) and is enacted through contributions to committee meetings, reports, and helping make decisions about particular directions of the campus. Faculty play a key role in maintaining the vitality, well-being, and institutional fitness of their campuses through participation in service to the campus (Berberet, 2002).

Another element of faculty service on campus that is included under the rubric of internal service is work that is done to support students. Typically, direct advising of students falls under the rubric of teaching (although it certainly has a service element), yet there are other aspects to working with students that can fall under the categorization of internal service. For example, if a faculty member provides oversight for a graduate student group in their college or an undergraduate interest group in their department, this area of contribution could be included in the service category.

Internal service can also be enacted through certain types of administrative and "quasi-administrative" positions (Berberet, 2002). Faculty often take on responsibilities for oversight of particular aspects of their programs. For example, the faculty member who is the graduate coordinator for his or her particular program can be viewed as carrying out internal service through this type of administrative role. The administration work is not the primary focus of the faculty position, yet through the service he or she carries out an important support function of the department. Faculty bring particular and unique perspectives that play an important role in helping their units. The expertise faculty bring from working directly in the areas of teaching, research, and student advising is needed to foster healthy decision making and functioning in departments. As campuses seek to do more with less and also respond to tight budgets and budget cuts, it is not unusual for faculty to take on increasing areas of campus and departmental service. Departments and their chairs rely on faculty support of particular function areas to help the departments run smoothly.

Another aspect of internal service is service to support the disciplines through association work. Like departments, disciplinary associations rely on the service of faculty from different institutions to support their functions.

Depending on the size and complexity of the disciplinary group, faculty members can play key roles in all aspects of running and managing their disciplinary organizations. While larger organizations (e.g., American Sociological Association, American Chemical Society) tend to have their own organizational structure with full-time leaders and support staff, many smaller organizations rely on the goodwill and expertise of their faculty membership to manage all aspects of the organization. Disciplinary service can include reading proposals and papers for conference presentations, editing journals and newsletters, and helping to organize the program for annual meetings.

All aspects of internal service can vary greatly depending on the career stage of the faculty member, individual inclination, the type of institution, and even particular areas of expertise. The key to this overview of internal service is to prompt prospective faculty and their advisors to think about graduate student socialization to faculty service roles as important work to be done with awareness about the nuances of internal service. Because of the nature of faculty meetings and departmental decision making, students typically are not privy to the inner workings of faculty service on campus, and they rarely witness faculty involvement in disciplinary service. The holistic socialization of graduate students involves making students aware of the internal service roles associated with faculty life. For doctoral students to be more fully prepared for faculty life, their preparation needs to provide understanding of the important role faculty play in shared governance and maintaining their disciplines (Plater, 2008).

Faculty Service External to Campus

Recent discussions of the civic mission of higher education (Checkoway, 2001), and the call for universities to contribute to the public good (Boyer, 1996; Kezar et al., 2005) bring attention to the continuing interest at all levels of academia to connect the resources of college campuses with the communities they serve. Such calls for community engagement also connect to faculty work because faculty are essential to carry out community-based missions of their campuses. Too often, however, faculty are not clear about what their role is or should be to support public service missions, and if faculty are unclear about their service roles then so are graduate students (O'Meara, 2007). While graduate students indicate an interest in the external service role of faculty, the majority of students are not clear about what this aspect of faculty work entails (Golde & Dore, 2001; O'Meara, 2007).

The external service role of faculty, just like the internal service role, has many nuances and complexities that faculty and graduate students would do well to recognize and understand. Most campuses have some type of public service or outreach mission that connects the campus to community and that contributes to the public good (Kezar et al., 2005; Lynton, 1995). Faculty play a key role in enacting the service role of their institutions. Faculty can share their disciplinary expertise with audiences beyond the campus through their external service roles. As calls have increased in recent years for colleges and universities to be more responsive to societal needs, and with an increased interest in the public service role of higher education, it is more important than ever to understand the dimensions of the external service role. If faculty and graduate students are to participate in external service, they need to have a better sense of what it is and how it is carried out through the faculty role.

The first step in defining the external service role is acknowledgment that it exists; the next is clarifying the terminology associated with external service. Lynton (1995) defined *professional service* as "work by faculty members based on their scholarly expertise and contributing to the mission of the institution" (p. 1). This definition assumes an outreach mission for higher education, because it is through professional service that faculty enact and realize; the outreach mission of their institutions. Public service, outreach, and engagement are all terms used to refer to different aspects of campus and community partnership and the ways the campuses extend their resources to meet the needs of the community (Ward & Moore, in press). That is, campuses serve their public, reach out to the community, and engage in the community. Regardless of the terminology, the service aspect of the higher education mission conveys connections between the knowledge and resources of the campuses and the needs of society. Given the current emphasis on public service and community engagement on many campuses, it is a topic that, in the words of Eugene Rice, has "soared to rhetorical heights" (as cited in Sandmann & Weerts, 2006, p. 182).

How is the service mission of the campus carried out by faculty? External service is not necessarily a stand-alone role for faculty in the same way as teaching or research. External service can be tied to teaching (e.g., service learning) and research (e.g., community-based research). One of the issues with ongoing integration of engagement is the continuing need to articulate what it means for faculty to do service and how that service intersects with the traditional tripartite faculty roles.

The original impetus for broadening understanding of faculty external service roles comes from Boyer (1990), who sought to expand the definition of scholarship to include more than traditional research. Boyer articulated four different types of scholarship: discovery, integration, application, and teaching. These categories transcend the traditional roles of teaching, research, and service by demonstrating that the four functions of scholarship he proposed are equally associated with research, teaching, or service. Boyer (1996) proposed a fifth function of scholarship: engagement. He called specifically for the harnessing of institutional resources to address issues and opportunities facing communities. Continued attention to what it means for faculty to be of service and what it means to engage is necessary to highlight the ways faculty can be scholarly and engaged with the community. Engagement as a form of faculty service is not so much about faculty doing more work in the service category as it is about working differently, thinking about how teaching and research may be used to connect with and serve communities outside of campus (Ward, 2003; Ward & Moore, in press).

An element of faculty involvement in external service that is often overlooked in higher education is consulting (Ward, Toma, & Gardner, 2004). Faculty involvement in consulting plays a key role in extending disciplinary-specific knowledge and expertise to corporate or community clients. The consulting activity of faculty falls under the rubric of external service and helps to support campus outreach and engagement missions by linking faculty expertise with community needs. The agricultural economics professor who meets with local farmers to talk about the economic benefits of new production techniques based on his or her research findings is meeting an important public service need and extending disciplinary expertise beyond the campus. In some fields, presentations to local and state government provide opportunities to extend faculty expertise into the realm of public policy and community decision making.

The Ph.D. is a research degree, and programs tend to emphasize research to the exclusion of other skills and abilities needed in the faculty role (Gaff, 2002; Golde & Dore, 2001; Walker et al., 2008), particularly its service aspect. Graduate students observe faculty teaching, they often see faculty researching or at least presenting the outcomes of their research (through journal articles or presentations), but the activities that faculty members engage in as part of their service responsibilities are not always apparent or transparent to their students. The holistic development of graduate students requires preparing students for all elements of the faculty career.

The Difference That Difference Makes

All faculty members encounter the aspects of the service role to a greater or lesser extent. There are two factors that often affect the way that faculty experience and enact their service roles—institutional type and demographic characteristics—that merit additional consideration here. How does institutional setting shape faculty involvement in service? How do personal characteristics influence faculty involvement in service?

Institutional Type

The mission and culture of an institution shape service expectations for faculty in particular contexts. Much faculty work is driven by the mission of an institution, yet often conversations about topics related to graduate student socialization and faculty work neglect consideration and analysis of institutional type. Doctoral education takes place in research universities, so frequently topics concerning graduate socialization are discussed using the research university as a frame of reference, even though many students will not attain faculty positions at research institutions (Austin & McDaniels, 2006; Gaff, 2002; Golde & Dore, 2001; Walker et al., 2008). Graduate students pursuing faculty careers may find themselves working at research universities, but they might also find positions at comprehensive universities, liberal arts institutions, or community colleges. Each context offers a different palette of service roles.

The community college setting tends to emphasize meeting local needs through workforce development and responsive curricular offerings (Austin & McDaniels, 2006) that are based on local community needs. The mission focus of the community college is teaching. The service role for faculty has two areas of emphasis. External service roles are manifest through faculty involvement in creating connections for workforce development (e.g., establishing partnerships with local industry) and, increasingly, service learning (Elsner, 2000). The internal service roles of community college faculty are shaped by the large number of part-time and adjunct faculty, who generally have limited involvement in campus service, leaving full-time faculty to take on additional responsibilities. In addition, these campuses often feature a managerial culture where administrators take a central role in decision making (Clark, 1987).

Liberal arts colleges are committed to undergraduate education, and faculty in these institutions maintain a focus on teaching and learning. The external role of service for faculty in the liberal arts college setting can be shaped by the small size and regional orientation of the campuses. Many liberal arts college campuses are located in small communities that create natural opportunities for faculty to work with students through research and teaching in community contexts (Prince, 2000). The internal service role of faculty in the liberal arts college is shaped by a collegial culture where faculty and administrators work together to create institutional policy (Tierney & Bensimon, 1996). Furthermore, the small size of many liberal arts colleges typically means that faculty work together in small units related to their specialization, which, in turn, can require more involvement in administrative service to support their disciplinary area.

Comprehensive colleges and universities have a strong commitment to their particular regions and their particular place in the community (Moore, 2008; Ramaley, 2000). Faculty involvement in external service, similar to the community college, is often related to workforce and community development. True to their name, comprehensive colleges provide a comprehensive education at the baccalaureate and master's level. For faculty, this can mean an internal service role that includes involvement in academic decision making at the departmental and campus levels.

The research university is a setting where knowledge production and discovery are a priority, but where teaching and outreach are also part of the culture (Austin & McDaniels, 2006). Faculty in the research university setting can find themselves challenged to manage the tensions between teaching, research, and service. The external service role for faculty in research universities is often ambiguous. Research universities have played a leadership role in calling for increased connection between campus and community (Checkoway, 2001), but for the faculty members on those particular campuses it is not always clear how to reconcile requests for increased involvement in external service and calls to be productive in the research arena and to maintain effectiveness in the classroom. The internal service role for faculty at research universities is marked by involvement in institutional decision making and shared governance. However, internal service involvement tends to be an activity that evolves with the development of the career. Junior faculty members are expected to limit involvement in service so they can establish themselves as scholars, with service being more prevalent after tenure (Neumann & LaPointe Terosky, 2007).

Where a faculty member works, including the type of institution, its location, and its level of prestige, can vary the service roles expected of faculty. As graduate students, and the faculty members who advise them, think about the faculty career, it is important to be cognizant of the different expectations for faculty work that exist in different types of institutional settings (Austin & McDaniels, 2006).

Personal Characteristics

Another area of difference to consider in any discussion of service (internal and external) is how personal characteristics shape involvement in service. Research findings related to different aspects of faculty life indicate that service roles vary depending on variables such as race/ethnicity and gender (Baez, 2000; Tierney & Bensimon, 1996). As campuses strive to diversify student and faculty ranks, faculty members from underrepresented racial and ethnic backgrounds and female faculty in disciplines that are traditionally male-dominated (e.g., engineering) can be asked to take on internal service responsibilities to "represent their group" on committees or service initiatives. For example, if a search committee wants to increase diversity with a new hire, it makes sense to have a search committee that is composed of a diverse faculty. This poses a challenge for the faculty member who is "the only one"; not only is the individual asked to represent his or her specialty, but the faculty member is also called on frequently to represent the racial/ethnic group and/or gender on campus and disciplinary committees. This type of representative service is not experienced the same by all faculty and creates a hidden workload (Kolodny, 1998) and form of cultural taxation (Padilla, 1994) for underrepresented faculty.

There is a tension here for new faculty. On the one hand, female faculty and faculty of color are often called to academic work based on their convictions to create more equitable educational environments and involvement in service is one way to play a role in creating change (Baez, 2000; Winkle-Wagner, Johnson, Morelon-Quanoo, & Santiague, chapter 9). On the other hand, service, regardless of institutional type, tends not to be rewarded to the same extent as teaching and research, leaving the faculty member who becomes overinvolved in service behind when it comes time for annual reviews and promotion and tenure (Fairweather, 1996; Tierney & Bensimon, 1996). This aspect of faculty life can be vexing for graduate students considering an academic career. Delineating how much service is too much service can be a challenge for underrepresented faculty who want to be a contributing member to their campus and their racial/gender community and to be successful as a faculty member (Winkle-Wagner et al., chapter 9).

The component of external service for minority faculty can pose similar challenges. Research suggests that female faculty and faculty of color are more involved in community service learning and community-based scholarship (Antonio, Astin, & Cress, 2000; O'Meara, 2002). As campuses focus more on their outreach missions, faculty work in the community is often high-lighted, but there is concern, especially in research universities, that faculty involvement in external service activities can jeopardize research productivity (Moore & Ward, 2008). As with internal service and faculty desire to create more diversity on campus, there is a similar challenge for minority faculty hoping to support their external communities. Faculty of color are sometimes called upon to support issues and concerns for communities of color (on-campus and off-campus), and they need to do so in ways that are consistent with their values and consistent with campus expectations for productivity.

As graduate students think about academic careers they need to be aware of the tensions that can be created by wanting to be involved in different elements of the life of the mind, the life of the campus, and the life of the community beyond the campus. Awareness of demographic differences and how they can shape involvement in service is important for all faculty to consider. Faculty who are White and male tend not to be called on to represent their ethnicity or their gender in the same ways as faculty of color or female faculty. It is just as important for a senior White male or female faculty member to be aware of how personal characteristics shape different aspects of faculty life, just as it is important for a junior African American female to be aware of how these characteristics privilege some and challenge others when it comes to managing workload and service responsibilities.

Institutional type and demographics are highlighted here because these are important variables that shape involvement in service, especially in the early stages of the faculty career, and they are important considerations for prospective faculty. Stage in career and discipline can also shape faculty in-volvement in service. Typically, faculty who are more established in their careers become more involved in service, and this is something faculty need to be aware of as their careers evolve (Neumann & LaPointe Terosky, 2007). Discipline can also shape involvement in service, as particular disciplines (e.g., social work, education) have more of a community orientation and thus call on faculty members to be more involved in initiatives involving external service. Many different concerns influence what faculty do, both on a day-to-day and career-long basis (Diamond, 1999), and graduate students are not always aware of these factors and how they shape the faculty career. Efforts to socialize graduate students to the academic profession need to be mindful how context, personal characteristics, discipline, and stage of career shape faculty career development.

The goal of this chapter has been to highlight how the service role is manifest in higher education and how different variables influence involvement in service internal and external to the campus. Recommendations follow to help graduate students and the faculty and administrators who support them to think about graduate socialization and preparation to take on the service aspect of faculty life.

Graduate Students and Service: Recommendations for Practice

Create campus level workshops or classes that focus on faculty life and faculty development for graduate students from all disciplines to learn more about the specifics of faculty life. Topics to include in these workshops related to service include the following:[2]

- Institutional type. Invite faculty who work at different types of institutions to talk about their service role and how it is incorporated into their faculty life in their particular campus setting. Provide opportunities for students to visit other types of campuses to see firsthand how this is done.
- Civic involvement. Present topics related to faculty work in the community and the civic mission of higher education. Invite faculty who do work in the community to present their work and how it is related to their teaching, research, and service.
- Documentation of service. Provide examples of how faculty document their work. Often faculty have very complex and integrated careers, but graduate students see only a glimpse of what it is that faculty do.

Workshops or class sessions can include specific examples of faculty vitae to see how faculty represent their internal and external service.
- Reward structures. Review examples of faculty handbooks and promotion and tenure guidelines from different institutions and disciplines, so graduate students can see the specifics of faculty work and how service is part of it.

Incorporate topics related to faculty development and the transition to the faculty career into departmental (or college) graduate colloquia, seminars, or orientations, so students can learn about the nuances of faculty life in particular disciplines. Suggestions for sessions include the following:

- Faculty examples. Faculty presenting their research that ties with community needs in the same way they would present a research seminar. If no faculty member in the department integrates the research with community issues, invite faculty from outside campus to present.
- Successful faculty. Recently tenured or promoted faculty presenting their dossier, so students can see how successful faculty represent their work (including service).
- Personal characteristics. Topics related to personal characteristics (gender, race/ethnicity) and how they shape faculty work in a particular discipline and specific examples of how faculty members have navigated the service aspect of their careers. If there are no faculty of color or female faculty who can speak to these issues, invite someone from another campus or a related discipline.

Encourage faculty to make the service aspect of their work transparent so graduate students can see what is involved in external and internal service. This can be done by

- appointing students to departmental, college, campus, and disciplinary committees. The nature of some committees (e.g., admissions) precludes student involvement, but other types of committees (e.g., curriculum revision, conference planning) could benefit from a student perspective. Such service would provide a student voice and let students see firsthand what is involved in internal service.

- encouraging involvement in disciplinary associations/meetings. Many associations have opportunities for graduate students to participate. Share these opportunities with students, encourage them to participate, and support them to do so.

Include topics related to service in mentoring and advising sessions between faculty and graduate students. Topics to include are as follows:

- Incorporating service into a work plan. Encourage frank discussions between faculty and graduate students (and between junior and senior colleagues) about how to be a contributing member of the unit, participate in the community, and succeed as a faculty member.
- Discussing what it means to "just say no." Faculty and graduate students are frequently advised to "learn how to say no" to succeed, yet this advice is not always realistic or easily applied. Graduate students and their advisors can gain from having conversations about service and what role service plays in career development.
- Document review. Detailed review of the curriculum vitae and dossier, so graduate students can see the complexity of the faculty career, how service is part of faculty life, and how it is documented.

Conclusion

Faculty involvement in service is important to help institutions to maintain vitality and to help campuses meet their societal obligations. Without faculty involvement in decision making and shared governance through internal service, campuses would be one-dimensional and lacking multiple perspectives. Campuses need the participation of faculty to be fit and functional to meet the needs of students, to create and disseminate knowledge, and to meet community needs. Faculty involvement in external service activities plays a key role in meeting community needs and realizing the public service and engagement missions of their campuses. In spite of their importance to the health and vitality of the academic profession and to colleges and universities, faculty service roles are often overlooked and ill defined.

If new cohorts of faculty are to take on their faculty roles with an awareness of what will be involved in their career choice, graduate student educators need to be attentive to all aspects of the academic career—teaching, research, *and* service. Graduate students need to understand the dynamic and creative tensions and rewards that come from developing and maintaining an integrated view of the faculty career that involves service to the campus and profession as well as service to the communities beyond the campus.

Notes

1. I use my work from the monograph Ward, K. (2003). *Faculty service roles and the scholarship of engagement*. San Francisco: Jossey-Bass, as the basis for the discussion about internal and external service roles.
2. The materials available from the Preparing Future Faculty program are a great resource to utilize for campuses moving in this direction (see http://www.preparing-faculty.org/ for more information).

References

Antonio, A. L., Astin, H. S., & Cress, C. M. (2000). Community service in higher education: A look at the nation's faculty. *Review of Higher Education, 23,* 373–397.

Austin, A., & McDaniels, M. (2006). Preparing the professoriate of the future: Graduate student socialization for faculty roles. In J. Smart (Ed.), *Higher education: Handbook of theory and research* (Vol. XXI, pp. 397–456). New York: Agathon.

Baez, B. (2000). Race-related service and faculty of color: Conceptualizing critical agency in academe. *Higher Education, 39,* 363–391.

Berberet, J. (2002). The new academic compact. In L. A. McMillin & J. Berberet (Eds.), *The new academic compact: Revisioning the relationship between faculty and their institutions* (pp. 3–28). Boston: Anker.

Boyer, E. (1990). *Scholarship reconsidered: Priorities of the professoriate.* Princeton, NJ: Carnegie Foundation for the Advancement of Teaching.

Boyer, E. L. (1996). The scholarship of engagement. *Journal of Public Service and Outreach, 1,* 11–20.

Burgan, M. (1998). Academic citizenship: A fading vision. *Liberal Education, 84*(4), 16–21.

Checkoway, B. (2001). Renewing the civic mission of the American Research University. The Journal of Higher Education, *72,* 125–147

Clark, B. R. (1987). *The academic life: Small worlds, different worlds.* Princeton, NJ: Carnegie Foundation for the Advancement of Teaching.

Colbeck, C. L., O'Meara, K., & Austin, A. E. (2008). Educating integrated professionals: Theory and practice on preparation for the professoriate. In *New directions for teaching and learning* (pp. 113). San Francisco: Jossey-Bass.

Diamond, R. M. (1999). *Aligning faculty rewards with institutional mission: Statements, policies and guidelines.* Boston: Anker.

Elsner, P. A. (2000). A community college perspective. In T. Ehrlich (Ed.), *Civic responsibility and higher education* (pp. 211–226). Phoenix, AZ: The Oryx Press.

Fairweather, J. S. (1996). *Faculty work and public trust: Restoring the value of teaching and public service in American academic life.* Boston: Allyn and Bacon.

Fear, F. A., & Sandmann, L. R. (1995). Unpacking the service category: Reconceptualizing university outreach for the 21st century. *Continuing Higher Education Review, 59,* 110–122.

Finsen, L. (2002). Faculty as institutional citizens: Reconvening service and governance work. In L. A. McMillin & J. Berberet (Eds.), *The new academic compact: Revisioning the relationship between faculty and their institutions* (pp. 61–86). Boston: Anker.

Gaff, G. (2002). The disconnect between graduate education and faculty realities: A review of recent research. *Liberal Education, 88,* 6–12.

Golde, C. M., & Dore, T. M. (2001). *At cross purposes: What the experiences of doctoral students reveal about doctoral education* (www.phd-survey.org). Philadelphia: A report prepared for The Pew Charitable Trusts.

Kerr, C. (1963). *The uses of the university.* Cambridge, MA: Harvard.

Kezar, A. J., Chambers, T. C., & Burkhardt, J. C. (2005). *Higher education for the public good.* San Francisco: Jossey-Bass.

Kolodny, A. (1998). *Failing the future: A dean looks at higher education in the twenty-first century.* Durham, NC: Duke University.

Lynton, E. A. (1995). *Making the case for professional service.* Washington, DC: AAHE.

Moore, T. L. (2008). *Placing engagement: Critical readings of interaction between regional communities and comprehensive universities.* Unpublished doctoral dissertation. Washington State University, Pullman, WA.

Moore, T. L., & Ward, K. A. (2008). Documenting engagement: Faculty perspectives on self-representation for promotion and tenure. *Journal of Higher Education Outreach and Engagement, 12,* 5–27.

Neumann, A., & LaPointe Terosky, A. (2007). To give and to receive: Recently tenured professors' experience of service. *Journal of Higher Education, 78,* 282–310.

O'Meara, K. A. (1997). *Rewarding faculty professional service.* New England Resource Center for Higher Education (NERCHE), Working Paper 19. Boston: NERCHE.

O'Meara, K. A. (2007). *Graduate education and civic education.* New England Resource Center for Higher Education (NERCHE), Policy Brief 20. Boston: NERCHE.

Padilla, A. M. (1994). Ethnic minority scholars, research, and mentoring: Current and future issues. *Educational Researcher, 23,* 24–27.

Plater, W. M. (2008). The twenty-first century professoriate: We need a new vision if we want to create a positive future for the faculty. *Academe, 94*(4), 2–12.

Potts, D. B. (1977). 'College enthusiasm!' as public response: 1800–1860. *Harvard Educational Review, 47*(1), 28–42.

Prince, G. S., Jr. (2000). A liberal arts college perspective. In T. Ehrlich (Ed.), *Civic responsibility and higher education* (pp. 249–262). Phoenix, AX: Oryx Press.

Ramaley, J. A. (2000). The perspective of a comprehensive university. In T. Ehrlich (Ed.), *Civic responsibility and higher education* (pp. 227–248). Phoenix, AZ: Oryx Press.

Tierney, W. G., & Bensimon, E. M. (1996). *Promotion and tenure: Community and socialization in academe.* Albany, NY: SUNY Press.

Veysey, L. R. (1965). *The emergence of the American university.* Chicago, IL: University of Chicago.

Walker, G. E., Golde, C. M., Jones, L., Conklin Bueschel, A., & Hutchings, P. (2008). *The formation of scholars: Rethinking doctoral education for the twenty-first century.* San Francisco: Jossey-Bass.

Ward, K. (2003). *Faculty service roles and the scholarship of engagement.* San Francisco: Jossey-Bass.

Ward, K. & Moore, T. (in press). Defining the engagement in the scholarship of engagement. *Handbook of engagement.* Lansing: Michigan State University.

Ward, K., Toma, D., & Gardner, S. K. (2004). *Faculty as consultants: Private gain or public good?* Paper presented at the annual meeting of the American Education Research Association. San Diego, CA.

Weerts, D. J., & Sandmann, L. R. (2008). Building a two-way street: Challenges and opportunities for community engagement at research universities. *Review of Higher Education, 32*, 73–106.

PART THREE

CONTEXTUALIZING SOCIALIZATION

4

ENTERING DIFFERENT WORLDS

Socialization Into Disciplinary Communities

Chris Golde

There is no more stunning fact about the academic profession anywhere in the world than the simple one that academics are possessed by disciplines, fields of study, even as they are located in institutions.

Burton Clark (1987, p. 25)

When their mutual friend Chris comes to town, Nate and Jennifer, both fourth-year doctoral students at Prestige University, meet for dinner. The three were undergraduates at the same college, and Nate and Jennifer both came to Prestige University to pursue Ph.D.s. Chris initially assumes that their experience as graduate students must be nearly identical, since they are students at the same university, but over the course of dinner they discover how different their lives in graduate school actually are. What accounts for this? One thing more than any other: Nate is a chemist and Jennifer is in the English department.

Nate recounts how thrilled he was when Professor Green agreed to take him into his organic chemistry group. Despite having what he thought was a strong undergraduate preparation, including two summers working in a lab, Nate confesses that he felt completely unprepared once he started graduate school. He had to work much harder than expected just to get average grades. Recalling his first year in graduate school, Nate tells Chris and Jennifer about his first (rather

79

unsuccessful) efforts to learn the experimental techniques used in the Green lab. One of the postdocs took Nate under her wing and coached him on the techniques and conventions of the group. For example, Professor Green had definite ideas how each student in the lab should be presenting work and giving each other feedback.

Nate confides that it took nearly a year for him to get the hang of his weekly meetings with Professor Green. "I just couldn't figure out how to prepare. Now I know that he wants a one-page summary of the experiments conducted in the last week and three or four suggestions for what I plan to accomplish in the next week. Together, we refine that plan, which forms the basis for my report the following week. It has certainly taught me to keep making research progress."

Hearing this, Jennifer is stunned. "You mean to tell me that you meet alone with your advisor on a weekly basis in addition to weekly group meetings, and that you've been doing this since you started graduate school?" When Chris asks about Jennifer's relationship with her advisor, Dr. Cook, Jennifer explains that she came to Prestige in part because Dr. Cook was on the faculty, but without any assurance of working with her as an advisee. In fact, there were several other faculty members who also focus on 20th-century U.S. literature with whom Jennifer considered working. During her third year, after her qualifying exam, Jennifer remembers how nervous she was when she approached Professor Cook and asked if she would be Jennifer's advisor. At the same time, Jennifer has composed the rest of her dissertation committee with another English professor and one from the drama department. "I meet with Professor Cook for about an hour two or three times a term, with each other committee member about once a term, and I've met with the entire committee as a group once so far. But unless I have at least 20 pages of new text to give her, which takes me at least two months, my advisor doesn't want to meet with me. And honestly, I don't know what we would talk about."

That is just the start of the conversation. As dinner progresses, it seems like there isn't a single part of their experiences that is similar. Teaching assistantships (Jennifer's experience surpassed Nate's), funding packages, presenting at conferences (Nate had to explain what a scientific poster was), coursework, relationships with the other students who had started when they did—none of them are remotely similar.

Not surprisingly, then, Nate and Jennifer also have different expectations for their futures. Nate is confident that he will be working as a research chemist, but he isn't sure whether he is bound for a job in industry or academia. "Given that my research has biomedical implications, I know I'll be able to find interesting work doing chemistry research. Part of my dilemma is figuring out what I really want to do. I like to teach, but as a research chemist I would spend a lot of my time communicating and selling my work. I'm just not sure I am cut out for the tenure track." Jennifer, on the other hand, yearns for a tenure-track faculty position. But she is not confident that she will get what she wants, despite the fact she will have a degree from Prestige and has gotten a lot of positive response to her work at a recent conference. When Chris asks what she would do if, given the economic downturn, she can't find a faculty position, she simply looks anguished. She confesses, "I have no idea. I really don't feel like I know how to do anything but be an English professor—spending my life teaching literature and writing books."

By the time dinner is over, Jennifer and Nate feel like they are two alien species inhabiting two different planets. Chris can't believe that their offices are actually located in neighboring buildings. The only thing they do have in common is that they both believe that they are getting a great education. Compared with other graduate students they know at other universities, both feel they are well on the way to being a full-fledged chemist and English professor, respectively.

This fictional account tries to illustrate a few of the ways in which doctoral programs are structured differently in different fields and how those structures both reflect and reinforce expectations and norms for how to be a productive member of a professional community. In other words, throughout their graduate programs doctoral students are socialized into being disciplinary professionals. And their view of the discipline and disciplinary competence is shaped by the experiences they have and the people they learn from.

Earlier chapters in this book have described how doctoral students are socialized into faculty roles and expectations in the arenas of teaching (see McDaniels, chapter 1), research (see Weidman, chapter 2), and service (see Ward, chapter 3). This chapter takes an orthogonal perspective, describing how graduate students become members of disciplinary communities, regardless of their career goals or destinations. Each of these communities has its own particular expectations for what it means to engage in teaching, research, service, and other components of professional life, whether inside or out of the academy. Regardless of the career path chosen by each student, in a well-structured doctoral program all students should be well socialized into the professional habits, norms, and practices characteristic of that field. (As other chapters in this book explore, a student's experiences, identity, and preexisting values interact to influence their reaction to their educational experiences. As a result, some students may adopt the normative values and behaviors more readily than do others.)

The next section of this chapter provides an overview of the ideas of disciplinary expertise and doctoral education, and the connection between them offered by socialization theory. The chapter concludes by returning to Nate and Jennifer and explaining their different experiences.

Conceptual Underpinnings

Academic disciplines have been defined as "a body of knowledge with a reasonably logical taxonomy, a specialized vocabulary, an accepted body of theory, systematic research strategy, and techniques for replication and validation" (Donald, 2002, p. 8). In addition to organizing and delineating bodies of knowledge, they are the primary organizing structure, along with institutional homes, that define the life of practicing academics. In fact, for many, disciplinary allegiances trump institutional affiliation (Clark, 1987).

As several researchers have demonstrated, disciplinary communities are complex social organizations (e.g., Becher, 1989; Becher & Trowler, 2001; Donald, 2002; Parry, 2007). They are distinct from one another. The knowledge, skills, and habits of mind expected of members in the disciplinary guild of historians are like those of other historians (for an excellent analysis, see Cronon, 2006) but are quite different from those of mathematicians, and both are quite different from those of neuroscientists. (Of course, various subfields have specific knowledge requirements, but broadly speaking, there are "shared ways of asking questions, interacting with each other and making sense of the world" (Cronon, 2006, p. 330).) Each field has its own "habits and practices;" they are quite "different worlds" (Clark, 1987, pp. 25, 44). In order to be a fully accepted member of a disciplinary community, disciplinary experts must possess more than content knowledge. "*Being* a member of the disciplinary community," said Becher and Trowler (2001), "involves a sense of identity and personal commitment, a 'way of being in the world,' a matter of taking on 'a cultural frame the defines a great part of one's life'" (p. 47, quoting Geertz). So, logically, *becoming* a member of a disciplinary community requires learning how to think and act like a member.

Socialization theory can be applied to many organizational contexts, but this book focuses on the process (how) and outcomes (for what) of doctoral student socialization. *Socialization* is the "process through which

2nd definition of socialization

newcomers learn to fit an expected role and pattern of behavior" (Austin & McDaniels, 2006, p. 400). The outcome of socialization is "identification with and commitment to a professional role" (p. 399).

The outcome of this learning process is professional competence and confidence. Proficient members of disciplinary communities, competent professionals, have learned how to think like a member of the discipline, have developed technical proficiency in research and teaching, and have adopted the beliefs and attitudes of experts. Experts are able to ask important questions, to competently conduct research, to assess others' work, to understand the important ideas of their field, to communicate what they know, and to apply their knowledge and understanding to solve important problems. This bundle of knowledge and skills was dubbed developing into a "steward of the discipline" by the Carnegie Initiative on the Doctorate (Golde, 2006, pp. 9–14). Expertise also requires facility with the tacit understandings, habits, and beliefs that underlie expert practice. This sort of savvy entails, for example, knowing how to talk in different settings (in a classroom or at a disciplinary conference or with classmates) and when to deploy each speaking style (Gerholm, 1990).

Learning any complex practice—such as becoming a midwife, tailor, physician, or historian—requires more than book learning. In general, those joining a community of practice must have many opportunities to actually try to do the work in real-world settings, and then get feedback from those more expert. This sort of learning, situated in settings of authentic practice, has been called *legitimate peripheral participation*. This term calls attention to the processes through which novices slowly develop the expertise necessary to become full participants in their community of practice. This sort of learning requires access to "a wide range of ongoing activity, old-timers, . . . information, resources, and opportunities for participation" (Lave & Wenger, 1991, p. 101).

For the purposes of joining a disciplinary community, the critical induction phase is the doctoral program. This is the training period during which novices become immersed in the formal procedures and informal customs of the intellectual community (Parry, 2007, p. 39). Doctoral education is a quintessential form of legitimate peripheral participation, and it differs from other forms of schooling that precede it. Learning is no longer classroom-centered. The development of doctoral students as researchers often relies on apprenticeship-learning principles. Advanced graduate students, Brown, Collins, and Duguid (1989) observed,

Acquire their extremely refined research skills during the apprenticeships they serve with senior researchers. It is then that they, like all apprentices, must recognize and resolve the ill-defined problems that issue out of authentic activity, in contrast to the well-defined exercises that are typically given to them in textbooks and on exams throughout their earlier schooling. It is at this stage, in short, that students no longer behave as students, but as practitioners, and develop their conceptual understanding through social interaction and collaboration in the culture of domain, not of the school. (p. 40)

This happens through immersion in the actual work of knowledge production and transmission—in the lab, the classroom, the library, the archive, the field site, departmental seminars, and professional conferences. Learning by doing is well suited to adult learners (see Kasworm & Bowles, chapter 11). It also has the benefit of teaching the culture. "By immersing doctoral students in the process of knowledge production, supervisors also immerse them in the dominant values and attitudes of specific disciplinary fields" (Parry, 2007, p. 56).

Doctoral study takes place over an extended period of time and allows apprentices (graduate students) to learn about membership in the community, what members do, what their everyday lives are like, and "what learners need to learn to become full practitioners" (Lave & Wenger, 1991, p. 95). Graduate school provides a setting in which graduate students have access to masters (faculty members), finished products (completed research projects, well-taught classes), and more advanced apprentices (other graduate students).

So, what are the salient features of doctoral education that contribute to the development of disciplinary expertise? Arguably, most of the experiences that a student has while enrolled in the program contribute to identity development. The formal requirements and curriculum have certainly been structured to teach necessary disciplinary content knowledge and skills. For most doctoral programs these requirements include coursework, candidacy or qualifying examinations, teaching requirements (in many, but not all departments), and independent research project(s) culminating in the written dissertation. In addition, much of the learning in doctoral programs takes place in activities that do not resemble formal schooling but in which students are generally expected to participate. Examples include participating in departmental seminars, reading leading journals, attending conferences, writing grants, making presentations, asking questions, and mentoring the next generation of students. Many of the experiences, again, are adapted to the dictates of the field. Students may learn the most of all in one-on-one or small group settings where feedback is provided and advice is given: with the faculty advisor, with other faculty members, in lab group meetings, with more advanced students, and with other scholars beyond the confines of campus.

Connecting these two ideas—disciplinary communities are distinct cultures and one learns to be a disciplinary expert through doctoral study—leads to the conclusion that strategies for socialization must of necessity be different in each field in order to inculcate different habits and skills. The normative doctoral student experience is different from field to field but is similar within a field. There are similarities within an area: humanities students share some common experiences, but philosophers and historians will also have some different experiences. Of course, there are differences across programs, and indeed, among individual students. Nevertheless, a common disciplinary identity—that which makes a chemist a chemist and distinguishes a chemist from a physicist or a biologist or an historian—is forged during doctoral studies.

The argument of this chapter is this: within a given discipline most doctoral programs in the United States bear striking resemblance to one another, they are distinct from those in other fields, and these normative ways of structuring a doctoral program in a given field teach proficiency in disciplinary practice. In other words, the prevalent educational experiences in each discipline are not randomly occurring or haphazardly selected; instead, they are reasonable and pedagogically sound mechanisms to meet the desired outcome of developing disciplinary expertise, in all of its complexity.

Specifics and Examples

Returning now to the example of Nate and Jennifer, I will touch briefly on a few elements of each of their doctoral programs and show how these features prepare each of them for their future professional lives. I am restricting my discussion to a few elements related to the research enterprise and scholarly discourse. (A more comprehensive description would require a thorough ethnographic analysis.) I refer readers who are interested in this topic to the work of Sharon Parry (2007). I selected chemistry and English because these are two disciplines with which I am very familiar. Doctoral students in both disciplines were included in the Survey of Doctoral Student Experience and Career Preparation (hereafter DSECP) conducted in 1999 and funded by The Pew Charitable Trusts (Golde & Dore, 2001, 2004). Both disciplines were part of the Carnegie Initiative on the Doctorate (CID); they were featured in a book of commissioned essays on the future of doctoral education (Golde & Walker, 2006), and faculty and students in CID-participating departments were surveyed as part of the CID (Walker, Golde, Jones, Bueschel, & Hutchings, 2008). Readers will recognize that many of the features of Nate's chemistry doctoral program are similar to those of other laboratory sciences, and likewise Jennifer's experiences echo those in other humanities fields.

What does it mean to be a chemist or an English scholar?

What are these lives to which Nate and Jennifer

Chemistry, often called "the central science," is the atom-level view of matter. Chemistry involves making molecules, measuring their properties, and modeling their features and uses. The discipline has a practical bent and is connected to the chemical sciences industry. Knowledge advances incrementally through experiment; each small study builds on ones that came before. Knowledge building is also competitive, as researchers in other labs are working on the same set of questions; success demands speed, accuracy, and beating others to the punch.

Chemistry research is conducted in a team-oriented, laboratory-based setting. Labs typically have 6–20 members, faculty members, postdoctoral scholars, graduate students, technicians, and perhaps undergraduates. Most Ph.D. chemists work in industry, not academia: nearly 60% in industry, 33% in academia, and about 5% in government (American Chemical Society, 2002). The academic research enterprise is funded by research grants from federal and industry sources, and most faculty members spend much of their time in pursuit of grants to further their research and fund the students, staff, and expenses for their labs.

English studies is one of the classic liberal arts and is generally practiced only in academic settings. It embraces the study of the English language and literature of the English-speaking world. It is a relatively solitary scholarly pursuit that relies upon writing, reading, and interpretation to illuminate the human condition. "Good work in the humanities is judged by its completeness, subtlety, and insight. Doing work quickly, beating others to the punch, is less important than getting it right and being thorough. The humanities emphasize the written word, so scholars value nuance and elaboration" (Golde, 2007b, p. 348).

Nearly all of the professional work of English scholars involves either teaching or writing. Engendering in others a love for literature and the written word is an important mission for most English scholars. Likewise, teaching others to write and communicate clearly is part and parcel of the work of the field. Doctoral study in English is geared to the preparation of future faculty, and the majority of Ph.D. recipients can expect a faculty position, although it may not be on the tenure track (MLA Ad Hoc Committee on the Professionalization of PhDs, 2002; Modern Language Association, 2003).

Keeping these outcomes in mind, I will now describe a few features of a typical chemistry and English graduate program and explain how they help prepare students for disciplinary practice. At the same time, the contrasts between disciplines are intended to make the case that fields differ both in their professional practice and, thus by necessity, their professional preparation.

Dissertations

Today, most dissertations take one of two common forms, either the single study book or the multi-paper compilation (Lovitts, 2007, p. 35). The humanities, including English, use the book form, which is well suited to a field in which most scholars are judged by their ability to produce books. Books are the predominant form in fields that allow for a slower research pace in part because there are few instances of direct competition. Scholars are working in their own area, and a scholarly reputation comes from making a contribution that changes the conversation, not from scooping someone else (Parry, 2007, p. 59). Dissertations in English provide an opportunity for students to practice the dominant form of scholarly output under tutored conditions. Under ideal conditions, when a new Ph.D. enters a faculty position, the dissertation will be reworked into a book published by a university press. "Each chapter of the dissertation follows a particular line of thought; taken together, it forms a coherent whole, and the dissertation is, ideally, ultimately published as a book by a university press" (Golde & Walker, 2006, p. 352). Thoroughness, nuance, and completeness of argument are more important than speed. As a result, the fact that it may take a student two to four years to write the dissertation is not problematic.

By the same token, but in a very different way, the dissertation in chemistry also provides apprenticeship in the dominant forms of scientific communication. A dissertation will comprise a set of articles, some of which may have already been published, with the remainder in various stages of the publication pipeline. Most will be co-authored with others from the student's lab and will in all likelihood carry the name of his advisor. The dissertation is likely to include a summarizing or introductory chapter that provides the scientific underpinnings and links the various articles. Collaborative authorship is common in lab sciences, because it accords credit to all of the members of the team. Over time, a student takes greater responsibility for the work, and moves up the authorship ranks. The work for which the student has primary intellectual responsibility will appear in the dissertation. Articles (not books) are the primary form of scholarly communication in the sciences. Articles communicate sufficient information to move the field forward incrementally. And, they have the added advantage of appearing in print quite quickly. So, the dissertation has evolved to reflect what is common and valuable. This is both efficient and teaches how to publish articles, which is a necessary skill. This is why coauthored articles are accepted in dissertations. This system has mutual benefits: the student is linked to the advisor's reputation, which certifies him or her as a rising researcher, and the advisor's vita continues to grow as well.

Topic Identification and Development

Just as Nate and Jennifer's dissertations will have different forms, they each have selected and developed their dissertation topics in a different way. Nate has developed the research projects in his dissertation while working in Professor Green's lab, and in close consultation with Green. The questions and experimental techniques he uses are part of the Green Lab's research aims and approaches. In some measure, the projects in his dissertation will be "his," he will have demonstrated some independence in asking a novel question or mastering a new technique. But his work will be within the boundaries of the research group. In the DSECP, 94% of chemists said that their topic related to their advisor's work and only 43% said that their topic was solely of their own choosing.

This hierarchical dependence on the advisor's line of research, funding, and intellectual expertise is well suited to a system in which research is resource intensive. As a result of being affiliated with a lab, students can embark on only those topics for which the necessary resources can be found. Parry (2007) called this a "production line ethos" and calls attention to the metric of efficiency. "Time is not wasted on topics that do not meet the research aims of the group, or those that cannot be funded" (p. 41). The highly competitive funding environment requires that resources (people, equipment, and chemicals) be prudently allocated in order to maximize results as quickly as possible. Expecting students to work within the parameters of the research group also teaches them how to run a group and how to shape research to the dictates of funders, which they will ultimately be called upon to do in the future. It is impossible to imagine being a chemist without a lab or multiple hands at the bench; even those teaching in small teaching-centered colleges involve undergraduate students as junior researchers. To many students, this university-based federally funded research system feels like indentured servitude: students are apprenticed in a lab and provide highly skilled but poorly compensated labor. The payoff for students is that they learn the ins and outs of lab management; students also get reputational certification. Nate will forever be known as one of Green's students.

Jennifer looks askance at Nate's experience, "No one handed me my topic," she says. In English, a student is expected to develop an original topic and perspective. Their work may well relate to their advisor's scholarship only by century, continent, or genre. Many students struggle to define the topic; in fact, the process of writing a project prospectus (English scholars "work on projects," they do not have "research problems") may take up to a year. One step on the way to defining the project is a comprehensive examination on a foundational "list" of 50–100 works (defined by the student consulting with the faculty committee) that the student has mastered. The examination tests the student's understanding of the evolution of the literature, themes, and ideas; the broad contexts in which works are located; and the theories that motivate analysis. Students are guided at each step by their dissertation committee members who provide feedback on the evolving project. But the intellectual captain is the student; s/he is intellectually quite independent from the faculty. Among respondents to the DSECP, 43% said that their topic related to their advisor's work and a whopping 96% said that their topic was solely of their own choosing.

Students develop a dissertation topic in the same way that faculty members create their projects. An English scholar conceptualizes a new project slowly, enlarging the argument through conference papers and articles over a period of several years until the project comes to fruition. Parry (2007) described this form of scholarly investigation as "highly individualized," requiring "independence of mind from experienced scholars," "often conducted in physical isolation," and notes that it expects "intellectual independence" (p. 41).

The process of preparation for the comprehensive examination is a period of intensive reading and usually stretches over several months, if not an entire year. The experience of list creation, mastery, and examination on it has three well-understood purposes. First and foremost, students must self-define and defend their location in the field. To do so, scholars enter into the discourse and commentaries around the works of literature, which have grown and evolved over time. Mastery of the list(s) is one step along the way toward definition of a professional identity, which has instrumental purposes in terms of getting a job but is more importantly about entering into a disciplinary community. Second, the list and the examination on the list are explicit preparation for the dissertation. Third, the development of the list is intimately related to the ability to teach within a broad swath of the discipline (Golde, 2007a, 2007b). The iterative process of defining and writing a dissertation prospectus, with input from senior faculty members, is a chance for students to engage in authentic practice with some support.

Advising and Dissertation Supervision

The different relationships that Nate and Jennifer have with their advisors should be obvious. Doctoral studies in chemistry exhibit close but hierarchical relationships, whereas in English the relationships are less tightly bound but arguably more collegial. Again, this reflects not only the traditions of the fields but also their demands on faculty members and students.

Chemistry labs are hierarchical environments, with the faculty principal investigator (PI) as the head. Indeed, most chemistry students refer to their advisor as "my boss." In the CID survey, 65% of chemistry students said that they had one faculty mentor or advisor, and 21% identified two (Walker et al., 2008, p. 95). Nevertheless, the relationship involves close collaboration and regular interactions from the start of graduate studies. Most faculty said that they met with their advisees (those within a year of graduation) either "two to three times a week" (50% of respondents) or "daily" (20%) (Walker et al., 2008, p. 108). Parry (2007) described patterns of relationships in laboratory sciences this way: "meetings with supervisors may be frequent and fairly informal, with students being encouraged to learn from and be responsible to the research groups" (p. 50). There is a premium placed on visibility and presence. Students are expected to be present in the lab every day (and most weekends), to participate in weekly lab meetings, and to report regularly to the PI. Close communication also allows the advisor to adjust expectations to changing circumstances, such as an experimental difficulty or dead end, or a personal situation that renders a student less productive for a period of time.

This system of close supervision, more like a workplace than a classroom, is dictated by the research science system. Fast science demands speed and productive output. The advisors' productivity, reputation, and ability to compete for new grants are all bound up in their students' productivity. By the time a student has graduated, the PI (and the university) may well have invested over $100,000 in the student, who was funded on the PI's grant for most of the student's tenure in graduate school. The way science and students are funded closely couples the student and the advisor, and implies ownership of and personal responsibility for what most faculty members call "my students."

Faculty-student relationships in English are likely to be more collegial than hierarchical. Faculty members tend not to supervise student scholarship closely. Instead, faculty take a hands-off posture; they are on call when a student needs advice. English faculty members responding to the CID survey said they typically met monthly with their advisees nearing degree completion (58%), others said "once or twice a term" (19%) or weekly (23%); none selected the more frequent response categories that predominated in chemistry (Walker et al., 2008, p. 108). Most English graduate students draw on a team of advisors; the most prevalent survey response was to identify two (30%) or three (33%) faculty advisors or mentors, and another 14% identified four or more advisors (Walker et al., 2008, p. 95).

This reflects the fact that the faculty members are not intimately familiar with the student's niche of inquiry, since the project is more loosely linked to the advisor's expertise than in chemistry. In addition, these guiding relationships presage professional relationships within the disciplinary community. Scholars are not directly in competition with one another to find answers; instead, they are part of larger scholarly conversations. Productive relationships are marked by supportiveness and by questions springing from curiosity.

Parry (2007) said of research in the humanities, "Ideas may be slow forming and the autonomous nature of research requires strong commitment to the doctoral topic and to its completion, as well as intellectual and emotional support from supervisors" (p. 49).

Conclusion

These three elements of a doctoral program—the dissertation structure, dissertation topic development, and relationships with advisors—are only three of many parts of a program. The foregoing discussion was merely a cursory overview; it does not reflect any of the three in depth. For example, advisor-student relationships change over time. However, these three elements illustrate how the structure and norms of a doctoral program shape doctoral students' disciplinary identities. The entire program and the interactions among the elements, which reinforce each other, exert a powerful socializing force on students. They internalize the norms and the cultural assumptions of expert practitioners. They learn what chemists know, and they learn to do what chemists do. The outcome of a doctoral program should be the facility, comfort, and ability to do and be a member of the disciplinary community. It is intended to move them from students to scholars.

However, there is a shadow side to disciplinary socialization. For one thing, disciplinary perspectives can become disciplinary blinders. Overallegiance to a discipline can make it difficult to embrace new perspectives or ideas that come from other fields. Often the naïve-sounding question coming from nonspecialists can lead to new insights or techniques. Creativity often requires questioning prevailing assumptions or trying something hitherto rejected.

The socialization process can also seem to fail. A large proportion of doctoral students leave before completing the Ph.D. and many of these students leave because they cannot or choose not to meet the expectations of their doctoral program (Golde, 2005; Lovitts, 2001). For example, attritors express varying degrees of dismay and disinclination to assume the life of a research faculty member that they see around them. (Many currently enrolled students share these feelings; (Golde & Dore, 2001).)

One interpretation of attrition is that those who leave were not cut out for the work. Others argue that the organizations (departments and disciplines) themselves should change. Optimistically, theorists contend that as new members enter organizations they help change the communities they join. They maintain that socialization is not solely a one-way process but that students can help reshape their programs, and thereby help change the norms of their discipline (Austin & McDaniels, 2006). This means that students who are underrepresented in the academy (e.g., racial and ethnic minorities, women in STEM fields, working-class students) may be leaders in reshaping the norms of the academy or of their discipline. (See further discussion by Sallee in chapter 7 and Winkle-Wagner et al. in chapter 9.)

However, a strong system of socialization and intergenerational formation is also inherently conservative. Current practices for disciplinary socialization may be maladapted for present or future needs. One place to see the tensions and fault lines is in reports and recommendations for changes in practices of doctoral education. For example, the field of chemistry has struggled with the dominance of the single advisor. On occasion, students can be very badly treated, resulting in disaffection or, more tragically, even suicide (Brennan, 1999; Hall, 1998). It is also alleged that this system does little to spur creativity. Looking within the field for suggestions shows suggestions loosening the dependence of students on one advisor or one line of inquiry (e.g., Moore, 2002; Stacy, 2006). In English, to take another example, it is debated whether students should learn to work in collaborative and interdisciplinary teams (e.g., Lunsford, 2006; MLA Executive Council Task Force on Graduate Education, 1999).

The world around doctoral education may be changing more rapidly than the programs that prepare the next generation are evolving in response (indeed, that was one premise of the recent Carnegie volume by Walker and his colleagues, (2008). It behooves those who administer doctoral programs to be on the lookout for new ideas in an ever-changing environment. Ideas can come from other disciplines, from other departments, or from students.

I have one final thought about disciplinary socialization. It is difficult to imagine doctoral education that is not firmly grounded in a field of study. Generic or homogeneous study at the doctoral level is an inherently inconsistent idea. However, it is possible that the stark disciplinary differences, and the attendant emphasis on the development of a disciplinary identity, may begin to erode a bit in the face of increasingly levels of interdisciplinary inquiry. It is entirely possible that as disciplinary boundaries blur and overlap, that strong disciplinary socialization will come to be seen as doing a disservice to students or even to the future of the discipline.

Note

1. These descriptions are drawn largely from the descriptions of chemistry and English in Golde & Walker, 2006, *Envisioning the future of doctoral education* (pp. 135–139 and 351–355). The citations in those sections provide the underlying data.

References

American Chemical Society. (2002). *Early careers of chemists*. Washington, DC: Author.

Austin, A. E., & McDaniels, M. (2006). Preparing the professoriat of the future: Graduate student socialization for faculty roles. In J. C. Smart (Ed.), *Higher education: Handbook of theory and research* (Vol. XXI, pp. 397–456). The Netherlands: Springer.

Becher, T. (1989). *Academic tribes and territories: Intellectual enquiry and the culture of disciplines*. Stony Stratford, UK: Open University Press.

Becher, T., & Trowler, P. R. (2001). *Academic tribes and territories: Intellectual enquiry and the culture of disciplines* (2nd ed). Buckingham, UK: The Society for Research into Higher Education & Open University Press.

Brennan, M. (1999). Graduate school: Smoothing the passage. *Chemical and Engineering News, 77*, 11–19.

Brown, J. S., Collins, A., & Duguid, P. (1989). Situated cognition and the culture of learning. *Educational Researcher, 18*(1), 35–42.

Clark, B. R. (1987). *The academic life: Small worlds, different worlds*. Princeton, NJ: The Carnegie Foundation for the Advancement of Teaching.

Cronon, W. (2006). Getting ready to do history. In C. M. Golde & G. E. Walker (Eds.), *Envisioning the future of doctoral education: Preparing stewards of the discipline. Carnegie essays on the doctorate* (pp. 327–349). San Francisco: Jossey-Bass.

Donald, J. G. (2002). *Learning to think. Disciplinary perspectives*. San Francisco: Jossey-Bass.

Gerholm, T. (1990). On tacit knowledge in academia. *European Journal of Education, 25*(3), 263–271.

Golde, C. M. (2005). The role of the department and discipline in doctoral student attrition: Lessons from four departments. *Journal of Higher Education, 76*(6), 669–700.

Golde, C. M. (2006). Preparing stewards of the discipline. In C. M. Golde & G. E. Walker (Eds.), *Envisioning the future of doctoral education: Preparing stewards of the discipline. Carnegie essays on the doctorate*. San Francisco: Jossey-Bass.

Golde, C. M. (2007a). Signature pedagogies and disciplinary stewardship: Observations from the Carnegie Initiative on the Doctorate. *ADE Bulletin, 36*(141–142), 16–23.

Golde, C. M. (2007b). Signature practices in doctoral education: Are they adaptable for the preparation of education researchers. *Educational Researcher, 36*(6), 344–351.

Golde, C. M., & Dore, T. M. (2001). *At cross purposes: What the experiences of doctoral students reveal about doctoral education*. Philadelphia, PA: A report for The Pew Charitable Trusts.

Golde, C. M., & Dore, T. M. (2004). The Survey of Doctoral Education and Career Preparation: The Importance of Disciplinary Contexts. In D. H. Wulff & A. E. Austin (Eds.), *Paths to the professoriate: Strategies for enriching the preparation of future faculty* (pp. 19–45). San Francisco: Jossey-Bass.

Golde, C. M., & Walker, G. E. (Eds.). (2006). *Envisioning the future of doctoral education: Preparing stewards of the discipline. Carnegie essays on the doctorate.* San Francisco: Jossey-Bass.

Hall, S. S. (1998, November 29). Lethal chemistry at Harvard. *The New York Times Magazine,* pp. 120–128.

Lave, J., & Wenger, E. (1991). *Situated learning. Legitimate peripheral participation.* Cambridge, UK: Cambridge University Press.

Lovitts, B. E. (2001). *Leaving the ivory tower. The causes and consequences of departure from doctoral study.* New York: Rowman and Littlefield.

Lovitts, B. E. (2007). *Making the implicit explicit: Creating performance expectations for the dissertation.* Sterling, VA: Stylus.

Lunsford, A. A. (2006). Rethinking the Ph.D. in English. In C. M. Golde & G. E. Walker (Eds.), *Envisioning the future of doctoral education: Preparing stewards of the discipline. Carnegie essays on the doctorate* (pp. 357–369). San Francisco: Jossey-Bass.

MLA Ad Hoc Committee on the Professionalization of PhDs. (2002). Professionalization in perspective. *Profession 2002,* 187–210.

MLA Executive Council Task Force on Graduate Education. (1999). Conference on the Future of Doctoral Education. *PMLA, 115*(5), 1136–1278.

Modern Language Association. (2003). 2000–01 survey of PhD placement. Personal correspondence.

Moore, J. (2002). Graduate education. *Journal of Chemical Education, 79*(1), 7.

Parry, S. (2007). *Disciplines and Doctorates.* Dordrecht, The Netherlands: Springer.

Stacy, A. (2006). Training future leaders. In C. M. Golde & G. E. Walker (Eds.), *Envisioning the future of doctoral education: Preparing stewards of the discipline. Carnegie essays on the doctorate* (pp. 187–206). San Francisco: Jossey-Bass.

Walker, G. E., Golde, C. M., Jones, L., Bueschel, A. C., & Hutchings, P. (2008). *The formation of scholars: Rethinking doctoral education for the 21st century.* San Francisco: Jossey-Bass.

5

DOCTORAL STUDENT SOCIALIZATION IN INTERDISCIPLINARY FIELDS

Karri Holley

Ling has a B.S. and an M.S. in Physics. However, most of her peers and professors are engineers and chemists. Thus, although her graduate work in China was in applied physics, she finds it difficult to follow her classmates's and professors's approach to research and academic tasks in general. Not only does she use different terms and nomenclature, but she also tends to be too mathematical and see problems too idealistically when compared to her colleagues. She worries that by trying to catch up with all the different approaches involved in a given problem, she is giving up depth in understanding. Her engineering peers keep telling her, "Don't worry, it doesn't have to be elegant; you don't have to understand it all. What matters is that it works." This is something hard to swallow for a physicist like her.

Nate's advisors call him on a Sunday afternoon to share the great news that they got the multimillion National Science Foundation (NSF) grant to start a neuroscience center with the medical school and a newly formed biotechnology company. His advisor tells him that they need to start right away with the first phase of the project and asks him to become familiar with the articles he just emailed for their meeting on Wednesday. Nate starts reading the articles right away and discovers that he can hardly understand a word. "This is like a different language! How am I supposed to learn how a neuron works in three days?" He goes to the library and starts browsing the neuroscience section and sighs, "These are going to be the three longest days of my life . . ."

Over the last three decades, *interdisciplinary* degree programs have become increasingly commonplace across American colleges and universities (Brint, Turk-Bicakci, Proctor, & Murphy, 2009). Such curricula include self-designed undergraduate courses of study, interdisciplinary master's degree programs planned with a focus on professional development and application, and doctoral education that incorporates coursework from multiple disciplines. For doctoral curricula, the concept of an interdisciplinary program is a paradox within the historical and cultural norms that dominate American higher education. Long considered a disciplinary endeavor, the goal of doctoral education is to produce scholars with an extensive depth of knowledge within a well-defined field of inquiry. By acquiring knowledge of the field and contributing research that furthers the advancement of the discipline, students become members of the disciplinary community (Golde, 2005). In contrast, the goal of interdisciplinary education is to produce scholars capable of engaging with multiple communities of practice. These individuals possess facilities with a range of disciplines, and focus on the integration of knowledge to advance a problem or topic. The challenge of interdisciplinary doctoral education is the balance required between the depth of disciplinary knowledge and the breadth of interdisciplinary engagement.

The interest in interdisciplinary doctoral education can be traced to calls for universities to produce scholars capable of participating in the emergent knowledge-based society (Council of Graduate Schools, 2007). Certainly, a symbiotic connection exists among American graduate education, knowledge production, and social needs. An inherent value to the graduate model is its provision of highly trained experts and leaders in a host of fields. Since the end of the Second World War, the federal government, private foundations, and research universities have invested in doctoral programs to extend economic competitiveness, social advances, and the public good (Geiger, 2004; Kezar, 2004). The rigorous training provided through doctoral education, however, is not always seen as capable of supporting the flexibility and innovation needed for a 21st-century society. A near-universal consensus exists regarding the disparity between the training provided in graduate school and the kinds of future activities in which scholars engage (Austin & McDaniels, 2006; Golde & Dore, 2001). This consensus suggests that the challenges of modern society demand faculty capable of crossing socially constructed disciplinary boundaries in their thinking and application of ideas. The question of *how* to produce interdisciplinary scholars through the existing doctoral model, however, is less clear.

In this chapter, I examine the question of doctoral student socialization in an interdisciplinary field. I begin by briefly outlining the implicit assumptions of disciplinarity that have shaped models of socialization, focusing on the significance of knowledge acquisition, investment, and involvement (Weidman, Twale, & Stein, 2001). I then present a sociocultural perspective regarding the components inherent to interdisciplinary doctoral student socialization. I conclude with examples from doctoral programs in a range of fields that provide implications for interdisciplinary practice.

The Disciplinary Influence on Doctoral Student Socialization

Any discussion of academic knowledge and degree programs must begin with the role of the disciplines (see Golde, chapter 4, for further discussion). I emphasize the role that disciplines play as a key anchor for academic behavior, knowledge production, and institutional logic. "Bodies of knowledge variously determine the behavior of individuals and departments," Clark (1989, p. 4) observed. Areas of disciplinary differentiation are evident in hiring and tenure decisions (Baldi, 1995), communication patterns among scholars (Lee & Bozeman, 2005), patterns of grant funding (Abrams, 1991), engagement in teaching (Neumann, 2001), and the dissemination of research (Cole & Cole, 1973). When examining doctoral student experiences, the question of "socialization to *what?*" is always answered in relation to the disciplinary field of inquiry (Becher & Trowler, 2001). For doctoral students, their experiences in graduate school require the acquisition of formal and tacit knowledge related to disciplinary norms. Doctoral education not only shapes an emerging scholarly identity that differentiates scholars in English from their colleagues in chemistry or engineering but also provides a community of practice that validates knowledge and behavior. Students engage in extensive courses of study, working alongside established faculty scholars and like-minded peers. The traditional view of doctoral education has assumed that, upon degree completion, these students will assume faculty careers, continuing the promulgation of disciplinary behavior (Clark, 1989; Golde, 2005).

Through knowledge acquisition, investment, and involvement, doctoral students develop a commitment to their particular field of practice, and align their work and beliefs in support of this commitment (Weidman et al., 2001).

Knowledge acquisition occurs as students move through the formal doctoral curriculum. The curriculum identifies those concepts, authors, and bodies of literature most salient to the field. The acquisition of specialized knowledge, held by only a few, contributes to the development of a professional identity. Students admitted to a doctoral program in physics may choose to specialize in astrophysics, experimental nuclear/particle physics, atomic physics, or theoretical nuclear/particle physics. Those in astrophysics further specialize in the study of compact objects or cosmology, which is also differentiated by a range of foci: optical, radio, x-ray, and so on. Participation in these small research groups contextualizes the socialization experience and encourages the development of a professional identity (Holley, 2009). The formal curriculum is supplemented by the research experience, where students work closely with a faculty advisor. Tacit, informal knowledge is shaped through interaction with disciplinary peers and other colleagues, all of whom contribute to student understanding of the discipline and the expected role of scholars within it.

Doctoral student investment as part of the socialization process transpires as students commit their time, financial resources, intellectual energies, and alternative career options to graduate education. Moving through the doctoral curriculum, and passing such milestones as qualifying or comprehensive exams, the dissertation proposal, the end of formal coursework, data collection, and the dissertation defense, requires increased responsibility on the part of the student and faculty. "During the informal and personal stages of socialization," Weidman et al. (2001) concluded, "more specialized knowledge is acquired that creates an even greater investment" (p. 17). Investment in the field occurs as students become more involved in the discipline. This involvement is facilitated not only on the departmental and institutional level but also through the network of scholars that comprise the discipline. Increasingly, graduate students are expected to participate in formal acts of knowledge production, such as conference presentations or journal articles. These expectations entail participation in academic meetings and dialogue with journal editors.

The disciplines, of course, should not wholly be viewed as monolithic scholarly communities (Donald, 2002; Lattuca, 2001; Toma, 1997). Disciplines are also defined by the pluralistic diversity of scholarship within their boundaries. Many disciplines overlap with neighboring fields, and scholars can frequently find greater kinship with researchers in other disciplines than their own. Disagreement exists even among those individuals in the same area related to epistemologies, paradigms, or the implications of research. Inquiry paradigms or theoretical models fall in and out of favor with community members. A unique characteristic of the academic discipline is the accepted cultural channels through which members articulate their differences: journal articles, conference presentations, and the like (Hyland, 2004). These channels are normative in nature and provide a point of reference through which scholars can understand and participate in the community. Areas of specialization are many for those affiliated with the field, and although some areas carry more social privilege than others, all coexist within the disciplinary umbrella.

Challenges Related to Doctoral Student Socialization in Interdisciplinary Fields

Since the socialization process for doctoral students is largely experienced as a disciplinary endeavor (Clark, 1989), the question of how to facilitate interdisciplinary socialization is an uncertain one. This uncertainty can in part be attributed to the multiple definitions of the term. In the truest example of *Humpty Dumpty language*, where words can mean only what the speaker intends them to mean, the term *interdisciplinarity* is frequently reduced to a popular catchphrase, synonymous with all things progressive, innovative, and creative. An observer of contemporary U.S. higher education would be hard-pressed to find an institution that is not engaged in some sort of interdisciplinary project, in whatever ways the parameters might be defined. Borrowing from Newell and Green (1982), I consider interdisciplinarity as "inquiries which critically draw upon two or more disciplines and which lead to an integration of disciplinary insights" (p. 23). The process consists not only of the integration of multiple disciplines but also the application of this knowledge toward a shared problem, topic, or theme (Klein, 1990; Lattuca, 2001). While the disciplines can be defined as a body of knowledge or a collection of like-minded scholars, interdisciplinarity is an active, deliberate process that relies upon resources and people from separate communities.

Unlike multi-disciplinary or cross disciplinary endeavors, those researchers involved in interdisciplinary efforts seek to foster understanding related to an area not served by traditional structures of inquiry. Interdisciplinary work can be accomplished by a single individual, or by teams of researchers working in collaboration. Klein's (1990) typological analysis highlighted the degree of integration between bodies of knowledge as a hallmark of defining interdisciplinarity. The application of knowledge of one area to another is at the center of interdisciplinary inquiry. Also, the outcome of interdisciplinary work is an important indication of the activity. To what end do scholars engage in interdisciplinarity? Klein noted the external motivations for such work concluding, "Interdisciplinarity is not a theoretical concept, but a practical one, one that arises from the unresolved problems of society rather than science itself" (p. 42). The interdisciplinary area of women's studies is but one example. The field developed from the interaction of scholars who did not feel that their respective disciplines provided an appropriate foundation for studying issues of gender and society. Through the interaction of selected methodological and cognitive tools from such disciplines as sociology, economics, and English, a more focused study of gender can be fostered.

Developing this type of engagement requires scholars to connect with researchers, literature, and topics outside their own field of study. For doctoral students, the nature of disciplinary silos can prove to be a formidable obstacle for participating in interdisciplinary work. The graduate model for higher education isolates scholars structurally and culturally. This isolation is, to some extent, by design. In the spirit of situated learning (Brown, Collins, & Duguid, 1989), developing disciplinary expertise requires immersion in the community of practice. The clustered nature of doctoral education renders the vast landscape of the university more manageable, and makes intellectual and financial resources easily available to scholars. Disciplines provide order to the inherent complexity of higher education organizations, although they do little to foster engagement across boundaries. The skills needed to participate in interdisciplinary work are not wholly compatible with the design and intent of doctoral education. Where such programs develop specialization, interdisciplinary scholarship requires the skill of integration and collaboration. In the following sections, I consider the challenges of interdisciplinary socialization related to knowledge acquisition, investment, and involvement for doctoral students (Weidman et al., 2001).

Knowledge Acquisition

A significant challenge for interdisciplinary doctoral education relates to the skills and knowledge needed to successfully integrate multiple fields of inquiry. Students entering a doctoral program have typically proceeded down an increasingly narrow path throughout their educational career, culminating in the intensive study of a particular area. Individuals engaged in interdisciplinary work are required to possess a facility with multiple ways of knowing. Klein (1990) referred to this dilemma as the "burden of comprehension," noting that interdisciplinary scholars must possess a basic understanding of how ideas are used in their original context before applying them in a new setting (p. 88). Understanding the cognitive map of each contributing discipline allows scholars to make reasoned applications of ideas, concepts, and paradigms from one field to another. Such a skill recognizes that ideas do not exist in isolation, but rather take shape in the unique context and history of the discipline. The more complex an interdisciplinary problem is, the more depth of knowledge a scholar is required to possess in order to actively engage in problem solving. The skill of borrowing necessary for this work is twofold: first, evaluating the strength of concepts in their original disciplinary context; and second, determining how best to apply those concepts to an interdisciplinary topic. When compared to the initial years of the doctoral curriculum, which are structured to develop foundational knowledge and expertise in a single or primary area of inquiry, the gap looms large.

The challenges of language and communication are embedded in the interdisciplinary experience. Perhaps all scholars at one time or another have experienced the sense of discomfort associated with reading a journal from a neighboring field, replete with its own language, cultural artifacts, and norms. These differences underscore the language researchers use to describe a study as well as the constructs through which such studies are assembled. For example, the sociologist begins a study of school children by considering them individual agents within overlapping social and cultural settings, while the economist begins a study by defining the same children as a collection of state expenditures or an example of human capital. Terminologies assume unique meaning based on the disciplinary boundaries in which they are applied. These differences change the way in which researchers convey ideas and meaning in their work. Interdisciplinary researchers are skilled in translating these multiple interpretations of the world, are aware of the pitfalls associated with doing so, and work on developing a common interdisciplinary vocabulary. Ultimately, in any academic community, language serves as a boundary object (Bowker & Star, 1999), mediating interactions between groups of people by providing a shared point of reference. Doctoral students are challenged to develop skills that enable communication and application between multiple disciplines.

Investment

Investment for doctoral students occurs on multiple levels—to the discipline, to the profession, and to a research topic or agenda. A challenge for interdisciplinary researchers is the length of time and investment of resources required to facilitate an interdisciplinary research agenda (Rhoten & Parker, 2004). Traditional norms of the academy do little to accommodate the time or effort needed to develop interdisciplinary or collaborative skills. Reflective of the changing influences which dominate faculty life, the mandate of "publish or perish" also permeates the culture of graduate education. While some debate exists over the demands placed on young scholars early in their career, students in traditional disciplinary programs have the advantage of a well-defined set of scholarly outlets. Students may attempt to model the career of a faculty advisor, or be encouraged by their advisor to attend particular disciplinary conferences from the beginning of the graduate school experience. Academic journals and conferences serve as disciplinary landmarks, helping to orient an emerging scholar's perception of the field.

Interdisciplinary scholarship creates unique connections among academic journals, conferences, and associations, requiring researchers to create and evaluate their communities as they proceed with their work. Such a commitment is often a detriment for developing interdisciplinary scholars, who can perceive negative consequences for their endeavors because they lack a defined set of disciplinary guideposts in terms of scholarly activities. In addition, the challenge of integrating disciplines may impact scholarly productivity relative to more traditional research. Not only does interdisciplinary research often take longer to develop compared to more established fields, but the work is also removed from a core community of like-minded scholars and researchers. Doctoral students may feel challenged to identify a network of peers who share research interests when they are not immersed in the daily activities of an institutional department. These networks serve as important sources of support for doctoral students in all fields (Golde, 2005). Rhoten and Parker (2004) highlighted "the tension between the scientific promise of the interdisciplinary path and the academic prospect of the tenure track" (p. 2046). Scholars pursue courses of action because of possible cognitive advances and social benefits as well as career advancement, recognition, and job security; that is, the academic profession holds both the reward of producing new knowledge and gaining personal benefits. The professional costs of interdisciplinary research, either real or perceived, can be a deterrent to doctoral students seeking to establish a foothold toward an academic career.

Involvement

During enrollment in a graduate program, students become progressively more involved with faculty, peers, the institution, and the discipline. The university structure and culture facilitates this involvement. As one example, doctoral programs are commonly housed within a single building on campus, separate from other departments. The location fosters clusters of researchers around various topics and areas of knowledge. Informal gatherings among peers help students decipher cultural norms and engage in disciplinary activities. Involvement facilitates a disciplinary identity, which fosters a sense of shared networks among researchers. The process also differentiates one group from another. Doctoral students come to see themselves as anthropologists, for example, or biologists, which are distinct identities compared to other disciplines. For doctoral students interested in interdisciplinary involvement, an immediate challenge is the disparate and frequently far-flung nature of the interdisciplinary community. Students must often bear the responsibility of locating faculty in particular disciplines who can contribute to their interdisciplinary development, especially related to mentoring, an understanding of career options, and the acquisition of teaching skills (Holley, 2006). Involvement in interdisciplinary research can be particularly problematic. In natural and laboratory science disciplines, as one example, doctoral students frequently work under the close supervision of a faculty advisor. The research is typically grant supported, and students may take a part of a larger project for their dissertation work. The socialization process works through the network of peers and faculty associated with the research laboratory. The flexibility needed to identify an interdisciplinary research project and construct a unique course of action to pursue such questions is not a part of the common graduate school model.

Embedded within the challenge of involvement is the notion of an interdisciplinary identity. Because the interdisciplinary process relies on the integration of two or more disciplines, such scholars must construct a sense of self that is responsive to multiple communities. No single reference group exists to anchor the experience of doctoral students engaged in interdisciplinary work, nor do clear expectations related to scholarly participation in the field operate as a guide to individual behavior.

Components of Interdisciplinary Doctoral Education

In order to meet the challenges outlined above and facilitate interdisciplinary graduate education, faculty and administrators must understand the disciplinary structures that dominate the contemporary academy. In this section, I consider examples of interdisciplinary doctoral programs in U.S. research universities. Students interested in interdisciplinary work are frequently bound to their discipline or department through funding. Research and teaching assistantships are almost always departmentally based, requiring students to participate in teaching or research that is directly related to their field. The provision of funds to doctoral students in exchange for undergraduate course instruction positions students as integral members of the discipline fulfilling a crucial cultural role. Students acquire those disciplinary norms associated with pedagogical functions. Through research assistantships, students ideally work under the close supervision of a faculty advisor or mentor, acquiring those skills needed for a future research career. Graduate student assistantships operate as a basic exchange between the student and the department, and leave little room for interdisciplinary support. This exchange is inherent to the function and organization of the university, which delegates management for most daily tasks to the departmental level. The provision of financial support for interdisciplinary graduate education allows students to fully utilize an array of institutional resources, and also offers a symbolic commitment to this work.

As opposed to the graduate school model, which fosters specialization and a narrowing of interests, interdisciplinary work relies on integrative networks and a breadth of coordinated skills. Successful interdisciplinary programs recognize the multiple venues in which doctoral students acquire knowledge and become engaged with an academic community. Faculty, doctoral students, and administrators are well served to consider alternative ways in which these structures can accommodate interdisciplinary interests. Not only do students participate in a formal curriculum delivered in the classroom, but they also take part in research activities, informal peer interactions, and academic conferences. I consider each of these components of the doctoral student experience, highlighting examples from interdisciplinary programs, and conclude with implications for interdisciplinary practice.

The Interdisciplinary Curriculum

The curriculum provides a core reference point for all doctoral students as they progress through their program of study. Regardless of specific research interests or faculty relationships, students share a common learning experience that provides a foundation for their future participation in the discipline. Different curricular approaches allow for the type of student proficiencies needed for interdisciplinary work. One approach is for doctoral students to complete a course of study in a primary discipline, and also participate in a colloquium, seminar project, or supplemental course structure that focuses on interdisciplinary integration. This model not only prioritizes the disciplinary foundation needed for interdisciplinary work but also allows for facility with integrative topics and skills. At Texas A&M University, the Integrative Graduate Education and Research Traineeship program (IGERT) concentrates on next-generation computational and analytical tools for materials science. Sponsored by the NSF, the program requires doctoral students to complete a common core, which develops expertise in analytic and computational abilities. The program also features a two-semester interdisciplinary core that prioritizes the language and concepts needed to communicate across the various participating disciplines.

Another model for interdisciplinary graduate education requires the construction of an integrative core curriculum supplemented by student-selected elective courses from relevant disciplines. In neuroscience programs, doctoral students commonly complete an interdisciplinary core curriculum during their first year of study. For example, the interdisciplinary training program in cognitive science at Duke University features a first-year immersion structured around an intensive seminar, workshops, and discussion groups. The seminar introduces students to fundamental concepts related to cognition and brain function, including anatomy, memory, vision, and the nervous system. Faculty identify key areas of neuroscience research, and supplement those areas of the curriculum with related workshops or discussion groups. The curriculum is designed to cultivate an interdisciplinary foundation for participation in the neuroscience community. During the second and third years of the program, students complete elective courses specific to their research interests, supplementing their interdisciplinary foundation in the field. A similar approach is evident in doctoral programs that concentrate on area studies, such as gender or race/ethnicity. The interdisciplinary doctoral program in gender studies at Indiana University in Bloomington requires five core courses that examine feminist theory, concepts of gender, and sexuality while the Ph.D. program in ethnic studies at the University of California, Berkeley, demonstrates a comparable structure, requiring students to complete an interdisciplinary core sequence before selecting elective courses relevant to research interests.

While the curricular models may appear similar, each presents a unique philosophical approach toward interdisciplinary behavior. To what degree does interdisciplinary scholarship rely on expertise and integration of the disciplines, and how much depth of disciplinary expertise should scholars possess to facilitate this scholarship? The answers to these questions are particularly problematic for doctoral students, who lack the depth of disciplinary expertise relative to more established scholars. Students also lack the cultural competencies necessary to navigate the institutional structure in pursuit of resources relative to interdisciplinary work. Each model not only offers an advantage for interdisciplinary development but also presents a negative consequence. For example, requiring doctoral students to complete an interdisciplinary core curriculum detracts from the depth of knowledge associated with a particular field of study, a depth that has long been assumed to be at the core of the graduate school experience. Students who enter an interdisciplinary graduate program without exposure to the multiple constituent disciplines lack the basis to understand and integrate the information presented in such a curriculum. As one example, students in a neuroscience program may be expected to understand fundamental neurological behaviors and brain functions. But without basic proficiencies in brain anatomy, the relationship between various components would be unclear. These obstacles are countered by a more disciplinary approach, which facilitates interdisciplinary proficiencies through elective courses and supplemental instruction. The distinction between an interdisciplinary student and a disciplinary peer, however, is blurred. How can the unique process of interdisciplinary socialization be fostered when the student is embedded within the disciplinary structure? In this case, particular attention is required toward research activities and other interdisciplinary learning opportunities outside the classroom in order to cultivate a holistic interdisciplinary curriculum.

Interdisciplinary Research Opportunities

Developing proficiencies as an interdisciplinary researcher requires participation in an institutional culture that values such work. For doctoral students, an initial challenge is identifying a faculty advisor and research topic that allows for engagement across disciplinary boundaries. Students in graduate programs rely on socialization by faculty to develop a rigorous and realistic research agenda. The model common in the laboratory and natural sciences, where doctoral students assume a grant-funded research assistantship in a laboratory, socializes students to work as a member of a research team. The skill of collaboration is particularly valuable for interdisciplinary research, which often necessitates networks among institutions, academics, and industry. When doctoral students work as part of a research team, they acquire valuable skills in the purposeful act of cognitive integration so crucial for interdisciplinary work.

The interdependent nature of academic science, however, does not necessarily equate to an interdisciplinary nature. For instance, doctoral students in a range of scientific disciplines participate in laboratory rotations during their initial years of study. These rotations provide some exposure to various research topics, and also permit students to work closely with faculty before selecting a permanent advisor. Students who participate in the research/rotation model enable interdisciplinary connections by carrying research topics and techniques from one laboratory to another, serving as a bridge between faculty researchers. However, as I outlined earlier in this chapter, the process of interdisciplinarity is not one that happens solely by circumstance. Students must be engaged in making explicit connections between bodies of knowledge by an active and deliberate process, a need that is not always reflected in the attitude toward laboratory rotations (Holley, 2009); that is, rotations might be primarily viewed as a way for students and faculty to sample fit and compatibility rather than an introduction to an array of research topics and skills.

Doctoral students across disciplines must also identify faculty advisors, mentors, and committee members with the requisite expertise and stance toward interdisciplinary research. Interdisciplinary researchers must ultimately master the steep learning curve associated with participation in multiple disciplines. This challenge is particularly acute for doctoral students, who are expected to produce a dissertation that is assessed by its contribution to a disciplinary field of study.

A push toward interdisciplinary research training is increasingly evident across a variety of higher education institutions, although largely evident in traditional scientific fields of study. The examples of interdisciplinary research at the doctoral-level principally focus on collaborative teams or research networks. The computational science and engineering program at the University of California in Santa Barbara, as one example, places students as part of research teams, who work on integrated questions related to micro-scale engineering, complex fluids, and computational science. The Bioinformatics and Computational Biology doctoral program at Iowa State University functions through a collaborative faculty network, where students work on projects that span an interdisciplinary structure. Also common is a postdoctoral interdisciplinary research training fellowship that builds upon proficiencies gained in a graduate program. The Center for Interdisciplinary Research on AIDS at Yale University provides fellowship support, as does the program in interdisciplinary informatics at the University of Minnesota. The goal of these programs is to build upon disciplinary expertise gained through a doctoral program. Outside the natural and laboratory science disciplines, however, interdisciplinary research is frequently an individualized endeavor. Doctoral students may construct an interdisciplinary dissertation through a committee composed of faculty who represent multiple disciplinary perspectives. Others may pursue an interdisciplinary studies doctoral degree.

Conclusion

Existing research on the doctoral experience has demonstrated the significance of peer support and participation in scholarly communities to student success (Weidman et al., 2001). When scholars go outside the boundaries that define disciplinary communities, the established network of peers is greatly diminished and much less accessible. Interdisciplinary graduate programs should supplement formal curriculum and research experiences with informal, social groups that celebrate like-minded interdisciplinary researchers. Since the traditional departmental structure is frequently absent from these sorts of programs, a proactive group of faculty and administrators should assume responsibility for these processes.

Academic disciplines serve a crucial function in the vast landscape of higher education. As a community of practice, they provide for training of future scholars as well as advancement in terms of bodies of knowledge. Yet, even as the boundaries between knowledge become increasingly blurred, disciplinary structures remain a restriction on the engagement of academics with each other. Interdisciplinary socialization for doctoral education requires attention to the elements of knowledge acquisition, investment, and involvement that are inherent to the U.S. graduate education model. Fostering interdisciplinary development entails recognition of the work as an active, deliberate process. Bringing doctoral students from different fields together does little to facilitate conversations across the disciplines, unless an integrative framework and plan for engagement is put into place. The framework for interdisciplinary doctoral education should concentrate on the curriculum, providing students with a knowledge foundation adequate for participation in multiple fields of study. The curriculum should be complemented by opportunities to partake in interdisciplinary research. Students should complete assistantships with established interdisciplinary scholars, and also be afforded the opportunity to acquire techniques and methodologies associated with a range of constituent disciplines. Recognizing the formative nature of the doctoral experience for a student's future academic career, fostering interdisciplinary socialization requires deliberate attention to the processes of learning, research, and service inherent to the graduate model.

References

Abrams, P. (1991). The predictive ability of peer review of grant proposals: The case of ecology and the U.S. National Science Foundation. *Social Studies of Science, 21*, 111–132.

Austin, A., & McDaniels, M. (2006). Using doctoral education to prepare faculty to work within Boyer's four domains of scholarship. *New Directions for Institutional Research, 129*, 51–65.

Baldi, S. (1995). Prestige determinants of first academic job for new Sociology Ph.D.s 1985–1992. *The Sociological Quarterly, 36*, 777–789.

Becher, T., & Trowler, P. (2001). *Academic tribes and territories: Intellectual inquiry and the culture of disciplines* (2nd ed.). Buckingham, UK: Open University Press.

Bowker, G., & Star, S. (1999). *Sorting things out: Classification and its consequences.* Cambridge, MA: MIT Press.

Brint, S., Turk-Bicakci, L., Proctor, K., & Murphy, S. (2009). Expanding the social frame of knowledge: Interdisciplinary, degree-granting fields in American four-year colleges and universities, 1975–2000. *Review of Higher Education, 32*, 155–183.

Brown, J., Collins, A., & Duguid, P. (1989). Situated cognition and the culture of learning. *Educational Researcher, 18*, 32–42.

Clark, B. (1989). The academic life: Small worlds, different worlds. *Educational Researcher, 18*(5), 4–8.

Cole, J., & Cole, S. (1973). *Social stratification of science.* Chicago, IL: University of Chicago Press.

Council of Graduate Schools. (2007). *Graduate education: The backbone of American competitiveness and innovation*. Washington, DC: Author.

Donald, J. (2002). *Learning to think: Disciplinary perspectives*. San Francisco: Jossey-Bass.

Geiger, R. (2004). *Research and relevant knowledge: American research universities since World War II*. New Brunswick, NJ: Transaction Publishers.

Golde, C. (2005). The role of the department and discipline in doctoral student attrition: Lessons from four academic departments. *Journal of Higher Education, 76*, 669–700.

Golde, C., & Dore, T. (2001). *At cross purposes: What the experiences of today's doctoral students reveal about doctoral education*. Madison, WI: University of Wisconsin, Madison.

Holley, K. (2006). *The cultural construction of interdisciplinarity: Doctoral student socialization in an interdisciplinary neuroscience program*. Unpublished doctoral dissertation, University of Southern California.

Holley, K. (2009). The challenge of an interdisciplinary curriculum: A cultural analysis of a doctoral-degree program in neuroscience. *Higher Education, 58*, 241–255.

Hyland, K. (2004). *Disciplinary discourses: Social interactions in academic writing*. Ann Arbor, MI: University of Michigan Press.

Kezar, A. (2004). Obtaining integrity? Reviewing and examining the charter between higher education and society. *Review of Higher Education, 27*, 429–459.

Klein, J. T. (1990). *Interdisciplinarity: History, theory, and practice*. Detroit: Wayne State University Press.

Lattuca, L. (2001). *Creating interdisciplinarity: Interdisciplinary research and teaching among college and university faculty*. Nashville, TN: Vanderbilt University Press.

Lee, S., & Bozeman, B. (2005). The impact of research collaboration on scientific productivity. *Social Studies of Science, 35*, 673–702.

Neumann, R. (2001). Disciplinary differences and university teaching. *Studies in Higher Education, 26*, 135–146.

Newell, W., & Green, W. (1982). Defining and teaching interdisciplinary studies. *Improving College Teaching, 30*(1), 23–33.

Rhoten, D., & Parker, A. (2004). Risks and rewards of an interdisciplinary research path. *Science, 306*(5704), 2046.

Toma, J. D. (1997). Alternative inquiry paradigms, faculty cultures, and the definition of academic lives. *Journal of Higher Education, 68*, 679–705.

Weidman, J., Twale, D., & Stein, E. (2001). *Socialization of graduate and professional students in higher education: A perilous passage?* San Francisco: Jossey-Bass.

6

ACADEMIC CAPITALISM

A New Landscape for Doctoral Socialization

Pilar Mendoza

Ling's main source of funding for her research assistantship comes from a company. Although the material she is working on has some interesting properties from the physics perspective, she is disappointed by the lack of interest on the part of the industry representatives. They simply don't seem to be interested in the basic science behind this material. All they care about is that it responds properly under certain conditions so they can patent it. Ling fears that the company is not going to let her publish the properties that she has discovered in this material. Her only hope is that her advisor can convince them to allow publishing the basic science behind the material in a timely manner; otherwise, her graduation may be delayed up to six months.

Nate has a new office in the new neuroscience center at the University's industrial park downtown. After being on campus for a year, he was used to having his weekly lab meeting with other students and faculty all from the chemistry department. Now, his lab meetings are with industry representatives, physicians, as well as faculty and graduate students from several disciplines. Although the meetings can be chaotic at times and difficult to follow, given the variety of perspectives and expertise involved, Nate highly appreciates the opportunity to interact with scientists from outside academia and from other departments. Each time they meet he learns something new about the world in industry, in medical research labs, and in other disciplines. He is excited about the job opportunities that he anticipates from these interactions. However, he complains about the amount of work that he has to do now, especially because of the quarterly reports for the company and the anxiety of industry representatives for fast, concrete results. Sometimes he misses the ability to let go and follow science for the sake of science.

M any faculty and doctoral students are heavily involved in research with potential commercial applications in fields such as engineering and biotechnology, and in many cases, through industry-sponsored research. In some cases, doctoral students become involved in patent applications and spin-off companies (e.g., Campbell & Slaughter, 1999; Gumport, 2005; Krimsky, 2003; Slaughter, Archerd, & Campbell, 2004; Slaughter, Campbell, Hollernan, & Morgan, 2002). In 1997, Slaughter and Leslie published a groundbreaking book titled *Academic Capitalism: Politics, Policies, and the Entrepreneurial University,* inspiring a host of scholars with new ways to conceptualize these current trends affecting higher education as the global economy continues to dominate. Slaughter and Leslie defined academic capitalism as the new competitive environment in which universities engage in market-like behaviors competing for external resources. Later in 2004, Slaughter and Rhoades developed the theory of academic capitalism to explain the process by which higher education integrates into the new economy. This theory sees faculty, students, administrators, and academic professionals as actors using public resources to participate in the new economy. In the United States, academic capitalism has been promoted by the federal government since the 1980s through a series of policies and laws that can be synthesized into three categories: (1) commercialization laws that allow universities to patent and sell knowledge developed by their faculty and graduate students as well as to start spin-off companies; (2) federal financial aid policies that give funds to students rather than universities increasingly in the form of loans; and (3) copyright and information technology laws and policies that provide universities with opportunities to commercialize curricula and develop new programs through distance education. On the basis of the knowledge I have gained through my own research, in this chapter I focus on commercialization of research because these trends have direct implications for doctoral students and their socialization (Mendoza, 2007a, 2007b, 2009; Mendoza & Berger, 2005, 2008; Mendoza, Kuntz, & Berger, forthcoming).

Doctoral Socialization and Academic Capitalism

Doctoral students impacted by academic capitalism are those who work in research sponsored by industry or in areas that might lead to patents. The life of doctoral students affected by academic capitalism resembles the life of Nate in chemistry (see Golde, chapter 4). In these fields, research is expensive and faculty heavily depend on grants from the government, foundations, or the private sector to advance their research agendas. These research agendas are conducted in teams of doctoral students, postdocs, and even several scholars around well-defined problems. Doctoral students also depend on this funding for their dissertation research, usually in the form of research assistantships, which limits their research options to those groups with funding available. Unfortunately, this could discourage students to continue pursuing their doctorates (Golde, 1998). The same way doctoral students in these fields depend on research funding to complete their doctorate, faculty also heavily depend on doctoral students hired as research assistants to advance their research agendas. From the firm's perspective, research assistants are more than just labor but potential future recruits. In fact, having students working on a project directly related to a problem faced by the sponsoring company offers a unique opportunity to assess the skills of the student and educate her in areas of interest for the company (Mendoza, 2007a; Mendoza & Berger, 2008). These mutual benefits for faculty and firms were well articulated by Slaughter et al. (2002) in their quote, "Graduate students [as tokens of exchange] were the faculty members' 'gifts' to industry; industry's gifts to the faculty were resources for research, ranging from equipment to money, which was most often attached to the support of graduate students" (p. 285).

Faculty with industrial grants are likely to have to conform to contractual agreements involving specific deliveries in a relatively short period of time (up to a year), which means that doctoral students, the working bees of these grants, might end up being pushed for results in a timely manner and involved in several projects of this kind throughout their doctorate (Gumport, 2005; Slaughter et al., 2002). Moreover, secrecy of knowledge is still a delicate issue in establishing relationships with industry. Patenting and secrecy of knowledge is critical for the competitiveness and viability of private firms, while free dissemination of knowledge and the peer-review process are cornerstones of the academic profession. However, given that there is always basic, general science behind products and technologies, faculty in these collaborations tend to focus on the basic science that is too general for product development and, hence, focus away from intellectual property issues. Generally, there is a contractual agreement between faculty and the sponsored firm in which the latter has the right to file patents before publication, which might delay publications for up to six months. Doctoral students might be co-authors of such publications or even dissertations, which might represent delays in graduation or inability to show a publication record while on the job market. However, in all my interviews with faculty and students (Mendoza, 2007a; Mendoza & Berger, 2008; Mendoza et al., forthcoming), these delays are rare and normally students are not affected by intellectual property issues. In some cases, students are hired by the company that sponsored their dissertation research, boycotting any intellectual property complications.

There is a common downside of industrial funding, which is the short-term nature of industrial grants due to fiscal constraints of the sponsoring companies. While federal grants tend to cover at least three years of funding, industrial grants might be one-year long in best cases and as little as months in some instances. There have been cases where industry abruptly cut funding, leaving students halfway through their dissertations (Mendoza, 2007a; Mendoza et al., forthcoming). This discrepancy in funding timelines creates a challenge for faculty members who have to support doctoral students for at least four or five years, which is the normal duration of doctoral programs in these fields (National Science Board, 2008). The short-term nature of industrial grants also interferes with the longer timelines in academia, where results take longer than industry representatives desire due to the additional obligations that both students and faculty must assume such as teaching, service, coursework, and examinations.

The negative implications of industrial sponsorship mentioned above are less likely to occur in departments or research groups with high prestige. Mendoza et al. (forthcoming) demonstrated that top-ranked departments within a given discipline have access to both high levels of symbolic resources (such as prestige) and material resources, which gives them a greater advantage attracting federal block grants, thereby allowing them to conduct research in line with their professional and scientific interests. In these cases, faculty are in a better position to protect their core academic goals when negotiating the terms and conditions of contracts with industry. In some cases, they can afford to reject industrial money at odds with their scientific and educational interests. However, less advantaged departments or less established faculty with fewer block grants are more likely to compromise core academic values such as the proper education of doctoral students and free dissemination of knowledge in exchange of restrictive industrial funds.

In sum, if faculty engage in collaborations with industry that do not jeopardize the core values of the academic profession such as academic freedom in inquiry, free dissemination of knowledge, the peer-review process, and education of the next generation of scientists, these collaborations offer benefits to both industry and academia (Mendoza, 2007a; Mendoza & Berger, 2008). By giving grants to faculty, industry gains access to a talent pool of potential recruits, expertise, basic knowledge related to the science behind their products, and scientific breakthrough for future technologies. Faculty obtain funds to maintain their research labs and support students, opportunities to learn about the scientific needs of industry as an inspiration for both their teaching and research, as well as educational and career opportunities for students.

Finally, the level of involvement of faculty and doctoral students in this form of academic capitalism varies across disciplines and types of institutions (Gumport, 2005; Isabelle, 2008; Mendoza, 2007a; Mendoza & Berger, 2008; Mendoza, 2009; Mendoza et al., forthcoming; Zusman, 1999). On the one hand, industry–academia collaborations and commercialization of research are more common in fields involved in research with direct research and development (R&D) applications. On the other hand, within disciplines, the level of involvement in academic capitalism by departments or even by faculty in one single department also varies. A variety of circumstances ranging from proximity to industrial hubs, specific departmental cultures, and personal characteristics influence the level of involvement in academic capitalism (Mendoza, 2009; Mendoza et al., forthcoming). In particular, some faculty and doctoral students are more interested in basic research than are others and some faculty and doctoral students are more interested in industry-sponsored research than their peers. Level of prestige also matters when assessing the impact of academic capitalism because it influences the ability of faculty or departments to attract funds in line with their scientific interests.

Parts II and III of this book discuss the socialization of doctoral students to all aspects of academic work, which are necessary to consider if we are to train doctoral students to the complexities of the academic profession (Austin & McDaniels, 2006; Golde & Dore, 2001). On the basis of these chapters, I discuss the implications for the socialization of doctoral students who are involved in academic capitalism.

Disciplinary and Interdisciplinary Socialization in Light of Academic Capitalism

In Golde's chapter 4, she illustrates different ways in which doctoral programs are structured based on disciplinary norms and cultures. In her chapter, Golde narrates how doctoral students are socialized to the academic profession, but more importantly, to the specific habits and practices of disciplines beyond mere content knowledge. This socialization translates into a sense of identity for members of a given discipline as they internalize its culture. For complete socialization into a discipline, Golde argues that doctoral students should have opportunities to engage in real-world situations related to their disciplines. Thus, besides formal coursework, examinations, and the writing of the dissertation, students learn the ropes of their disciplines through informal experiences such as seminars, attending professional conferences, reading scholarly documents, as well as through interactions (formal and informal) with faculty, peers, and other scholars in the field.

In fields where research is inspired by application, industry-sponsored research as well as formal and informal interactions with industry representatives through these sponsorships are important ways in which doctoral students learn the ropes of their disciplines. This is true because, in these fields, peers in industry are part of the community of practice, and even the purest form of basic research in these disciplines is always motivated by applicability and technological innovations (Mendoza, 2009). Therefore, regardless of students' career aspirations, the involvement with industrial research and industry representatives, if well managed, offers significant socialization opportunities for students (Debackere & Veugelers, 2005; Gluck, 1987; Mendoza, 2007a; Salminen-Karlsson & Wallgren, 2008; Stephan 2001). The ties to industry in these fields are a natural source of inspiration for academic work to the point that it is common for students and faculty in these fields to work in industry a number of years before or after their academic careers (Mendoza, 2007a; Mendoza & Berger, 2008).

Academic capitalism is most likely to happen in interdisciplinary fields such as biotechnology, materials science, optical science, and cognitive science because most technological applications draw from several fields (Slaughter & Leslie, 1997). Holley, in chapter 5, discusses the increasing trend of interdisciplinarity in higher education and its effects on doctoral education. Interdisciplinarity in higher education is normally manifested in research centers of networks of scholars from different disciplines focusing on a single problem or technology. In less common instances, doctoral students engage in a dissertation that requires knowledge and committee members drawing from several disciplines. According to Holley, the main goal of interdisciplinary education is to produce scholars capable of engaging with multiple communities of practice and respond to scientific problems that depend on several disciplinary perspectives. The challenge with this approach is to balance depth versus breadth of knowledge given that interdisciplinary education requires the acquisition of knowledge, skills, practices, and habits in more than one discipline.

For example, materials science is an interdisciplinary field concerned with the properties of matter and its applications to various areas using applied physics and chemistry as well as chemical, mechanical, civil, and electrical engineering. It originated in the 1970s from industry employers who needed graduates with the skills to apply science and engineering to the understanding and creation of materials. In recent years, the field has been at the forefront of nanoscience and nanotechnology, which have the potential to create many new materials and devices with wide-ranging applications in medicine, electronics, and energy production. Clearly, scholars in fields such as materials science have ample opportunities to engage in research with technological applications competitive in the global market, including with doctoral students. And, so, doctoral students in these fields are likely to experience the challenges of interdisciplinarity as described by Holley, such as breadth versus depth of knowledge and dealing with different cultures and habits from various disciplines. In particular, Mendoza (2007a) found difficulties among doctoral students in materials science interacting with their lab members and faculty with different disciplinary backgrounds in terms of not only different knowledge bases but also related to different ways of thinking and approaching a research problem.

Socialization to Research in Light of Academic Capitalism

Becoming an independent researcher is considered the hallmark of doctoral education (Gardner, 2008; Lovitts, 2008). Normally, doctoral programs are designed to turn students into researchers, and, so, most of the students' time is devoted to activities related to research or knowledge necessary to conduct research. Weidman, in chapter 2, discusses the different ways in which students are socialized into research, including courses in research design and methodology, interpersonal interaction with faculty and peers, including mentoring, participation in professional activities related to the academic field of study through associations, and hands-on experiences actually conducting research either through research assistantships or through dissertation work. These are essential components needed to socialize students into research, but as Golde explains in chapter 4, there are important differences among disciplines that need to be acknowledged.

Furthermore, I argue that even within disciplines, there are significant differences in the socialization of doctoral students in light of academic capitalism. These differences depend not only on the characteristics of advisors but also on the source of funding for dissertations. In other words, two doctoral students in the same discipline, in the same department, and with the same advisor can have very different socialization experiences with research if the support for one student comes from a block, unrestrictive governmental grant and the support for the other student comes from a company expecting specific deliverables within established deadlines. This scenario is plausible in certain fields involved in academic capitalism given that faculty normally have several sources of funding at the same time. In sum, as I illustrate in this section, within disciplines and academic departments and even with the same advisor, those students socialized through research aligned with academic capitalism are subject to a set of unique experiences in addition to those emanating from specific disciplinary characteristics (Mendoza, 2007a).

Without doubt, the idea of faculty entrepreneurs engaging in research with commercial potential, starting spin-off companies, or simply partnering with the private sector in the research and development of products competitive in the market clashes with the traditional, Mertonian (1957) notion of faculty members engaged in research for the sake of pure scientific curiosity. Moreover, the idea of betraying the value of free dissemination of knowledge by keeping knowledge secret through patents in the name of monetary returns is also an image that contrasts the ideal of altruistic scientists, at least in the materialistic sense. Questions have been raised about the values that doctoral students might acquire socializing in environments engaged in academic capitalism (Gumport, 2005; Mendoza, 2007a). For example, are students in these contexts being socialized to value more secrecy of knowledge over free dissemination? Are they becoming more interested in research that would lead to profitable products than in basic science without palpable, immediate results? Are they internalizing a business-like culture of habits and practices emphasizing managerialism, bottom-line results, and material rewards? As these students enter the academic profession, are we seeing a shift in the academic culture in those fields engaged in academic capitalism?

The answer to these questions depends on the specific academic context of the doctoral student involved in industry-sponsored research as well as on the individual characteristics and goal aspirations of both faculty and students. For example, for doctoral students interested in careers in industry, working in industry-sponsored projects and interacting with industry representatives offer advantages for their training as future scientists in industrial settings such as learning about scientific problems relevant to industry and the culture in industry. These opportunities allow students to learn first-hand about potential job environments after graduation and to be exposed to job opportunities. In fact, many students in these fields end up being hired by the companies that sponsored their dissertations (Mendoza, 2007a; Mendoza & Berger, 2008; Mendoza et al., forthcoming). For these students, these benefits are likely to shadow potential issues around the ability to publish their dissertations due to intellectual property conflicts or research too focused toward applied ends. By the same token, the opposite is true for doctoral students working on industry-sponsored research who want to pursue careers in academia. In this case, publishing, inquiry in basic science, and socialization to academic roles become a priority, which can be undermined by working on industry-sponsored projects (Mendoza, 2007a; Mendoza & Berger, 2008; Slaughter et al., 2002).

In addition to these personal preferences related to career goals, level of prestige or recognition of students' departments and advisors play a role in shaping their socialization in light of academic capitalism. For example, those students who work for an advisor who is successful at attracting funding for research, especially from the federal government in the form of unrestrictive block grants, and who has a strong commitment to education, are likely to engage in research with an educational component. This is possible in great part due to advisors' intentional protection of these students from the pitfalls that may occur when students' research projects are sponsored by a private company. Such pitfalls may include overemphasis on applied research and intellectual property conflicts (Mendoza et al., forthcoming). These successful faculty members have enough funds and leverage to delineate the terms and conditions of collaborations with industry protecting the core values of the academic profession and doctoral education (Mendoza, 2007a; Mendoza et al., forthcoming).

On the other hand, given the high costs of research in these fields due to the need for expensive equipment and facilities as well as intensive labor (normally by postdocs and doctoral students), faculty with low levels of prestige and recognition are more likely to engage in contractual work with industry in projects of little scientific value due to their disadvantage in securing block grants to sustain a research program. In these cases, doctoral students end up caught in work with little academic value and away from their dissertation. This type of contractual work is normally closer to actual specific products, which require significant secrecy of knowledge and applied research, thereby continuing to undermine the educational and career opportunities for graduate students. Unfortunately, for many doctoral students in these less prestigious institutions or with less established advisors, this is the only way they can fund their doctoral degree. The exploitation of doctoral students documented in the literature (e.g., Campbell & Slaughter, 1999; Slaughter & Leslie, 1997; Slaughter & Rhoades, 2004; Slaughter et al., 2002, 2004) is likely to happen under these circumstances (Mendoza et al., forthcoming).

Socialization to Teaching in Light of Academic Capitalism

The literature on academic capitalism has mainly focused on its potential negative influences on teaching. For example, Gumport (2005) argued that in these cases, faculty behave more like project managers and supervisors pushing for results than as mentors and educators. Another concern has to do with the additional time that faculty have to spend finding resources to sustain their research writing grants or establishing trustworthy relationships with private sponsors (Mendoza & Berger, 2008; Mendoza et al., forthcoming). This burden might deter faculty from time spent teaching and advising students (Lee & Rhoades, 2003).

However, if we expand and elaborate the definition of teaching using the framework presented in McDaniels' chapter 1, it becomes clear that under the right circumstances, industry-sponsored projects are an effective means to socialize doctoral students into teaching roles in their respective fields. Given that research in fields engaged in academic capitalism is inspired by use, having doctoral students formally working on projects with real-life industrial applications is an effective mechanism for socializing them to the conceptual underpinnings of applied research in their field. This corresponds to the first desired outcome in McDaniel's framework, which refers to students' conceptual understandings about their role as scholars as well as their disciplinary and institutional differences within which the academic profession takes place. In fact, students reported that those faculty who have close ties to industry have the ability to easily incorporate that practical knowledge into their teaching, which makes their classes and advising more engaging and relevant to their career aspirations (Mendoza, 2007a). Thus, doctoral students as future teachers benefit from learning first-hand about "the real world" if involved in research and interactions with industry representatives. However, to make this opportunity an educational and socializing experience for doctoral students, advisors should choose carefully projects or aspects of projects sponsored by industry in which doctoral students will be involved, making sure that there is enough basic science and room for the development of skills essential in the profession in these projects.

Also, the interactions of doctoral students with industry representatives have been identified as one of the primary benefits of industry–academia collaborations for students, especially because students are exposed to the culture in settings that are likely to be students' future employment as well as to different ways of communication and collaboration (Mendoza, 2007a; Stephan, 2001). Even if students aspire to academic careers, these interactions are useful to learn how to interact with industry representatives for their future careers as sources of inspiration and funding for research. Clearly, these benefits relate to McDaniels' third component of her framework related to the development of interpersonal skills, such as written and oral communication skills, collaboration skills, and ability to interact with diverse students and colleagues.

Socialization to Service in Light of Academic Capitalism

Ward, in chapter 3, offers a broader view of the role of service in the academic profession beyond the well-understood committee work that faculty do in the name of shared governance. According to Ward, service includes a variety of roles and responsibilities to support faculty members' institutions, disciplines, communities, and society at large. Faculty service to the mission of higher education is normally tied to the mission of universities in their local, state, regional, and national communities. In this sense, both teaching and research are part of that social service through the generation and dissemination of knowledge and education of the youth and a skilled workforce. In addition, universities, especially land grant institutions, fulfill more specific social service through outreach programs to communities. Finally, an indirect form of service is the fact that universities are normally engines of economic growth and cultural and social activity to their surrounding communities.

This approach to service clearly agrees with what proponents of academic capitalism have argued to fuel commercialization of research, spin-off companies out of faculty research, and industry–academia collaboration (Geiger, 2004). In fact, the main motivation for the federal government to promote academic capitalism was based on the belief that universities partnered with the private sector in the development of knowledge with direct technological implications and products competitive in the global market, which are all powerful engines of economic growth (Geiger, 2004; Slaughter & Leslie, 1997). This logic is also the main justification for university administrators and faculty to engage in these activities beyond the obvious monetary rewards from these activities. For academic administrators, academic capitalism is a major form of service to society, not only because of the creation and transfer of knowledge for immediate societal and economic needs but also as a means to prepare the scientists who will create the technological advances of the future. For example, University of Florida's President Machen made a recent announcement meant to seek public support in the state for higher education. He said:

> Florida faculty bring into the state an estimated $1.2 billion annually in federal and private research grants. That money does far more than pay for the purchase of equipment or the salaries of graduate students. It leads to innovations that become the seeds of new startup companies and expansion of existing companies. That boosts high-skilled, high-paying jobs and helps Florida stay in front of important industry trends. For example, biotechnology—and especially now, green energy technology. (University of Florida, 2009, p. 14)

However, critics have argued that service defined in purely economic terms undermines the social charter between higher education and society (Kezar, 2004; Kezar, Chambers, Burkhardt, & Associates, 2005; Newman, Couturier, & Scurry, 2004; Slaughter & Rhoades, 2004; Teixeira, Jongbloed, Dill, & Amaral, 2004; Tierney, 2006). In a nutshell, the argument against academic capitalism is that it places an overemphasis in applied research that is guided by the specific needs and objectives of corporate America neglecting other pressing social issues that do not represent monetary gains.

One of the hallmark programs from the U.S. government to encourage industry–academia collaborations are the Industry/University Cooperative Research Centers (I/UCRCs) sponsored by the National Science Foundation (NSF) since the late 1970s. These centers start with a seed grant to a faculty member to create partnerships with industry between his or her department and relevant industries. Doctoral students are active participants of these venues. Normally, industries become members of the center via a fee that is then directed to support research in the department. Through formal and informal venues such as conferences, workshops, and meetings, the center grants industries access to the expertise and science of their faculty and doctoral students as potential recruits. Also, through these interactions, faculty are more likely to secure research funds for research and research assistants. The Canadian government pioneered a different approach to foster these interactions through its Canadian Networks of Centers of Excellence (NCE). While the American I/UCRC program normally supports regional research centers between one academic department and several companies, the NCE networks are nationwide webs of different types of organizations such as universities, hospitals, governmental agencies, nonprofit organizations, and companies around common technologies. For example, the Canadian Advanced Food and Materials Network is concerned with the development of food and the health implications of genetically modified foods as well as the factors affecting consumer acceptance of these foods with regard to moral, religious, and cultural issues. These ideas resonate with the concept of social entrepreneurship, which focuses on the social gains of the entrepreneurial endeavors typical of academic capitalism, such as benefits for communities in terms of quality of life (Mars & Metcalfe, 2009).

Mendoza (2007b) argued that networks of knowledge such as the Canadian approach are a better model to promote the social service of higher education and socialize students toward a scholarship of engagement as explained in Ward's chapter and also by Ramaley (2005). Doctoral students' socialization through research projects in networks of knowledge is likely to engage them in projects less focused on the bottom line and specific corporate needs and more oriented toward societal needs. Also, with less emphasis on research directed to products, students and faculty are less likely to have intellectual property issues and overapplied research. In addition, these networks have the potential to expose doctoral students to a greater variety of organizations and thus gain broader educational and career opportunities.

Recommendations

Academic capitalism affects doctoral students and faculty as well as departments, universities, and other external agencies, such as the federal and state governments. In this section, I provide recommendations to each of the above about how to engage in productive and meaningful ways for collaborations with industry for both the private and the public good.

Recommendations for Doctoral Students

- If options are available, join a research group with the right balance of federal and industrial grants according to your professional goals. In other words, if your goal is a career in industry, you will have better opportunities to advance if you choose a group heavily involved with industry, but if your career goal is an academic career, it is more desirable to work in a research group mainly supported by unrestrictive block grants such as those from the NSF or the National Institutes of Health (NIH). However, keep in mind that regardless of your career goals, it is good to be exposed to both types of funding and research because both are interrelated and depend on each other in many ways.
- If you work in an industry-sponsored research and have to interact with industry representatives, do not feel intimidated or frustrated by their different practices and habits. Instead, frame your interactions with industry representatives as an educational experience. Pay attention to their culture, their communication styles, and to the scientific problems they are facing as an inspiration for your own work, even if your goal is an academic career. Remember that industry might become a significant source of funding and research projects throughout your career.
- If your career goals are in industry, do your best in your work and interpersonal skills when working on an industry-sponsored research. The sponsoring firm might be interested in recruiting you after graduation and it is likely to be assessing your fit in the company both as a researcher and as a potential colleague throughout the duration of the research project. Even if you are not interested in working for that

particular firm sponsoring your research, the community of practice is normally small and so you should always be professional in all your interactions with them.

- It is important to establish clear criteria, goals, objectives, and deliverables with associated timelines from the beginning with the sponsoring firm. Intellectual property agreements regarding publications should also be clearly established from the beginning. In doing so, work with your advisor in finding balance between what the firm wants from your research and what is required to complete your dissertation and other scholarly milestones. Also, with your advisor, reach a comfortable agreement with the company about intellectual property issues including what you can publish and within what parameters.

Recommendations for Faculty Members

- Diversify your grant portfolio maintaining a healthy balance of unrestrictive grants (such as those from NSF or NIH) and restrictive funding with specific deliverables and focused on applied projects. Various sources of funding and types of funding avoid overdependence on one single granting agency and give you greater flexibility to juggle your scientific interests and funding opportunities for students.
- Recruit doctoral students for your research whose career goals match the type of research available for funding. Ideally, students should be exposed to projects relevant to industry and technological applications but with sufficient basic science. However, basic science is more important for students interested in academic careers.
- Stay true to your academic goals and values. If possible, reject collaborations with industry that compromise your ability to properly educate students involved in those collaborations or that undermines your scientific interests, your ability to publish, or your academic freedom.
- Given the different objectives, cultures, and practices between industry and academia, it is important to establish clear parameters, boundaries, goals, and deliverables from the beginning. For this, you must be clear in your early negotiations with industry representatives about your broader responsibilities as a faculty member, which involves educating students and other commitments such as teaching and service that may translate into longer timelines of work than in industry. Make industry

realize that processes in academia are slower given the other demands and challenges that faculty and students face. By the same token, be mindful that students are apprentices and are likely to take longer to obtain results, even more so if they are still in the midst of coursework and doctoral examinations.

- Realize the educational and employment benefits of industry–academia collaborations for students. Find opportunities for students to directly interact with industry representatives and learn about the world of industry through visits to companies, presentations to industry representatives, and other formal and informal ways of interaction. Highlight for students the importance of learning the ways industry interacts and operates as well as the real-life applications of research that these interactions offer. Stress the importance of professional interpersonal skills to students when interacting with industry representatives and assist students in polishing those skills.

Recommendations for Departments

- The development of healthy and productive industry–academia collaborations involve a considerable amount of time networking, establishing trustful relationships, and developing contracts that protect the values and interests of all involved, including doctoral students. Departments should provide support and resources to faculty members to facilitate the development of these collaborations such as full-time staff dedicated to identify potential partners and arrange the nuances around the establishment of these relationships. Other support mechanisms include assisting faculty negotiating contracts that protect the core mission of academic institutions as well as creating venues to facilitate encounters with industry such as in-house conferences, symposia, open-house days, and newsletters.
- Departments can establish consortiums modeling the I/UCRCs around the knowledge base of given technologies, in which industries become members by means of a fee. The resources collected from that fee can be used as seed money to support faculty research. In return, industry members have access to doctoral students and the expertise of faculty and to a variety of structured venues such as workshops and conferences.

- Establish mentoring programs where established faculty mentor junior faculty on ways to establish partnerships with industry. Also, established faculty can be encouraged to invite junior faculty to collaborate with industry.
- Establish rewards and incentives for faculty members who have successfully partnered with industry while maintaining the integrity of the academic profession, including providing educational and job opportunities for doctoral students and for those who actively mentor and assist junior faculty in establishing healthy industry–academia collaborations.

Recommendations for Universities

- Facilitate the development of industry–academia collaborations with adequate resources and support for departments and faculty including staff dedicated to help the development of these relationships.
- Reward those departments and faculty members who have successfully engaged in collaborations with industry while protecting the integrity of education of doctoral students, academic freedom, free scientific inquiry, and free dissemination of knowledge.
- Provide specific mechanisms to assist junior faculty in establishing healthy collaborations with industry.
- Implement intellectual property policies that do not impede the formal establishment of collaborations with industry by carefully assessing the real returns of commercialization of research versus attracting funds from industry (Mendoza & Berger, 2005). In considering this, university administrators should weigh whether it is worth losing industrial sponsorship because of restrictive intellectual property policies designed to cash in royalties in the future from potential successful licensing options.

Recommendations for External Agencies

- Federal R&D policies should be designed not only in the name of economic prosperity but also to foster scientific and technological innovation to improve broader societal needs as well as adequately train scientists and a skilled workforce in those technologies.

- Initiatives such as the I/UCRCs are successful in promoting industry–academia collaborations. However, the federal government should consider expanding these types of programs to networks of knowledge, such as the ones in Canada, including nationwide interdisciplinary and interorganizational webs around critical technologies and societal issues.
- Government programs should reward and encourage collaborative programs that protect the public good of higher education while bringing economic prosperity to communities, regions, and nations.
- While supportive of R&D collaborations between the private and the public sector, the federal government should continue investing in basic research through block grants to help scientists develop their research agendas with full academic freedom, detached from contractual arrangements with private firms. A healthy stream of unrestrictive grants for research from the federal government improves the ability of faculty members to establish contractual arrangements with industrial sponsors that do not compromise the pillars of the academic profession and the education of doctoral students.
- The federal government should increase the level of federal research funding in order to guarantee equal opportunity of access to these funds across different types of institutions. If federal grants are concentrated in a few institutions, those departments with less federal funding might be compromising their core values in order to service industrial sponsors in exchange for industrial funds that compromise the values and goals of the academic profession.

References

Austin, A. E., & McDaniels, M. (2006). Preparing the professoriate of the future: Graduate student socialization for faculty roles. In J. C. Smart (Ed.), *Higher education: Handbook of theory and research* (Vol. XXI, pp. 397–456). New York: Agathon Press.

Campbell, T., & Slaughter, S. (1999). Faculty and administrators' attitudes toward potential conflicts of interest, commitment, and equity in university-industry relationships. *Journal of Higher Education, 70,* 309–352.

Debackere, K., & Veugelers, R. (2005). The role of academic technology transfer organizations in improving industry science links. *Research Policy, 34,* 321–342.

Gardner, S. K. (2008). "What's too much and what's too little?": The process of becoming an independent researcher in doctoral education. *The Journal of Higher Education, 79,* 326–350.

Geiger, R. L. (2004). *Knowledge and money: Research universities and the paradox of the marketplace.* Stanford, CA: Stanford University Press.

Gluck, M. E. (1987). *University-industry relationships in biotechnology: Implications for society.* Unpublished doctoral dissertation, Harvard University.

Golde, C. M. (1998). Beginning graduate school: Explaining first-year. In M. S. Anderson (Ed.), *The experience of being in graduate school: An exploration* (pp. 55–64). San Francisco: Jossey-Bass.

Golde, C. M., & Dore, T. M. (2001). *At cross purposes: What the experiences of doctoral students reveal about doctoral education.* Philadelphia, PA: The Pew Charitable Trust.

Gumport, P. J. (2005). Graduate education and research: Interdependence and strain. In P. G. Altbach, R. O. Berdahl, & P. J. Gumport (Eds.), *American higher education in the twenty-first century: Social, political, and economic challenges* (2nd ed., pp. 425–461). Baltimore, MD: The Johns Hopkins University Press.

Isabelle, M. (2008). Proprietary vs. open-access dimension of knowledge. In B. Laperche & D. Uzunidis (Eds.), *Genesis of innovation: Systemic linkages between knowledge and Market* (pp. 56–81). Northampton, MA: Edward Elgar.

Kezar, A. (2004). Obtaining integrity? Reviewing and examining the charter between higher education and society. *The Review of Higher Education, 27,* 429–459.

Kezar, A. J., Chambers, T. C., Burkhardt, J. C., & Associates (2005). *Higher education for the public good: Emerging voices from a national movement.* San Francisco: Jossey-Bass.

Krimsky, S. (2003). *Science in the private interest: Has the lure of profits corrupted biomedical research?* Lanham, MD: Rowman & Littlefield.

Lee, J. J., & Rhoads, R. A. (2003). *Faculty entrepreneurialism and the challenge to undergraduate education at research universities.* Paper presented at the American Educational Research Association (AERA), Chicago, IL.

Lovitts, B. E. (2008). The transition to independent research: Who makes it, who doesn't, and why. *Journal of Higher Education, 79,* 296–325.

Mars, M. M., & Metcalfe, A. S. (2009). *The entrepreneurial domains of American higher education.* San Francisco: Jossey-Bass.

Mendoza, P. (2007a). Academic capitalism and doctoral student socialization: A case study. *Journal of Higher Education, 78,* 71–96.

Mendoza, P. (2007b). *Educating for the public good through comprehensive federal research & development policies.* ASHE/Lumina Policy Briefs and Critical Essays

No. 3. Ames: Iowa State University, Department of Educational Leadership and Policy Studies.

Mendoza, P., & Berger, J. B. (2005). Patenting productivity and intellectual property policies at Research I universities: An exploratory comparative study. *Education Policy Analysis Archives, 13*(5). Retrieved June 17, 2009, from http://epaa.asu.edu/epaa/vol13.html

Mendoza, P., & Berger, J. B. (2008). Academic capitalism and academic culture: A case study. *Education Policy Analysis Archives, 16*(23). Retrieved June 17, 2009, from http://epaa.asu.edu/epaa/vol16.html

Mendoza, P. (2009). Academic capitalism in the Pasteur's Quadrant. *Journal of Higher and Further Higher Education, 33*(3), 301–311

Mendoza, P., Kuntz, A., & Berger, J. B. (forthcoming). The effects of market forces on faculty work in science and engineering.

Merton, R. K. (1957). *Social theory of science.* Chicago: University of Chicago Press.

National Science Board. (2008). *Science and engineering indicators 2008.* Arlington, VA: Author.

Newman, F., Couturier, L., & Scurry, J. (2004). *The future of higher education: Rhetoric, reality, and the risks of the market.* San Francisco: Jossey-Bass.

Ramaley, J. A. (2005). Scholarship for the public good: Living in Pasteur's quadrant. In A. J. Kezar, T. C. Chambers, & J. C. Burkhardt (Eds.), *Higher education for the public good: Emerging voices from a national movement* (pp. 166–182). San Francisco: Jossey-Bass.

Salminen-Karlsson, M., & Wallgren, L. (2008). The interaction of academic and industrial supervisors in graduate education: An investigation of industrial research schools. *Higher Education, 56*, 77–93.

Slaughter, S., & Leslie, L. (1997). *Academic capitalism: Politics, policies, and the Entrepreneurial University.* Baltimore: The Johns Hopkins University Press.

Slaughter, S., Campbell, T., Hollernan, M., & Morgan, E. (2002). The "traffic" in graduate students: Graduate students as tokens of exchange between academe and industry. *Science, Technology, and Human Values, 27*, 282–313.

Slaughter, S., & Rhoades, G. (2004). *Academic capitalism and the new economy: Markets, state, and higher education.* Baltimore, MD: The Johns Hopkins University Press.

Slaughter, S., Archerd, C. J., & Campbell, T. I. D. (2004). Boundaries and quandaries: How professors negotiate market relations. *The Review of Higher Education, 28*, 129–165.

Stephan, P. (2001). Educational implications of university-industry technology transfer. *Journal of Technology Transfer, 26*, 199–205.

Teixeira, P., Jongbloed, B., Dill, D., & Amaral, A. (2004). *Markets in higher education: Rhetoric or reality?* Boston, MA: Kluwer Academic.

Tierney, W. G. (2006). *Trust and the public good: Examining the cultural conditions of academic work.* New York: Peter Lang.

University of Florida. (2009). *University presidents make case for tuition increase.* Retrieved March 24, 2009, from http://budget.president.ufl.edu/2009/03/24/university-presidents-make-case-for-tuition-increase

Zusman, A. (1999). Issues facing higher education in the twenty-first century. In P. G. Altbach, R. O. Berdahl, & P. J Gumport (Eds.), *American higher education in the twenty-first century: Social, political, and economic challenges* (pp. 109–148). Baltimore, MD: The Johns Hopkins University Press.

PART FOUR

INTERSECTING
SOCIALIZATION
AND DEMOGRAPHICS

7

THE INDIVIDUAL AND THE INSTITUTION

Socialization and Gender

Margaret W. Sallee

Ling has been at Flagship University for over a year now. While she has adjusted to the expectations of her polymer science program and her assistantship, she is admittedly having a hard time meeting people. Being one of the few women students in the program, much less her entire college, she often feels excluded from her peers' conversations and get-togethers. While she knew she would have trouble finding other women faculty, she was surprised at how few other women students she has met in the sciences. When coupled with the language and cultural challenges she is facing, Ling feels isolated and often lonely. This is particularly problematic when it comes to group work. Most of the male peers get together on a regular basis to work on their coursework and constantly help each other with their respective experiments and issues they may face in research. However, things are different for Ling. Her lack of peer support means that she generally has to figure out things on her own, sometimes resulting in academic performance lower than that of her peers. She wonders if she made the right decision in coming to this country.

When asked how he feels he is doing in his program, Scott, now in the second year of his child psychology degree at Ivy U, just shakes his head slowly and sighs. One of the first things that come to mind for Scott is the attitude of his male buddies questioning his masculinity as they try to figure out why is he in such a "girly" field. As one of the few male students in his area of child psychology, and one of the few students of color, he often wishes he could be with other men. Scott

doesn't know with whom he can talk about this, so he starts looking around at
other psychology programs in his college, hopefully with more males.

I n this chapter, I describe the ways in which socialization is a gendered
process that compounds differences between men and women in different disciplines. I explore gender at both an individual and an institutional
level. Every individual will have a different experience in his or her doctoral
program; some of those differences may be attributed to gender. In addition,
men and women may be found in different disciplines that have different
norms and expectations. We can say that such differences are gendered. For
example, women do not have different experiences in science and engineering
because they are inherently less capable than their male counterparts, but
rather because the disciplines create a culture that promotes a particular set of
masculine norms.

I begin the chapter by providing an overview of the status of men and
women in doctoral programs. I then turn to a brief discussion of the gen-
dering of disciplines before further exploring how particular disciplines are
more welcoming to students of one gender than the other. I then consider
how three features of doctoral education—advisor–advisee relationship, type
of assistantship, and time-to-degree—play a critical role in students' success
and the degree to which such elements differ by discipline. I conclude with
recommendations for different constituencies interested in creating a more
welcoming climate for all students. To illustrate the differences both by discipline and by gender, I draw upon examples from a recent study (Sallee, 2008)
on the experiences of doctoral students in two disciplines—aerospace and
mechanical engineering (AME), a male-dominated discipline, and English, a
female-dominated discipline. As the literature suggests and the experiences of
these students illustrate, gender—both of individual students and of a discipline—shapes students' experiences and trajectories through their programs.

Gender Across the Disciplines

Over the past 30 years, women have moved from representing a fraction of
all doctorates earned to nearly half of all doctorates earned. In 1976–1977,
men earned 76% of the 33,126 doctorates conferred across all disciplines
in the United States. Fifteen years later, in 1992–1993, the total number of
doctorates conferred rose to 42,132. Of these, men accounted for only 62%

of the total. In 2006–2007, men and women had reached parity in terms of the number of doctorates earned. Of the 60,616 doctorates conferred, women actually accounted for a slightly higher number of the 60,616 doctorates conferred: women earned 30,365, or 50.1%, of all doctorates (Snyder, Dillow, & Hoffman, 2009).

While these numbers signal good news for those interested in promoting gender equity in the academy, men and women have still not reached true parity. The professoriate continues to be dominated by men, who accounted for 58% of faculty across all ranks in the United States in 2007. While women and men are represented in near equal numbers at the assistant professor rank (men accounted for 53% of all assistant professors), men outnumber women at the full professor rank by a margin of nearly three to one (Snyder et al., 2009). Although the focus of this chapter is on the experiences of doctoral students, the representation of male and female faculty play a critical role in shaping students' experiences in their programs.

Although men and women are now earning doctorates in equal numbers across the academy, disaggregating by discipline reveals inequities. Table 7.1 highlights the differences in doctoral degree completion by selected fields.

As the table indicates, men and women are earning doctorates in disproportionate numbers in various disciplines. Some fields mirror the national data. For example, approximately the same number of men and women are earning doctorates in the biological and biomedical sciences as well as the social sciences. Yet, there are other disciplines where the percentages are far more unbalanced. Women account for only 21% of doctorate recipients in engineering and only 29% in philosophy and religious studies. Similarly, women are overrepresented in the fields of psychology, accounting for 73% of all doctorates earned, and in education, earning 68% of all doctorates. They also hold a slight majority in English, accounting for 59% of all doctoral degrees in 2007. These disciplinary differences are significant, not only because they point to the continued inequities in outcomes for male and female students but also because they lead to the creation of gendered disciplinary cultures that privilege distinct sets of gendered values.

Gender in Organizations and Universities

Early scholarship in organizational studies assumed that organizations were gender-neutral. Since men composed the majority of employees in the workplace, the male perspective was taken to represent the human perspective

TABLE 7.1

Doctorates Conferred by Gender and Selected Fields of Study, 2006–2007

Fields	Total	Men	Women
All	60,616	30,251 (49.9%)	30,365 (50.1%)
Agriculture and natural resources	1,272	768 (60%)	504 (40%)
Biological and biomedical sciences	6,354	3,221 (51%)	3,133 (49%)
Business	2,029	1,188 (59%)	841 (41%)
Education	8,261	2,681 (32%)	5,580 (68%)
Engineering	8,062	6,377 (79%)	1,685 (21%)
English	1,178	478 (41%)	700 (59%)
Mathematics and statistics	1,351	949 (70%)	402 (30%)
Philosophy and religious studies	637	453 (71%)	184 (29%)
Physical sciences and science technologies	4,846	3,317 (68%)	1,529 (32%)
Psychology	5,153	1,382 (27%)	3,771 (73%)
Social sciences	3,037	1,627 (54%)	1,410 (46%)

Source: Snyder et al. (2009).

(Acker, 1991). Little scholarship considered the degree to which gender identity influenced the experiences of employees. As women entered the workforce in greater numbers, feminist scholars such as Kanter (1977) called attention to the challenges that women faced in the workplace and the degree to which they were expected to assimilate to male norms. Kanter's work led to a transformation of organizational studies, leading to work by many scholars (e.g., Acker, 1991; Collinson & Hearn, 2005; Hearn, 2002) who explored the gendered nature of organizations and the degree to which gender shapes organizational life.

Britton (2000) suggested that organizations are typically thought of as being gendered in three ways. First, an organization might be gendered to the degree to which it has been structured based upon a distinction between masculinity and femininity. Such organizational processes will continue to reproduce distinctions that privilege masculinity while marginalizing femininity. Second, an organization might be gendered by the extent to which it is either male- or female-dominated. For example, nursing is considered to be a feminized field, since women compose the overwhelming majority of nurses. Similarly, as the number of doctorates conferred indicates, engineering is a masculine field. Finally, an organization might be considered gendered in that it is "symbolically and ideologically described and conceived in terms of a discourse that draws on hegemonically defined masculinities" (Britton, 2000, p. 420). The use of such discourse and symbols helps to explain the marginalization of women in fields that are not male-dominated. Although women's representation has increased in a variety of organizations and careers, the majority of fields were designed to focus on the needs of the male worker. As a result, many organizational practices require employees to conform to particular norms that favor one definition of the ideal, masculine worker.

Like organizations, universities too can be thought of as gendered either to the extent that they are dominated by men or women or to the extent that they adopt practices that replicate a distinction between masculinity and femininity. As highlighted earlier, men continue to outnumber women in the ranks of the faculty. Given this disparity, we might expect that female faculty and students assimilate to the norms established by the male majority. My argument here is not just that men and women have different experiences but that women in engineering will have different experiences than women in English due to differences in disciplinary cultures and expectations.

The Impact of Gendered Disciplines on Doctoral Students

As Table 7.1 illustrates, men and women populate different doctoral programs in different numbers. While roughly equal numbers of men and women pursue degrees in the social sciences, engineering and mathematics continue to be dominated by men. Such structural disparities create an environment that favors masculine norms and male students. Much has been written about the "chilly climate" in academe. First coined by Hall and Sandler (1982), scholars over the past 25 years have explored how the chilly climate has differentially impacted female faculty (Hagedorn & Laden, 2002) and female students (Crawford & MacLeod, 1990) in a variety of disciplines (Fox, 1998; Wasburn & Miller, 2006). Most frequently, issues of chilly climate are noted among women pursuing doctorates in the sciences and engineering. In particular, scholars have found that women in these fields cite lower levels of self-confidence and satisfaction with their programs, issues of gender discrimination, and an emphasis on competition more than their male counterparts. I discuss these findings below.

women less
confident

While women and men are equally qualified to pursue their doctorates, several studies have indicated that women tend to have more negative experiences in their programs and lower levels of self-confidence. In her study of men and women in a chemistry doctoral program, Ferreira (2002) found that while students of both genders entered graduate school with similar undergraduate GPAs and levels of confidence, female students reported lower levels of self-confidence at the time of the study. Similarly, in their study of students in gender-balanced and male-dominated fields, Ülkü-Steiner, Kurtz-Costes, and Kinlaw (2000) found that women in male-dominated programs reported more negative perceptions of their own competencies throughout their doctoral programs. These studies point to processes in doctoral programs that affect women's beliefs in their ability to succeed.

Perhaps such self-doubt might be attributed to experiences with gender discrimination. While men may be oblivious to gender discrimination, women's experiences suggest that the sciences are anything but gender-neutral. In a survey of 574 doctoral students in STEM fields at the University of Washington, Litzler, Edwards Lange, and Brainard (2005) found that women reported greater experiences with gender discrimination than did their male colleagues. While their results did not probe the types of discrimination experienced, female AME doctoral students in my research discussed the subtle—and not so subtle—ways in which they were discriminated against and propositioned in their departments. For example, they frequently found themselves targeted as their male colleagues' objects of affection. Jenny told several stories about different men in the department who hit on her, including one who gave Valentine's Day cards to multiple women in the same class:

> It got to a really weird part where on Valentine's Day or the day before Valentine's Day or whatever, he gave us cards. But he gave me a card that, like a Valentine's card and it had, you opened it up and it played music. It had like a little squirrel with an ice cream cone and hearts everywhere and whatever. And it said something disturbing I thought. It was like, "I love you all over!" And it was kind of like, I don't know you at all.

While some might not construe this student's actions as being discriminatory, they created an uncomfortable environment for Jenny and the other female students in the class. Female students also shared stories about finding out that male advisors in the department had different conversations with their male advisees than they did with the women. I will return to these stories later in this chapter.

In addition to gender discrimination, women in the sciences and other male-dominated departments are also more likely to report a sense of isolation and a culture of competition in the department (Ferreira, 2002; Litzler et al., 2005). In the study of chemistry doctoral students, women reported that their advisors created a lab that promoted competition, leading to a sense of isolation particularly for the women (Ferreira, 2002). Many of the AME students in my own research echoed similar claims. However, both the female and the male students in the department criticized their advisors for trying to create a culture that promotes competition and minimizes collegiality. For example, Jeff described a lab meeting in which his advisor complained about the students' lack of competition with each other:

> He's actually complained to us that we don't argue. He's like, "You don't have a big enough ego." Every semester, we have one or two meetings where he kind of complains about us . . . "What I want to see is more ego. You guys have to have more pride." It's kind of what we don't like.

While advisors argued that the sciences require competition between scholars for success, the students had adopted a different set of norms. This example underscores my contention that gender is not simply a matter of differences between men and women but about different expectations that are associated with each discipline. While Jenny's experiences being aggressively pursued by a male classmate suggest that women are indeed treated differently in engineering, Jeff's story about an emphasis on competition suggests that the entire discipline is dominated by gendered norms—and perhaps outdated norms that may change as a new generation of scholars become faculty. I have briefly focused here on the ways in which the norms of a discipline might be gendered. I now concentrate on the ways in which men and women have different experiences within their doctoral programs.

Doctoral Education and Gender Differences

Although the numbers of women pursuing doctoral degrees have risen considerably over the past several decades, graduate school remains a difficult journey for many women. While all students are expected to navigate the same obstacles, such as passing comprehensive exams and writing a dissertation, women often face a disproportionate burden off-campus. While women may not be more likely to be married or have children, they typically assume greater responsibilities for childcare than do their male counterparts (Mason & Goulden, 2004). Here, I focus on the ways in which the features of doctoral education influence women's experiences, including three features that have been repeatedly cited as critical to students' progress in graduate school: relationship with advisor, assistantships and methods of financial support, and time-to-degree. Each of these features is related and impacts the other. A student's relationship with his or her advisor, for example, is shaped, in part, by the type of assistantship held; both the advisor–advisee relationship and the type of assistantship shape a student's time-to-degree. While each is discussed separately, the areas are interrelated and indeed impact each other. I discuss each in turn, devoting attention to both the obstacles for all students and the way in which women are differentially impacted.

Advising Relationships

The faculty advisor plays a critical role in a doctoral student's success (Austin, 2002; Baird, 1992; Golde, 2000, Golde & Dore, 2001). For example, Baird (1992) argued that "the graduate faculty is the critical agent conducting . . . socialization, serving as definers of knowledge and disciplinary values, models of the roles of academics in the discipline, and producers of practical help and advice" (p. 1). In a survey of 189 graduate students at UC Santa Cruz, Tenenbaum, Crosby, and Gliner (2001) identified three types of help that advisors might provide to students: instrumental help, psychosocial help, and networking help. Instrumental help focuses on learning how to do academic and research tasks specific to doctoral study (such as writing a paper). Psychosocial help focuses on care for the individual's well-being. Finally, types of networking help include assisting the student in making contact with others working in the field. As I discuss shortly, men and women tend to receive different types of help from their advisors.

While scholars agree that good advising is important, there is less attention as to what constitutes good advising. Although students must learn the skills necessary to complete their dissertations, good advisors are not charged solely with teaching their students' skills. Rather, good advisors provide emotional support as well. Golde (2000) suggested that good advising can be measured by the amount of time the advisor and student spend together, the quality of the interactions, and a sense of investment and care in the student's success. In part, good advising can be measured by student satisfaction. Tenenbaum et al. (2001) found that students who received more psychosocial help reported greater satisfaction with their advisors and with the graduate school experience in general. In another study, Girves and Wemmerus (1988) found that students who reported being treated as junior colleagues were more satisfied with their doctoral programs. In sum, the literature highlights the fact that students with positive advising relationships excel and feel more satisfied with their programs.

While good advising is critical to students' success, the antithesis is also true: poor advising contributes to students' failure (Golde, 2000; Moyer, Salovey, & Casey-Cannon, 1999; Nerad & Miller, 1996). Golde (2000) found that students who leave their doctoral programs often point to broken relationships with their advisor as a primary reason. Similarly, in their study of graduate students who dropped out of UC Berkeley, Nerad and Miller (1996) found that poor advising relationships contributed to students' decisions to leave. One study found that women in the sciences are far more likely to leave doctoral study than are their male peers. Over a nine-year period, the attrition rate for female students averaged 45% compared with 30% for men (Ferreira, 2002). Doctoral education depends considerably on the advisor–advisee relationship. However, men and women report having different types of relationships with their advisors.

While positive advising relationships are an indicator of satisfaction with the doctoral program, research has indicated that women are less likely to have positive advising relationships than do men. In a survey of 154 graduates of York University, Seagram, Gould, and Pyke (1998) found that female doctoral students had less satisfactory relationships with their advisors than did their male counterparts. The women reported that their advisors had less interest in their dissertation topics and were more likely to report conflict with members of their dissertation committees. There is less agreement in differences in research preparation. Some have reported that women are less likely to conduct research with their advisors than men (Tenenbaum et al., 2001), whereas others (Schroeder & Mynatt, 1999) have found no difference in the numbers of publications produced by male and female students.

In addition to differences in academic preparation, scholars have found that women have different levels of social interaction with their advisors. Nettles and Millett (2006) found that male doctoral students in education and engineering perceived social interactions with faculty to be better than that reported by female students. While this study does not disaggregate by gender of advisor, other studies do. Research by Schroeder and Mynatt (1993, 1999) indicated that male and female doctoral students have different experiences depending on the gender of their advisor. In a study of female doctoral students, Schroeder and Mynatt (1993) found that those who had female advisors reported higher quality interactions and felt that their advisors were more concerned with their welfare than did students with male advisors. In a later study, the authors found that female students with male advisors reported more negative psychosocial interactions than did female students with female advisors or male students with advisors of either gender (Schroeder & Mynatt, 1999). In my research, women in AME reported learning that their advisors interacted differently with them than with their male peers. While the women's (male) advisors occasionally joked around with them, Vanessa told me that her male classmates said that the same advisors made off-color jokes in all-male settings. While one could argue that the female students were better served by not being subjected to inappropriate humor, the fact remains that the women had different types of interactions with the faculty than did the men.

In addition to different quality interactions, Schroeder and Mynatt (1999) found that male and female students reported meeting with their advisors at different levels of frequency. Students of both genders met with their advisors more in academic versus nonacademic settings. However, male students with male advisors met more frequently in nonacademic environments than did male students with female advisors or female students with advisors of either gender (Schroeder & Mynatt, 1999). The authors also found that same-gender advisor–advisee pairings interacted more frequently in nonacademic settings than did other-gender pairings. Many of the English students in my study reported occasionally meeting with their advisors to talk about academic matters. The men, however, described meeting with their advisors on a more social basis. For example, Eric was invited out to dinner with his male advisor. Joe described a typical meeting with his advisor, also a man:

> We exchanged cigars. And we talked football and we talked about the paper that I'm writing now and if it's ready for publication. He says it looks very good and . . . we also talked about a conference that I'll be presenting at in the spring and gave me information for this other professor that might be able to help me with my work. I think we set up a date too, to go hang out at this bar and smoke more cigars.

As Joe indicated, his meetings with his advisor are both social and academic. They mix conversations about requirements for papers and conferences with discussions of football and cigars. Students and faculty in mixed-gender pairings may not have the same types of common discourse to draw upon, leading to an advising relationship that may be productive academically, but less so socially. Given that the frequency of advisor contact translates into increased satisfaction and retention, the literature suggests that men may be more likely to persist through their graduate programs than women.

Assistantships and Methods of Financial Support

While the advisor–advisee relationship shapes the doctoral student experience, it alone cannot account for the variation in student outcomes. Students' trajectories through their programs are also shaped by their level of financial support and the ways in which they pay for their programs. Receiving encouragement from faculty is critical to student success. However, many students do not persist in their programs without financial support. Some report that low graduate student stipends affect students' persistence (Maher, Ford, & Thompson, 2004; Moyer et al. 1999; Nerad & Miller, 1996). For example, Moyer et al. (1999) found that 38% of students reported stress during their doctoral programs due to low stipends and the process of acquiring funding. In their study of students who dropped out of graduate study, Nerad and Miller (1996) found that students also pointed to low levels of financial support as contributing to their decision to leave. As I discuss in the next section, adequate levels of financial support can play a significant role in students' trajectories through their program. Maher et al. (2004) found that students who took longer to finish their degrees were more likely to have erratic sources of funding from both inside and outside the university than those who finished their degrees in a more timely fashion.

While some doctoral students rely on outside employment, many rely on university assistantships to pay for their graduate programs. However, different types of assistantships lead to different demands on students' time and, indeed, different rates of progress through their programs. Nettles and Millett (2006) found that 67% of students were offered some form of financial support by their institutions at time of entry. The level of support differed by discipline; 90% of students in science and mathematics were offered an assistantship versus just 46% of students in education. However, the remaining 54% of students in education were not without any financial support, but rather relied upon external sources of employment to finance their education.

Students who are employed on-campus are more integrated into their degree programs than those with employment elsewhere. Girves and Wemmerus (1988) found that students who worked either as research assistants (RAs) or teaching assistants (TAs) reported greater involvement in their graduate programs and were more likely to persist to graduation than those without university employment. The type of assistantship differs by discipline. In Nettles and Millett's (2006) study, 44% of students who were offered financial support were offered research assistantships while 60% were offered teaching assistantships. Sixty-nine percent of engineering students but only 26% of education students and 14% of humanities students were offered research assistantships. Significantly, the authors found no gender differences across all fields of study in assistantships; men and women were equally likely to work as RAs. The percentages of students offered teaching assistantships were fairly equal across fields, though only 41% of students in education and 44% of students in humanities received such support. In my study, the differences in type of assistantship were more attributable to discipline than to gender. For example, most of the students in AME worked as RAs while most of the students in English, both male and female, worked as TAs. Coupled with Nettles and Millett's (2006) findings, this suggests that gender differences do not simply reside at the individual level, but at the institutional level as well.

Time-to-Degree

A student's progress through his or her doctoral program is shaped by the factors already discussed: advisor relationship and type of funding. In their study of 160 female graduates of Stanford's School of Education, Maher et al. (2004) found differences between women who finished their doctorates in under 4.25 years and those who took more than 6.75 years to finish their doctorates. Specifically, those who they classified as early finishers were more likely to report positive relationships with their advisors. The trends hold true for students of both genders. Ferrer de Valero (2001) found that departments with high completion rates and low times to degree were characterized by positive advisor–advisee relationships and more advisor involvement in doctoral education. Similarly, the type of assistantship also affects degree progress. Those with teaching assistantships take longer to complete their degrees than do those with research assistantships (Sallee, 2008; Seagram et al., 1998).

While teaching and research are both time-intensive undertakings, students employed as RAs are often able to work on research that informs their dissertations while a TA's teaching responsibilities rarely facilitate research progress.

In addition to advising and source of funding, there is some evidence that time-to-degree differs by discipline and gender. Abedi and Benkin (1987) found that the smallest average time to doctorate was 6.8 years for students in the physical sciences. Students in education averaged the longest time to doctorate at 11.0 years. While discipline appears to make a difference, there is less agreement as to whether gender does. Nettles and Millett (2006) found no difference in their sample of degree completion between men and women. However, Abedi and Benkin found that women had a longer time-to-degree than men; women averaged 9.51 years, whereas men averaged 8.32 years to complete their program. Twenty years later, data from the 2007 Survey of Earned Doctorates Differences echo these claims. The survey reports that, on average, men earn their doctorates in 7.7 years while women take 8.2 years to earn their degree (Welch, 2008). In my research, there was little difference in rate of degree completion between men and women in each discipline. However, across disciplines, the rates varied wildly. The engineers typically finished both their master's and doctorates in a total of five years, whereas the English students averaged eight to ten years to finish their Ph.Ds. These findings again point to the fact that while some have found slight differences in time-to-degree by individual gender, the larger differences arise from disciplinary differences, or institutional gender.

In this section, I have suggested that students' trajectories through their doctoral programs are particularly influenced by three factors: the advisor–advisee relationship, type of assistantship, and time-to-degree. While the literature indicates that men and women indeed have different experiences, there is similar evidence that differences also extend across disciplines. The woman in engineering may have less in common with her female counterpart in English than her male counterpart in her own field. Such findings extend the conversation about gender from merely an individual analysis to an institutional analysis.

Suggestions for Practice

Given the individual and institutional differences outlined above, I conclude this chapter with suggestions for five key stakeholders who are interested in improving the climate and experiences for male and female doctoral students across all disciplines.

Doctoral Students

- Find support networks. As this chapter has made clear, the advisor plays a critical role in doctoral student success. Doctoral students should aim to seek out an advisor who can provide guidance to help them successfully navigate their programs. Of course, different students have different needs; some students may feel that they need more emotional support than others. While advisors are designated to provide support, students should be encouraged to seek support from other sources as well, including other professors in the department or senior graduate students.
- Advocate for change if the culture is unfriendly. Too many studies have indicated that students fail to complete their doctoral programs due to poor advising relationships and perceptions of an unfriendly climate. While faculty and administrators are ultimately responsible for creating a friendly climate, doctoral students who feel that they are being discriminated against should not be complacent. Students are advised to seek out an ally—perhaps a professor or sympathetic administrator in the department. Other possible sources include faculty and administrators in other departments or members of the Graduate Student Senate.

Faculty

- Fulfill advisor responsibilities. Faculty advisors play the single most critical role to doctoral student retention and success. Being an advisor means more than simply chairing a dissertation. It entails advising students on potential classes to take, helping them refine their research interests, and providing them with opportunities for professional development. For some students, this may also include providing emotional support. Faculty who feel unable to provide all the support that a student needs should encourage students to seek out multiple mentors.
- Do not marginalize groups of students. As the data at the beginning of this chapter indicate, some departments contain equal numbers of

women and men while others are more heavily dominated by one gender or the other. Women in the sciences and engineering frequently report that they are marginalized or experience gender discrimination. Faculty are reminded to be cognizant of their behavior. While, of course, all faculty know to avoid sexual advances toward their students, gender discrimination takes more subtle forms, including socializing exclusively with students of one gender. Faculty should strive to treat all students equitably.

Departments

- Create opportunities for students to get to know faculty. Although students are usually assigned advisors, students can benefit from knowing multiple professors in the department. As the literature has indicated, students—particularly women in male-dominated fields—can benefit from having an advisor of the same gender. Male-dominated departments might consider creating a mentoring program to match female students with female faculty mentors. Where numbers of female faculty are particularly small, as they are in many science disciplines, departments may consider creating a joint mentoring program.
- Host monthly sessions to allow students to meet each other. Much of the literature reported that the female students complained that their science departments were isolating. Similarly, AME students of both genders in my research reported knowing few other students outside of their lab. Departments might consider offering monthly lunches to allow students to get to know each other. Such events would reduce isolation as well as create possibilities for collaboration on research projects.
- Be conscious of underrepresented groups. Men in the humanities and education and women in the STEM fields have a different experience in their programs than the other gender. Departments are encouraged to be cognizant of the needs of these underrepresented groups and to consider whether the culture discriminates against these students.

Universities

- Conduct periodic audits to evaluate gender equity of institutional and departmental practices. Such an audit might include attention to the gender distribution of research and teaching assistantships. Are more men than women serving as RAs while women are primarily TAs? Such an analysis should be disaggregated by department as science and engineering students are more likely to be RAs while those in the humanities and social sciences are more likely to serve as TAs. Similarly, the institution should examine differences in time-to-degree by discipline and by gender. Regular audits will ensure that students of either gender are not being unduly discriminated against.

- Create rewards for excellent faculty advisors. Faculty tend to be rewarded for their research productivity and occasionally recognized for their work as teachers. However, the one-on-one mentoring that faculty provide is often overlooked. Institutions might consider establishing a program that recognizes and rewards professors who create research opportunities for students and otherwise facilitate academic success. At the same time, institutions should also provide workshops and other assistance to help interested faculty develop the skills to become strong advisors.

External Agencies

- Professional associations should demonstrate their commitment to gender equity. Various disciplines take their cues from their professional associations, such as the MLA (Modern Language Association) for the humanities and AERA (American Educational Research Association) for education. Each professional association should issue a statement outlining its commitment to gender equity and the steps it will take to help women and men achieve parity in the field.
- Funding agencies might tie grants to demonstration of gender equity. Faculty in the STEM fields rely considerably on funding from NSF (National Science Foundation), NIH (National Institutes of Health), and NASA (National Aeronautics and Space Administration), among others. The federal government might issue guidelines that limit funding for departments and individual faculty members who have a history of attrition by female doctoral students. Departments might also be required to include a plan for how they plan to increase the representation of women.

Conclusion

Over the past 30 years, women have moved from representing a mere fraction of doctoral students to slightly over half. However, as the data illustrate, women have not yet reached parity in all fields—nor are men equally represented in others. To continue to ensure equitable outcomes for students of both genders, departments and universities need to pay attention to their practices and create a positive climate that enables all students to succeed.

References

Abedi, J., & Benkin, E. (1987). The effects of students' academic, financial, and demographic variables on time to the doctorate. *Research in Higher Education, 27,* 3–14.

Acker, J. (1991). Hierarchies, jobs, bodies: A theory of gendered organizations. In J. Lorber & S A. Farrell (Eds.), *The social construction of gender* (pp. 162–179). Newbury Park, CA: Sage.

Austin, A. E. (2002). Preparing the next generation of faculty: Graduate school as socialization to the academic career. *The Journal of Higher Education, 73,* 94–122.

Baird, L. L. (1992). *The stages of the doctoral career: Socialization and its consequences.* Paper presented at the annual meeting of the American Educational Research Association, San Francisco.

Britton, D. M. (2000). The epistemology of the gendered organization. *Gender and Society, 14,* 418–434.

Collinson, D. L., & Hearn, J. (2005). Men and masculinities in work, organizations, and management. In M. S. Kimmel, J. Hearn, & R. W. Connell (Eds.), *Handbook of studies on men & masculinities* (pp. 289–310). Thousand Oaks, CA: Sage.

Crawford, M., & MacLeod, M. (1990). Gender in the college classroom: An assessment of "chilly climate" for women. *Sex Roles, 23,* 101–122.

Ferreira, M. M. (2002). Context factors related to women attrition from a graduate science program: A case study. *Advancing Women in Leadership Journal,* 1–10.

Ferrer de Valero, Y. (2001). Departmental factors affecting time-to-degree and completion rates of doctoral students at one land-grant research institution. *The Journal of Higher Education, 72,* 341–367.

Fox, M. F. (1998). Women in science and engineering: Theory, practice, and policy in programs. *Signs, 24,* 201–223.

Girves, J. E., & Wemmerus, V. (1988). Developing models of graduate student degree progress. *The Journal of Higher Education, 59,* 163–189.

Golde, C. M. (2000). Should I stay or should I go? Student descriptions of the doctoral attrition process. *The Review of Higher Education, 23*, 199–227.

Golde, C. M., & Dore, T. M. (2001). *At cross purposes: What the experiences of today's doctoral students reveal about doctoral education.* Philadelphia, PA: The Pew Charitable Trusts.

Hagedorn, L. S., & Laden, B. V. (2002). Exploring the climate for women as community college faculty. *New Directions for Community Colleges, 118*, 69–78.

Hall, R. M., & Sandler, B. R. (1982). *The classroom climate: A chilly one for women? Project on the status and education of women.* Washington, DC: Association of American Colleges.

Hearn, J. (2002). Alternative conceptualizations and theoretical perspectives on identities and organizational cultures: A personal review of research on men in organizations. In I. Aaltio & A. J. Mills (Eds.), *Gender, identity and the culture of organizations* (pp. 39–56). London: Routledge.

Kanter, R. M. (1977). *Men and women of the corporation.* New York: Basic Books.

Litzler, E., Edwards Lange, S., & Brainard, S. G. (2005). *Climate for graduate students in science and engineering departments.* Proceedings of the 2005 American Society for Engineering Education annual conference & exposition, Center for Workforce Development, University of Washington.

Maher, M. A., Ford, M. E., & Thompson, C. M. (2004). Degree progress of women doctoral students: Factors that constrain, facilitate, and differentiate. *The Review of Higher Education, 27*, 385–408.

Mason, M. A. & Goulden, M. (2004). Do babies matter (Part II)? Closing the baby gap. *Academe, 90*(6), 10–15.

Moyer, A., Salovey, P., & Casey-Cannon, S. (1999). Challenges facing female doctoral students and recent graduates. *Psychology of Women Quarterly, 23*, 607–630.

Nerad, M., & Miller, D. S. (1996). Increasing student retention in graduate and professional programs. *New Directions for Institutional Research, 92*, 61–76.

Nettles, M. T., & Millett, C. M. (2006). *Three magic letters: Getting to Ph.D.* Baltimore: The Johns Hopkins University Press.

Sallee, M. W. (2008). *Socialization and masculinities: Tales of two disciplines.* Unpublished doctoral dissertation, University of Southern California.

Schroeder, D. S., & Mynatt, C. R. (1993). Female graduate students' perceptions of their interactions with male and female major professors. *The Journal of Higher Education, 64*, 555–573.

Schroeder, D. S., & Mynatt, C. R. (1999). Graduate students' relationships with their male and female major professors. *Sex Roles, 40*, 393–420.

Seagram, B. C., Gould, J., & Pyke, S. W. (1998). An investigation of gender and other variables on time to completion of doctoral degrees. *Research in Higher Education, 39*, 319–335.

Snyder, T. D., Dillow, S. A., and Hoffman, C. M. (2009). *Digest of Education Statistics 2008* (NCES 2009–020). Washington, DC: National Center for Education Statistics, Institute of Education Sciences, U. S. Department of Education.

Tenenbaum, H. R., Crosby, F. J., & Gliner, M. D. (2001). Mentoring relationships in graduate school. *Journal of Vocational Behavior, 59*, 326–341.

Ülkü-Steiner, B., Kurtz-Costes, B., & Kinlaw, C. R. (2000). Doctoral student experiences in gender-balanced and male-dominated graduate programs. *Journal of Educational Psychology, 92*, 296–307.

Wasburn, M. H., & Miller, S. G. (2006). Still a chilly climate for women students in technology: A case study. In M. F. Fox, D. G. Johnson, & S. V. Rosser (Eds.), *Women, gender, and technology* (pp. 60–79). Urbana, IL: University of Illinois.

Welch, V., Jr. (2008). *Doctorate recipients from United States universities: Selected tables 2007.* Chicago: National Opinion Research Center.

8

THE Ph.D. DEGREE AND THE MARRIAGE LICENSE

A Good Pairing for Socializing Students to Doctoral Education?

Catherine M. Millett and Michael T. Nettles

Scott began graduate school after he got married a few years ago. He feels he has adjusted well to his role in his marriage but now struggles with how to balance that with his graduate school peers. He is honestly surprised that his personal life would have any influence on his graduate education, but he finds that because he is married he hasn't found the opportunity to interact much with his peers. These peers, who are almost all single, want to socialize at times when he is busy with family obligations and in places meant for singles such as bars. On top of this, his wife isn't particularly keen on the idea of Scott hanging out with all the single women in his program. He gets the feeling that he is really missing out on a lot by not having this casual time with his colleagues in the program. In particular, he has realized that key information and insights about the program and how to be successful in the career are shared in these informal gatherings.

Eva is really excited about the program but is admittedly a bit worried about the isolation she already feels from her peers. Eva has found she is dramatically older than many of her peers, something she did not expect. Because of this difference in age and maturity she tends to shy away from much interaction with the other students in her classes. She has found, however, that she feels much more comfortable with her faculty members, who are closer in age and seem to

58   INTERSECTING SOCIALIZATION AND DEMOGRAPHICS

share similar life experiences. For now, while she feels a bit awkward with her classmates, she is happy that she at least has easy relationships with her faculty. She wonders to herself, which relationship is more important?

T his chapter is based upon work supported in part by the Lilly Endowment, Inc., under Grant No. 950437; the Spencer Foundation under Grant No. 9980004; the National Center for Postsecondary Improvement under Grant No. R309A60001; and the National Science Foundation under Grant No. REC 9903080. Any opinions, findings, and conclusions or recommendations expressed in this material are those of the authors and do not necessarily reflect the views of either the Lilly Endowment, Inc., the Spencer Foundation, the National Center for Postsecondary Improvement, or the National Science Foundation.

⚔ No Road is Long With Good Company. ~Turkish Proverb✈

With the national median time-to-degree being 7.8 years and in some fields nearly 12 years (Welch, 2008), one might ask if the road to the Ph.D. is different for those who have good company—namely, a spouse or a significant other—as opposed to those who travel the road alone. The tasks that lie ahead for students who enter doctoral programs are twofold: first, they must gain mastery of their subject; and second, they must make a unique contribution to their field. Hence, each student ultimately undertakes a personal journey to earn his or her doctoral degree. In their day-to-day experiences, faculty and their fellow graduate students typically have a very strong influence on doctoral students' experiences. Regardless of whether it is discussions during the structured hours of a seminar, discussions during a research team meeting, writing a paper with fellow students and/or faculty, discussing one's work with faculty over coffee, attending a professional association meeting, or attending the annual department holiday party, students are always learning from faculty and their contemporaries what it means to be a doctoral degree holder in their field of study. This is how students are socialized into their professions.

When we began the research that led to *Three Magic Letters: Getting to Ph.D.* (Nettles & Millett, 2006), student marital status was not a central interest. Our study began in our quest to answer such public policy questions about the doctoral student experience as "How do doctoral students find the financial resources to support their academic interests and see themselves through timely completion of their Ph.D. degrees?" Such demographic matters as gender and race/ethnicity within a field were the primary lenses through which we initially examined the data. Marital status emerged as an interesting personal characteristic of doctoral student socialization, and for this book we decided to take a closer look at this facet of doctoral students' lives in relation to their socialization experiences. Two questions guide our analyses of the doctoral experience:

1. What are the differences by marital status in doctoral students having an academic advisor, a mentor, academic interactions with faculty, academic interactions with their faculty advisor, student–faculty social interactions, peer interactions, and plans for a faculty career after completing their degree program?
2. What contributes to married or single doctoral students' academic interactions with faculty, academic interactions with their faculty advisor, social interactions with faculty, and peer interactions?

The Literature on Marital Status   ✶ multiple roles

On the basis of his review of the work of Levin and Franklin (1984) and Heins, Fahey, and Leiden (1984), Baird (1990) concluded that graduate students often have nonacademic roles that are as important to them as their roles as graduate students; many, for instance, are spouses or partners and parents. These multiple roles may compete for students' attention and may be accompanied by numerous demands on students' time and energy as well as financial resources. Researchers have sought to determine the relationship between marriage or partnership and success in doctoral programs (Feldman, 1973; Hawley, 1993); marital status and productivity (Feldman, 1973; Price, 2005); marital status and social interactions (Feldman, 1973); and marital status and degree progress (Girves & Wemmerus, 1988; Price, 2005). It may be helpful to review these studies in chronological order.

Feldman (1973) analyzed a Carnegie Commission on Higher Education data set with responses from 33,000 mailed questionnaires from a spring 1969 sample of graduate and professional school students in 158 colleges and universities. In his review of the productivity of students who planned a faculty career, Feldman concluded that the greatest difference in publication—presenting a paper or publishing an article—was between married men and married women, with married men being the most productive (19% vs. 10%). In questions about socialization, women of all three types of marital status (single, married, and divorced) reported higher rates of almost never socializing with their fellow graduate students than did men. In fact, single women (25%) had a higher rate of never socializing with fellow graduate students than did married graduate students (23%).

Girves and Wemmerus (1988) examined the correlates of degree progress in either master's-level or doctoral-level programs in their 1984 single institution study of 948 graduate students from 42 departments across 12 colleges who entered graduate school at a Midwestern university in 1977. Students' marital/couple status at the start of their program as well as getting married/couple status changed were included in the analytical models. Girves and Wemmerus determined that these two student characteristics were not related to degree progress for either master's or doctoral students.

In *Being Bright is Not Enough: The Unwritten Rules of Doctoral Study*, Hawley (1993) drew on her career experiences and the extant research to provide a comprehensive overview of the journey that doctoral students take over the course of their graduate careers. At the end of the monograph, Hawley considered the impact of the graduate school experience on one's relationships with spouses, family, and friends with an eye toward earning the doctoral degree and keeping relationships with family and friends intact.

Over 30 years after Feldman (1973) published his work, Price (2005) analyzed the Andrew W. Mellon Foundation's Graduate Education Initiative data set of 11,435 students from the entering cohorts of 1982 to 1996 to determine whether graduate students who were married at the start of their graduate programs do as well as or better than students who were single at the start of their programs. Price was particularly interested in within-gender differences. He determined that married men had better outcomes than single men on degree completion, time-to-degree, likelihood of publishing, the number of publications, and obtaining a tenure-track job six months after graduation. Married women were at a slight advantage over their single women peers in publishing (both likelihood of publishing and number of publications) and completing their degrees in less time.

Methodology and Data Analyses

The research presented in this chapter is based on research that we conducted for *Three Magic Letters: Getting to Ph.D.* (Nettles & Millett, 2006). The original intent of our work was to examine gender and race/ethnicity differences within fields of study.

The sampling plan involved a three-stage design. The first stage involved selecting 21 doctoral-granting universities and inviting them to participate, the second stage involved selecting the 11 fields of study, and the third stage involved selecting a stratified sample of students from the participating universities and the relevant fields of study. Doctoral students who were beyond the first year of their doctoral coursework, and who were actively engaged in their programs in the fall of 1996, were selected from the following 11 fields: (a) biological sciences, (b) mathematics, (c) economics, (d) physical sciences, (e) education, (f) political science, (g) engineering, (h) psychology, (i) English, (j) sociology, and (k) history. For analytic purposes, the fields were collapsed into the following: education, engineering, humanities, science and mathematics, and the social sciences.

The 88-item Survey of Doctoral Student Finances, Experiences, and Achievements was developed for this study. The survey consists of seven sections: (a) application and enrollment process, (b) current doctoral program experience, (c) attendance patterns, (d) financing your doctoral education, (e) future plans, (f) undergraduate experiences, and (g) background. The sample had 9,036 doctoral students representing a 70% response rate. Men and women were equally represented in the sample. The distribution of the sample by race/ethnicity and citizenship was U.S. African Americans (10%), U.S. Asian Americans (9%), U.S. Hispanics (7%), U.S. Whites (58%), and international students (16%).

Important Analytic Variables

"Mentors, unlike advisors, cannot be assigned to specific students. Advisors may be mentors, but many advisor–advisee relationships never evolve to the mentor–protégé relationship" (Willie, Grady, & Hope, 1991, p. 72). The quote by Willie et al. rang true for us in our writing of the Survey of Doctoral Student Finances, Experiences, and Achievements. Willie was one of Catherine's mentors during her master's program. We wanted to learn more about the experiences of today's doctoral students when it came to advising and mentoring. For us, advising and mentoring are two distinct activities. We also sought to learn about students' interactions with faculty and their fellow graduate students in a variety of settings. We developed four factors that cover the range of these different types of interactions: the Peer Interaction Index, Student Faculty Social Interaction Index, Academic Interactions with Faculty Index, and Advisor Interactions (see Table 8.1).

The conceptual framework for the study focused on how students navigate the doctoral experience, including their socialization experiences. The background characteristics include the student's gender, race/ethnicity, age, parent socioeconomic status (a measure of education and occupation), marital or domestic partner status, household income, and whether the student has children under 18. Two admission credentials, GRE General Test scores (Verbal, Quantitative, and Analytical) and the selectivity of the undergraduate college, are included in each of the analyses. For predicting each outcome (interactions with faculty advisor, academic interactions with faculty, student faculty social interaction, and peer interaction), we selected from among a variety of doctoral program experiences including the following: whether the student was attending a public or private graduate school, whether the current program was the first/only choice doctoral program, whether the student had a master's degree upon entry, whether the student ever had a fellowship, whether the student ever had a research assistantship, whether the student ever had a teaching assistantship, whether the student had a mentor, whether the student was always full-time, and whether the student expected the first job to be a faculty or a postdoctoral position.

Data Analysis

The statistical analyses are both descriptive and relational. The descriptive analyses include analysis of variance (ANOVA) for continuous outcomes and chi-squares (cross tabs) for dichotomous (binary) outcomes in order to reveal similarities and differences among the race and sex groups within fields of study on the various dependent measures (Table 8.2). The relational analyses consist of regressions by field of study (Table 8.3). At the graduate level, the norms and practices with respect to such issues as funding and scholarship vary considerably. Our goal is not to compare the experiences across the fields, but rather to observe whether there is parity within a field for single and married students. We performed separate regressions for each of the five fields (Tables 8.2 and 8.3).

TABLE 8.1

Survey of Doctoral Student Finances, Experiences, and Achievements Factor Analysis

Factors and Survey Items	Factor Loading	Internal Consistency (Alpha)
Peer Interaction (z-Scored)		.731
B3.2 It has been easy for me to meet and make friends with other students in my program	.642	
B15.1 Participated in an informal study group with other graduate students	.637	
B15.2 Participated in school- or program-sponsored social activities with other graduate students	.701	
B15.5 Socialized with graduate students of different racial/ethnic backgrounds	.706	
B15.9 Socialized informally with other graduate students	.789	
Student/Faculty Social Interactions (z-Scored)		.916
B3.5 It is easy to develop personal relationships with faculty in this program	.845	
B3.6 There is a great deal of contact between professors and students out of class in program	.800	
B4.4 There is a collegial atmosphere between the faculty and students	.886	
B4.5 Satisfaction with communications between faculty and students	.904	
B4.7 Satisfaction with quality of overall faculty–student relations	.900	
Academic Interactions With Faculty (z-Scored)		.853
B4.1 Quality of faculty instruction	.643	
B4.6 Availability of the faculty to meet with students	.742	

(Continued)

TABLE 8.1
(*Continued*)

Factors and Survey Items	Factor Loading	Internal Consistency (Alpha)
B4.8 Quality of academic advising provided by faculty	.840	
B4.9 Quality of feedback on scholarly projects or academic progress	.840	
B4.10 Quality of professional advising and job placement	.703	
B4.12 Faculty interest in my research	.765	
Advisor Interactions (z-Scored)		.873
B8.1 Advisor is accessible for consultation	.797	
B8.2 Advisor offers useful criticisms of my work	.843	
B8.3 Advisor has concern for my professional development	.911	
B8.4 Advisor is interested in my personal welfare	.852	

A Profile of Doctoral Students

As we indicated in the methodology, the students who completed our survey had completed the first year of their doctoral program. Our marital status measure may not be comparable to many prior studies because we included in our definition both students who were married and students who had domestic partners at the time that they completed the study. For ease of presenting and reading, we refer to this category of our sample as *married*, and both partners and spouses are referred to as *spouses*.

Across the sample, 54% of the doctoral students were married. The largest percentage of married students (62%) majored in the field of education (as one might expect from the higher ages of doctoral students in education), followed by humanities (54%), social sciences (52%), sciences and mathematics (50%), and engineering (49%). The only significant major field difference we observed in student marital status was between education and most other

TABLE 8.2
Summary Table of Descriptive Analyses

	All Fields	Education	Engineering	Humanities	Social Sciences	Sciences and Mathematics
Descriptive Analyses						
Having an advisor						Married
Advisor is same sex as student	Single					Single
Advisor is same race as student		Married				
Having a mentor	Married		Married	Married		Married
Mentor is same sex as student						Single
Mentor is same race as student		Married				
Advisor is mentor		Married				
Interactions with faculty advisor	Married	Married	Married		Single	
Academic interactions with faculty	Married	Married	Married			
Student–faculty social interaction	Married	Married	Married		Single	
Peer interaction	Single	Single	Single		Single	
Postdegree employment plans			Married			

Notes:

Blank indicates married and single students do not differ on this measure.

Married indicates that married doctoral students have an advantage.

Single indicates that single doctoral students have an advantage.

TABLE 8.3
Summary Table of Relational Analyses

	Education	Engineering	Humanities	Social Sciences	Sciences and Mathematics
Relational Analyses					
Interactions with faculty advisor					
Academic interactions with faculty		Married		Single	
Student–faculty social interaction				Single	
Peer interaction				Single	

Notes:
Blank indicates married and single students do not differ on this measure.
Married indicates that married doctoral students have an advantage.
Single indicates that single doctoral students have an advantage.

fields. When we viewed marital status by sex, we found that 68% of the men and 59% of the women in education doctoral studies were married. In the humanities, we observed a similar pattern, with 57% of men and 51% of women being married. In the sciences and mathematics, the percentages were reversed, with 53% of women married compared with 49% of men. Differences in the marital status of men and women in the other fields were minimal.

The spouses of doctoral students in our sample are best characterized as having a high level of educational attainment. Approximately 28% of the sample who were in domestic relationships had spouses whose highest attainment was a bachelor's degree; 45% of spouses had a master's degree, 16% had a Ph.D., J.D., or M.D., and 12% of the spouses of the doctoral students did not have a bachelor's degree. Although many doctoral students' spouses have attained high levels of education, many others are pursuing their doctoral degrees at the same time. We can think of these as dual-graduate student couples. Among the students who were married, nearly one-third (29%) had spouses who were also students.

Among our sample, it appears that students are foregoing parenthood, at least temporarily. Nearly three-quarters of students reported having no children under the age of 18. Two-fifths of married students had children under 18 compared with just 8% for single students. These differences held within each of the five fields of study.

The Socialization Experiences: Descriptive Analyses

We begin by examining the advising and mentoring experiences of single and married students and then examine each of the four socialization factors. The final section presents students' career expectations after the degree program.

Advising and Mentoring

As we indicated, we asked separate questions in the survey about faculty advising and mentoring. The good news is that 92% of doctoral students reported that they have an advisor. Overall, single and married students reported similar rates of having an advisor. The only within-field difference that we noted is that married students in the sciences and mathematics reported slightly higher rates of having a faculty advisor (91% vs. 86%).

Nearly two-thirds of doctoral students had advisors who were their same sex. Among single and married doctoral students, married students reported slightly lower rates of having an advisor of the same sex compared with their single peers (62% vs. 65%). When we looked at the five fields of study, this pattern of married students reporting lower rates of having advisors of the same sex was found in the sciences and mathematics (64% vs. 70%).

Students also provided information about the race/ethnicity of their advisors. Nearly two-thirds of students reported that their advisor shared their race/ethnic background. Overall, single and married students reported similar rates of having an advisor of their same race/ethnicity. Education was the only field in which married students reported slightly higher rates of having an advisor of the same race/ethnicity (70% vs. 63%).

Nearly 70% of all doctoral students in our study reported having a mentor. Married students had a slight edge in mentoring compared with their peers in the overall doctoral sample (71% vs. 68%). A closer look within fields finds that married students retained their slight advantage when it came to having a mentor in engineering (74% vs. 67%), the humanities (78% vs. 71%), and the sciences and mathematics (73% vs. 69%). Doctoral students' experiences of having a mentor of the same sex mirror their advising experiences. Nearly two-thirds of doctoral students had a mentor of the same sex. Overall, there were no differences by marital status and only within the field of sciences and mathematics did married students report a slightly lower rate of having a mentor of the same sex (64% vs. 69%). Similar patterns were found when we examined having a mentor of the same race/ethnicity. Overall, slightly more than two-thirds of doctoral students had a mentor of the same race/ethnicity. Single and married students reported the same access to same race/mentors. As we saw in their experiences with advisors, married students in education had a slight edge in reporting having a mentor of the same race/ethnicity.

The doctoral admissions process bears some similarities to the marriage courtship ritual. Just as one seeks a good fit with one's prospective life partner, graduate students as well as faculty need to be concerned about a good fit. When students and doctoral programs are courting each other in the admissions process, one of the key issues is having a good fit or match with regard to academic interests. Doctoral programs aim to match incoming students with the intellectual foci of their department overall as well as the academic interests of the particular faculty. One important reason for this is that students will need to recruit faculty to chair their dissertation committee or to serve on the dissertation committee. With this in mind, we asked students whether their faculty advisor and faculty mentor were the same person or two different people. Slightly more than 60% of students reported that their advisor and mentor were the same person. This held true for married and single students overall as well as within field of study.

We were curious as to how long it took students to find a mentor (within months, within the first term, within the first year, within the first two years, longer than two years). For the most part, doctoral students identified a mentor in the first term of their doctoral program (50%) and by the end of the first year that number rose to 70%. Single and married doctoral students reported some slight differences in the time that it took them to identify a mentor. Single students had somewhat higher rates of finding a mentor in their first term (17% vs. 15%) and within the first year (21% vs. 19%).

Aspects of Socialization

This section reports on the four factors that we developed for socialization. The first two are related to students' academic experiences and the other two are related to their social experiences.

Interactions with faculty advisor. The factor we have called "interactions with faculty advisor" brings together all the student perceptions about their faculty advisor that relate to the accessibility, care, and interest that faculty display about their advisees' welfare, progress, and careers. We found no differences in students' experiences with their faculty advisor among the fields of study. When we compared married students with single students overall, married students had higher ratings of their interactions with faculty. This rang true in the fields of education and engineering. Conversely, in the social sciences, married students had lower ratings than did their single peers. Married and single students reported similar ratings in the humanities and the sciences and mathematics.

Academic interactions with faculty. The factor that we are calling "doctoral students' academic interactions with faculty" combines all the aspects that relate to the quality of faculty instruction: faculty availability to meet with students, faculty academic advising, faculty feedback on projects and academic progress, faculty interest in student research and the quality of professional advising, and job placement by faculty. There were some variations by field in students' ratings of their academic interactions with faculty. Students in the social sciences rated their experiences lower than did their peers in each of the four other fields. Overall, married students rated their academic interactions with faculty higher than did their single peers. These differences were found within the fields of education and engineering. We found no differences in the humanities, the sciences and mathematics, or the social sciences when it came to marital status and academic interactions with faculty.

Student faculty social interaction index. Our measure of faculty social interaction reflects the general relationships that develop between students and faculty outside of classrooms. The five items that comprise the faculty social interaction factor reflect student perceptions of the quality, ease, and satisfaction of doctoral student relationships with faculty in their program. Doctoral students in the social sciences reported the lowest scores for this index. Their scores were lower than those of their peers in education, engineering, and the sciences and mathematics. Engineering and sciences and mathematics students were relatively similar in their perceptions of the student–faculty social interactions. In the aggregate, married students had higher ratings of student–faculty social interactions. This pattern was also seen in the field of education, engineering, and the sciences and mathematics. In the social sciences, however, married students had lower ratings than did their single peers. Married and single students in the humanities had similar views of their student–faculty social interactions.

Peer interaction index. Our peer interaction factor is broadly cast and includes five items that deal with the ease of meeting and making friends with other students, participating in informal study groups with other graduate students, participating in sponsored social programs, socializing with graduate students of different racial backgrounds, and socializing informally with other graduate students. When we look at doctoral students reporting on their peer interactions, students in education and engineering reported less positive experiences than did their peers in the social sciences and the sciences and mathematics. In a reversal of the patterns that we saw with faculty, overall, single students reported higher ratings for peer interactions than did their married peers. With the exception of the humanities, these differences held when we examined individual fields of study.

Postdegree employment plans. The final issue that we included in our exploration of married and single students' socialization during their doctoral programs is their career expectations after they earn their degree. One set of analyses looked at whether students expected to hold a faculty or postdoctoral position compared with other types of jobs (e.g., industry, government, and self-employment). Slightly less than half the students reported that they expected a faculty or postdoctoral position, which is in keeping with national trends (60% in 2006) (Hoffer, Hess, Welch, & Williams, 2007). Overall, single and married students were similar in their expectations to hold a faculty or postdoctoral position. Within fields, engineering was the only field in which married students reported a higher rate of expecting to hold a faculty/postdoctoral position than did their single peers.

Relational Analyses

Having a Mentor

In planning our approach to the relational analyses for *Three Magic Letters* (Nettles & Millett, 2006), we decided that since doctoral students identified their mentors so early in their doctoral careers that we needed to limit our predictive variables to the information that faculty had at the time of admission. Although we know the marital status of students when they completed the survey, we did not know whether it was the same at the time of admission. Therefore, we did not include marital status in the relational analyses for mentoring.

Interactions With Faculty Advisor

When we started the separate regression analyses by field to determine the important predictors of students' interactions with their faculty advisor, we included students' marital status. Our analyses found that when we held all other conditions constant, students' marital status was not a predictor of interactions with faculty advisors in any of the five fields.

Because this book focuses on socialization we thought it might be useful to report on what we found about two other aspects of students' socialization experience that contribute to students' positive perception of their interactions with their faculty advisor. One notable predictor is having one faculty member who serves as both a student's advisor and his or her mentor. With the exception of education, students who had the same person serving as both their advisor and mentor reported more positively on their interactions with their faculty advisor. Similarly, students in all five fields who aspired to a first job as either faculty or postdoctoral researcher compared with their peers with other initial career goals generally rated their interactions with their faculty advisor positively.

Academic Interactions With Faculty

This factor measures students' opinions about the overall quality and performance of their faculty in teaching, research, and advising and how accessible they are to students. In the social sciences, married students rated faculty academic interactions lower than did single students. The opposite experience was found in engineering, with married students rating their faculty academic interactions higher than did single students.

The most important correlates to predicting academic interactions with faculty are having a mentor, attending one's first/only choice doctoral program, expecting to achieve a faculty/postdoctoral position upon completing a degree, and spending less time progressing through their program. Having a mentor seems to be the key predictor of students' feelings about their academic interactions with faculty. In all five fields, having a faculty mentor results in between .45 to .73 SD increase in the academic interaction with faculty index.

Student Faculty Social Interaction Index

Student–faculty social interaction is a measure of the relationships that develop between students and faculty outside of classrooms. The four items that comprise the measure reflect student perceptions about the quality and ease of their social relationships with faculty. In many respects, this factor is quite similar to academic interactions with faculty. Married students in the social sciences had less favorable social interactions with faculty.

A variety of other characteristics and experiences are related to positive student–faculty social interactions, with the most prominent being students having a mentor, being enrolled at their first/only choice doctoral program, and spending relatively little time pursuing their doctoral degree. In all fields, students with mentors reported strong student–faculty social interactions. In fact, having a mentor may be the key to positive student–faculty social interactions. The size of the increases in student–faculty interactions by virtue of having a mentor were larger than increases based upon any other attribute we studied. Students with a faculty mentor compared with those without a mentor reported an increase in student–faculty social interactions ranging from a .44 SD increase in sciences and mathematics to as high as a .63 SD increase in education. Students who expect to be college or university faculty or a postdoctoral position also had more favorable views of student–faculty social interactions in education, the humanities, and in sciences and mathematics compared with students with alternative career plans.

Peer Interaction Index

Peer interaction is a measure of the students' experiences with their graduate school peers. It takes into account the nonclassroom experience with them. For the most part, marital status did not predict peer interaction. Only in the social sciences did married students report weaker social relations with peers. Expecting to have a career as a college or university professor or a postdoctoral position had a significant positive effect upon social participation in the humanities but a negative effect in education.

It should not be surprising that the type of funding doctoral students receive may contribute to peer interaction. In all fields except engineering, being a teaching assistant contributed favorably to students' social participation. Likewise, in two fields, engineering and sciences and mathematics, being a research assistant contributed favorably to students' social participation. A

common belief is that a byproduct of student participation as teaching or research assistants is a greater connection to their departments because students
are likely to have office space and be required to conduct their assistantship
assignments in their department. By contrast, fellowships have typically been
viewed as funding vehicles that may require students to engage in little contact with the department, since students may not receive office space or be
required to spend time in their department. Hence, we were surprised to see
that in all fields except humanities, having a fellowship contributed favorably
to students developing peer social interactions. It could be that the reduced
workload of fellowship recipients relative to research and teaching assistants
offers students more flexible schedules to establish peer connections, and
perhaps even a greater sense of belonging to their academic programs. Another hypothesis is that engineering and sciences and mathematics students
have more instances of working as part of a research group in their classes
than do students in other fields and this spills over to other aspects of their
relationships with peers.

Summary of Descriptive and Relational Analyses

Married students appear to be at an advantage on several aspects of doctoral
socialization in the descriptive analyses. Overall, and in each field, with the
exception of the humanities, single students have higher rates of peer interaction than do married students. In the humanities, the only difference appears
to be that married students more often have a mentor than do their single
counterparts. Married students also have a greater frequency of having a mentor overall and in engineering and in sciences and mathematics. Despite more
often having a mentor of the same race in the field of education, married students in that field do not have a mentor more frequently than do their single
contemporaries. Just as single students in education are dominant with peer
interaction, married students lead in both academic and social interactions
with faculty generally, and with their faculty advisor. These advantages for
married students are prevalent in the fields of education and engineering. In
the case of social interaction with faculty it also applies to the field of science
and mathematics. Married science and mathematics students also reported
having an advisor more often than did their single counterparts, but overall,
and in science and mathematics, single students report more often having an

advisor of the same sex as their own. Only in the field of education do married students more often report having an advisor of their own race.

In the relational analyses, in which we were able to hold constant other aspects of the doctoral student experience such as other background characteristics, admissions attributes and criteria, funding during doctoral program, and graduate school experiences, married and single students appeared to have many similar experiences. One exception was that married students in engineering reported higher scores for their academic interactions with faculty. In contrast, single students rated their academic interaction with faculty, student–faculty social interaction, and peer interaction higher than did their single peers.

A Cautionary Note

Our two groups of interest in this chapter were married and unmarried students and their experiences with different dimensions of doctoral socialization. We must make a cautionary note that there may be a self-selection effect in which married students have unobservable characteristics (e.g., motivation and outgoing nature) that make them more likely to participate in socializing opportunities, which makes it difficult to determine causation. There may be a number of differences between students who are married during their doctoral programs that we are not able to take into account.

Doctoral Student Socialization is Not Just an End Point

In this chapter, we focused on the different components of doctoral student socialization, the related student background, and behavioral characteristics, and examined whether and how the experiences were different for married and single students. As we demonstrated, doctoral student socialization experiences, in turn, have an influence on other critical aspects of the doctoral student experience. The types of analyses presented in *Three Magic Letters* (Nettles & Millett, 2006) reveal how aspects of the doctoral experiences influence other experiences and outcomes. For example, although not in each of the five fields, faculty mentoring is a predictor of other outcomes of doctoral education such as presenting a paper at a conference, publishing an article, students' overall research productivity, their rate of progress in doctoral programs, their degree completion, and their time to degree.

The relational analyses revealed a different story. Student marital status appears to make little difference in student achievement of the doctoral student socialization outcomes in education, the humanities, and the sciences and mathematics. In engineering, married students have an advantage in academic interactions with faculty. In the social sciences, the opposite patterns occurs, with single students having an edge over their married peers in academic interaction with faculty, student–faculty social interaction, and peer interaction.

Moving Research Into Practice—Implications for Doctoral Students

Our intent is for the research to inform students' experiences. Here are some suggestions for doctoral students that are based upon the analyses conducted for this chapter:

Connect With Other Doctoral Students:

- In order to keep social pace with single students, married students need to accelerate their peer relationships. Typical strategies might include the following: form study groups, work on assignments, or write conference papers together.
- Married students: seek out other doctoral students in your program or at your graduate school with spouses or families. Help connect your family to other families at your university.
- Invite peers to review your course papers or work that you do as part of your research team. Provide feedback about the work that you are conducting as well as the areas that you can improve.

For Expanding Academic Relationships With Faculty:

- Join student campus groups.
- Join professional associations in one's discipline.
- Join student–faculty committees on campus. For example, volunteer to serve on faculty or administrative search committees.

For Expanding Social Relationships With Faculty:

- Invite a faculty member for coffee. Explore common research interests and hobbies or social interests.

- Meet with a faculty member during office hours to discuss assignments or to think about your future academic and professional activities. Prepare for the meeting ahead of time so that you have an agenda for what you want to discuss.

Sustaining Relationships With Advisors:

- Read and discuss the different stages of the doctoral degree (see Mendoza & Gardner, Introduction). Discuss activities of the profession that you plan to enter after your doctoral program. Consider each faculty member in the department on what he or she contributes to your development.
- Ask other students about their experiences with a prospective faculty advisor. Ask students if the faculty member has different expectations of married and single students.

Expanding Mentor Relationships:

- Consider selecting or changing advisors to someone who can also serve as a mentor.
- When possible, student research interests should be aligned with faculty research interests.

References

Baird, L. L. (1990). The melancholy of anatomy: The personal and professional development of graduate and professional school students. In J. C. Smart (Ed.), *Higher education: Handbook of theory and research* (Vol. VI, pp. 361–392). New York: Agathon Press.

Feldman, S. D. (1973). Impediment or stimulant? Marital status and graduate education. *American Journal of Sociology, 78*, 982–994.

Girves, J. E., & Wemmerus, V. (1988). Developing models of graduate student degree progress. *Journal of Higher Education, 59*, 163–189.

Hawley, P. (1993). *Being bright is not enough. The unwritten rules of doctoral study.* Springfield, IL: Charles C Thomas.

Heins, M., Fahey, S. N., & Leiden, L. I. (1984). Perceived stress in medical, law, and graduate students. *Journal of Medical Education, 59*, 169–179.

Hoffer, T. B., Hess, M., Welch, V., Jr., & Williams, K. (2007). *Doctorate recipients from United States universities: Summary report 2006*. Chicago, IL: National Opinion Research Center.

Levin, R. B., & Franklin, A. L. W. (1984). Needs assessment and problem identification of first-year and second-year medical students. *Journal of Medical Education, 59*, 908–910.

Nettles, M. T., & Millett, C. M. (2006). *Three magic letters: Getting to Ph.D.* Baltimore, MD: The Johns Hopkins University Press.

Price, J. (2005). Does a spouse slow you down? Marriage and graduate student outcomes [Electronic Version]. Retrieved January 31, 2009, from http://ssrn.com/abstract=933674

Welch, V., Jr. (2008). *Doctorate recipients from United States universities: Selected tables 2007*. Chicago, IL: National Opinion Research Center.

Willie, C. V., Grady, M. K., & Hope, R. O. (1991). *African-Americans and the doctoral experience: Implications for policy*. New York: Teacher's College Press, Columbia University.

9

A SENSE OF BELONGING

*Socialization Factors That Influence the Transitions of
Students of Color Into Advanced-Degree Programs*

Rachelle Winkle-Wagner, Susan D. Johnson, Carla
Morelon-Quainoo, and Lilia Santiague

*"Why does everybody think that I am a genius?" Ling tells her mother over the
phone with frustration. "I am just a hard working student. I make mistakes and
fail sometimes too," she continues. Ling explains that she finds the pressure of being
the "model minority" overwhelming. Despite her success academically, she struggles
to live up to the expectations that others have placed upon her, just because she is
Asian. She wants people to see her as an individual, with qualities and defects,
rather than as a representative of her entire race. Tomorrow she has a final exam,
and as usual, she worries that she is not going to be able to sleep well because of
the anxiety of not being able to get the expected "A."*

*Scott is the only African American in the entire child psychology program right
now. "It just feels lonely here," he thinks to himself. The prospect of becoming a
faculty member is even more discouraging. He recently learned that only a handful
of African American faculty exist in the entire field, but he has yet to meet any.
"Why should I even bother? I don't belong here," he says to himself often. Scott
feels he is at the point of seriously considering not pursuing an academic career,
despite the encouragement of his advisor to do so.*

*Eva has lived her entire life in South Florida close to her extended family.
Indeed, family is the focus of Eva's life, and so she spends most of her weekends
with her relatives. This leaves her classmates frustrated because she is hardly ever
available on the weekends to work on group assignments. In fact, her classmates*

have a hard time understanding why it is so important for Eva to socialize with her extended family every single weekend. At the same time, Eva wishes that her classmates and instructors had more respect for her culture and values.

There is an increasing need for graduate or professional degrees. The National Center for Education Statistics (2008) estimates that 2.6 million students will be seeking advanced degrees over the next 10 years and many of them will be minority students. Yet, relatively few people actually earn advanced degrees—only about 2% of U.S. citizens earned master's degrees in the past 10 years and only 1% of the U.S. population attained a doctoral-level degree (Bauman & Graf, 2003). This relatively small percentage shrinks even more when examining people from racially underrepresented groups (Redd, 2007).

There has been an increase in the number of students of color enrolling in doctoral degree programs, approximately a 7% increase in the past 10 years (Redd, 2007, p. 1). Yet, large disparities persist when students of color are compared with their White peers (Harvey, 2002). The majority of the advanced degrees earned by students of color were most recently earned by women (Hoffer et al., 2005). There are also disparities in the fields of study for students of color. For example, most of the advanced degrees earned by African Americans were in the field of education (Hoffer et al., 2005). Even for those students of color and women who do earn advanced degrees, research demonstrates that many are "rejecting academic careers," for one reason or another, declining to pursue tenure-track or positions within the professoriate (Glazer-Raymo, 1999).

What leads to the "rejection of academic careers," particularly for students from underrepresented groups? While there is bourgeoning research on the graduate experience, scholarship examining the nuances of students of color in advanced-degree programs remains comparatively meager. Many students of color in advanced-degree programs learn that it is difficult to find academic, social, and emotional support during their degree programs (Gay, 2004; Howard-Hamilton, Morelon-Quainoo, Johnson, Winkle-Wagner, & Santiague, 2009). A growing body of evidence indicates that students of color are heavily influenced by a lack of faculty or peer support (Boice, 1992; Cosgrove, 1986; Cronan-Hillix, Gensheimer, Cronan-Hillix, & Davidson, 1986; Fox, 1984; Gay, 2004; Hancock, 2002). This gap in faculty support can lead to intellectual, physical, and cultural isolation (Gay, 2004).

Some of the other factors influencing the experiences and success of students of color in advanced-degree programs are a lack of socialization (Turner, Miller, & Mitchell-Kernan, 2002); involvement on campus (Gardner & Barnes, 2007); mentoring (Davidson & Foster-Johnson, 2001; Hinton, Grim, & Howard-Hamilton, 2009); religion or spirituality (Howard-Hamilton, Hinton, & Ingram, 2009); financial support, including assistantships, scholarships, and fellowships (Johnson, Kuykendall, & Winkle-Wagner, 2009); student–faculty interaction or a lack thereof (Hancock, 2002); marginalization/isolation (Beoku-Betts, 2004; Gay, 2004; Turner et al., 2002); and program culture and environment (Lovitts, 2004). The research findings presented here attempt to elucidate the factors that influence the transition and matriculation process (i.e., a sense of belonging) for first-year graduate and professional students into advanced-degree programs with particular attention toward socialization factors.

Theoretical Framework   belonging definition

Herzig (2006) reiterated a definition of *belonging* as "the extent to which each student senses that she or he belongs as an important and active participant in all aspects of the learning process" (p. 263). This is something that can be realized through various aspects of the learning experience, both in- and out-of-class. Herzig argued that the socialization process shapes the learning experience, as it often entails exposure to both academic and social activities designed to impart certain knowledge and impress upon the student the expectations of the major.

The academic and social communities, Herzig (2006) suggested, are instrumental in a student's development and learning. Herzig's study of graduate-level mathematics students led to the conceptualization of *academic* influences as "faculty beliefs about teaching and learning" as well as "both faculty and student beliefs about mathematics and mathematics epistemology" (p. 256). *Social* influences were described as "students' relationships with faculty both in- and out-of-class, encompassing teaching, mentoring and advising and informal interactions and relationships, in addition to students' relationships with other students" (p. 256). Herzig's delineation of academic and social influences informs the research in this chapter and provides a framework for understanding how these factors shape students' perception of their sense of belonging.

In advanced-degree programs, the department and its faculty are the locus of all primary socialization activities. As Austin (2002) explained, "Socialization is the process through which an individual becomes part of a group, organization or community. The socialization process involves learning about the culture of the group, including its values, attitudes and expectations" (p. 96).

The hierarchy of the faculty and department, and the apprenticeship model often used in graduate education, suggests that a student's ability to form meaningful and effective relationships and to partake in the socialization experience (especially with faculty) is imperative if he or she wishes to succeed. It follows that a student's capacity to successfully navigate such relationships will undoubtedly affect his or her ability to matriculate and graduate from the program. More specifically, developing the capacity to become involved in and make sense of the socialization process and becoming attuned to the ideal notion of a professional are daunting for most, and especially for students of color whose numbers are miniscule in comparison to their nonminority peers. This chapter attempts to reveal some of the factors that affect socialization for students of color in advanced-degree programs.

Methodology

The data for this research stem from a larger study examining factors that shape the way in which students of color choose and matriculate through their graduate and professional programs (see Howard-Hamilton et al., 2009). The primary research question guiding the larger study was "What factors influence the decision-making process for students to pursue and persist in graduate school?"

The inquiry followed a qualitative focus group study design as outlined by Denzin and Lincoln's (2003) conception of a focus group where the interviewer "directs the inquiry and the interaction among respondents" in an attempt to investigate a research problem (p. 71). This method afforded participants the freedom to choose aspects of their educational process on which to elaborate so that it was possible to collect foreseeable as well as unanticipated information about their experiences (Manning, 1992). Exploratory in nature, a semi-structured interviewing technique allowed for an in-depth examination of participants' experiences in the first year of advanced-degree programs (Miles & Huberman, 1994).

Participants

While the larger study was multi-institutional and included students from various academic disciplines, we chose in this chapter to focus particularly on first-year graduate and professional students in the Schools of Education and Law at a Midwestern State University (MWSU). Employing purposeful sampling techniques, researchers contacted administrators in the Schools of Education and Law at MWSU to obtain contact information for first-year graduate and professional students. The doctoral students incorporated into this chapter included four females: Anna, a Latina student; and three African American students, Naya, Alana, and Lisa. The four African American professional students included one male and three females: Tony, Kira, Yvette, and Stacey.

Design and Procedure

Invitation messages with the study purpose and contact information were sent via e-mail to all first-year graduate and professional students at MWSU. As students responded, researchers arranged focus groups at times and locations convenient for the students. During the focus groups, lasting approximately 90 to 120 minutes, one researcher directed questions to the students while the other recorded field notes and observed the interview process in an attempt to capture the meaning of participants' experiences during their first year as graduate and professional school students.

The data were analyzed using the constant comparative method, an inductive process for forming a categorical model to describe the data collected in a study (Glaser & Strauss, 1967; Lincoln & Guba, 1985). This iterative method of data analysis continuously develops a process for explaining individual units of information as compared to the large whole of the data in an effort to eventually construct a descriptive model. Following verbatim transcription, researchers examined interviews through an open-coding process identifying potential themes and meaningful categories from actual text examples (Denzin & Lincoln, 2003; Strauss & Corbin, 1998). After each transcript was coded, other researchers on the team checked the coding. In addition, coding software was utilized to electronically process the data.

Trustworthiness

To ensure the accurate interpretation of participant comments and responses, researchers employed member checking where they shared an initial draft of the interview transcriptions and findings with focus group participants. Through this process, participants provided feedback and revisions to the initial transcripts. In addition, all analyses were checked by multiple research team members, thus establishing reliable and replicable codes.

Limitations

The number of participants, the use of a single institution, and the ethnic composition of the focus groups are several notable limitations of the study. Despite the fact that qualitative research allows for and is designed to accommodate smaller sample sizes, we recognize that a larger number of participants would provide greater evidence that could be generalizable to a larger population. The work at hand, however, provides the context by which to further build research regarding graduate education socialization for students of color. Given the relative lack of diversity in the selected graduate and professional programs at the chosen institution, most students in the study were African American. To adequately and thoroughly discuss graduate students of color, a more diverse sample of students is needed. The incorporation of institutions of varying Carnegie classifications and the inclusion of White students for comparative purposes would further expand the limited literature on the socialization of graduate and professional students of color.

Findings

In the interest of understanding the factors that influence the extent to which first-year students are socialized in order to transition smoothly into their graduate or professional programs, the following emergent themes are discussed: (a) faculty and institutional socialization and support, (b) peer socialization and support, and (c) family and community socialization and support.

Faculty and Institutional Socialization and Support

Reflecting on the short amount of time that they had been enrolled in their programs, most of the students offered strong opinions about the need to feel a "sense of belonging," which was influenced by faculty interest in their academic and professional growth. Lisa and Alana, doctoral students in education, shared the sentiment that faculty interest in their research areas was instrumental in helping them to feel welcomed and competent as new scholars. Lisa specifically commented that validation from faculty was an indication that her physical presence and areas of interest were meaningful to the department and the field. This combination of faculty interest and support, Lisa noted, would be "the difference between me staying here and leaving." Support can be a key factor to both the initial transitions and ultimate persistence in advanced-degree programs. Lisa's comments intimate that faculty and department-level support of her research interests were integral to her decision to persist in her program.

The importance of faculty and peer support was also emphasized by Naya, a doctoral student in education, "In a lot of cases, for us . . . we are the first ones in our families. So, it's not like we have people we can talk to and say, 'How does this system work?' [White students] know how to work the system." Graduate school, for Naya, is a "system" that she needed to disentangle to better understand what was necessary to succeed academically. Faculty and peer support were commonly considered integral to demystifying the "system," to make it accessible for the students in this study, especially first-generation graduate students such as Naya. In this example, as was the case with the majority of the participants in this study, Naya felt that White students had an advantage when it came to figuring out the "system" of graduate school.

For many of the advanced-degree students in this study, their expectations of faculty support were not met once they came to campus. As students of color, the students had specific expectations of faculty of color. Alana expressed initial excitement about the possibility of interacting with the few African American faculty members in the school. However, she conveyed her disappointment in having little time and few opportunities to dialogue with them: "We don't really get the support that we see other students getting, but I'm determined to finish this program no matter what they do, what they don't do, no matter what happens." Alana felt that she did not receive the support she saw White students receiving. It was as if she felt like she had to find a way to succeed in the program despite the fact that she felt unsupported by faculty.

Some students longed for more faculty of color to help socialize them into the departmental and institutional norms. Naya noted, "Frankly, they don't have as many [minority faculty] as I thought they would have." Alana agreed and indicated that she had not received as much support from African American faculty as she had hoped. Although she did not fault the faculty members, it is clear that her expectations of faculty support were not met. Many students mentioned the lack of faculty of color and also explained that the presence of more faculty of color would have facilitated their adjustment to and socialization within their graduate programs.

Anna, on the other hand, had opportunities to form a relationship with a Latino faculty member in her department (in addition to her assigned advisor), and she maintained that having the professor as an unofficial advisor was integral to making her transition more comfortable. She explained that the professor offered advice that was especially valuable for a first-generation student who was unfamiliar with various aspects (i.e., the "system") of the doctoral program: "[The professor] has just been like, 'This is what you need to do,' and 'This is how [you need to do this],' and 'You need to stand up for yourself.'" In Anna's case, she described the way in which her faculty mentor was socializing her to the discipline and institutional norms. Her close relationship with her faculty advisor helped her to understand the "system" and to successfully transition into it.

The law students were not as conversant about the role of faculty support in their transition into the program. In a matter-of-fact tone, the law students acknowledged that faculty were there if they needed help. But they believed that as a law student, as noted by one student, one should "find your own way." However, this was the extent of their sentiments about faculty influence, suggesting that law students did not have high expectations for faculty support. Stacey was the only student who specifically stated that she desired close interaction with faculty. Conceding that the law student culture is more individualistic, she still expressed disappointment in feeling that she would not have the opportunity to develop more personal relationships with her faculty members as she progressed through the program.

While the law students were less likely to readily describe a need for faculty support, many of these students did describe this type of support as one of the reasons for their successful transition into the program. Many of the law students in this study were involved in a state need-based financial aid program, the Law Opportunity Fellowship. Participants explained that the Law Opportunity Fellowship program, which required students to matriculate on campus during the summer and offered early exposure to faculty, ultimately helped to socialize them to the norms of the law program. Stacey explained how the Law Opportunity Fellowship summer program helped her to get to know professors and students by stating that the program "helped in knowing who did what and, I guess, before that, being in contact [with] students and asking them what the professors are like and what are the students are like." This summer program allowed many of the students to learn the law school "system," initiating supportive relationships with faculty and other students before actually arriving on campus, therefore, easing the transition process.

Relative to the larger sentiment of institutional support, the advanced-degree students in this study often described their transition into graduate school using the word "shock." For instance, Anna recalled, "I was going through 'Midwest shock.' It's such a conservative, such a homogenous, a religious, you know, a remote location." Anna noted that forming relationships with other students of color reduced her "Midwest shock," although she still often struggled with the lack of diversity on campus. This was a prevalent issue for many of the participants because the lack of diversity led to a feeling of shock that ultimately made the institutional environment feel less supportive. At times, peers helped to alleviate these feelings, and the perception that the institution/faculty/department was not supportive.

Peer Socialization and Support

Upon arriving on campus, students formed new friendships and found social outlets to absorb the potential stress associated with becoming acclimated to a new environment. At times, these social outlets or peer relationships supplanted the perceived lack of faculty support. This peer support and socialization occurred both within and outside of academic programs.

At the program or department level, there was a sense among the law students that it was important to do well, especially as minority students. Some of their comments suggested that they were more reliant on their peers for support since there were few opportunities for close interaction with faculty. For example, one student noted, "You want [the other African American students] to do well so we will make sure that we are getting our work [done]. So there is a support network to kinda push you along." In this case, the law student was referring particularly to other students of color. This implies that in the law school, students of color find the greatest support among other students of color. Naya described the importance of her friendships within her department in the school of education, "Having a friend here . . . really has helped me having that bond. That network. [A friend who is also a student of color] kind of knows what you're going through." Other students used the term *network of friends* to describe their peer groups, often comprising other students of color. According to many of the participants, this peer network, consisting of peer support among and between students of color, was especially important in socializing the students to the departments, institutions, and disciplines. It was as if students (either consciously or subconsciously) socialized one another when they did not find support from faculty or the institution.

Outside of academic departments or programs, many of the students of color in this study sought out involvement in cultural activities. Perhaps this was a way to make the predominantly White campus seem more manageable, and to stay engaged with ethnic communities. At times, because students in advanced-degree programs were so busy, this involvement was not active involvement. Rather, involvement took the form of collecting information and staying aware of on-campus events and activities associated with a cultural group. For example, Anna actively sought evidence of a Latino culture on the campus and was relieved and happy to find a very active Hispanic culture center on campus. Although she did not have much time to consistently take advantage of the culture center's offerings, Anna said that she relied on the listserv to feel connected to the Hispanic community. She noted, "I'm updated through their emails which are constant, like weekly emails and it's like two pages of events . . . I still kinda keep my ear to the ground to see what they're up to." Thus, while Anna was unable to be actively involved in the Hispanic culture center, she felt comforted and supported by the weekly updates, knowing that there were others on campus with whom she could identify and to whom she could turn for support.

Law students identified organizations such as the Black Law Students Association (BLSA) as a facilitator for social interaction. In addition to this outlet, the Law Opportunity Fellowship was mentioned as a catalyst for students of color in law school as a place for students to find support from other underrepresented students.

Relative to campus involvement, some of the participants underscored the separation between minority and majority students. One student in education mentioned, "We tend to hang out with ourselves and not go out to other people's functions." This relates to the discussion above about the need for peer support from other students of color that many participants voiced. In general, the students of color in advanced-degree programs seldom mentioned meaningful peer interactions or peer support from White students on campus.

While there seemed to be comparatively less peer interaction between White students and students of color, there also appeared to be less interaction among various student of color groups on campus. For example, Tony was concerned about the racial separation on campus and in the local community: "I come from an area where Blacks and the Latinos kinda stick together and here it's different." Tony indicated that on this campus, African American students primarily spend time with African American students and Latino students mostly are friends with only Latino students. Thus, while both groups were in the minority on campus, they often did not interact.

The participants described mixed experiences relative to faculty and peer support. Thus, some students described their primary support as stemming from their families, friends, and communities off campus.

Family and Community Socialization and Support

Many of the participants described finding support from the surrounding community, churches, and friendships off-campus. Among law and education students in advanced-degree programs, there was often discussion about the "purpose" or "reason" for working toward the degree when discussing their religious beliefs/spiritual beliefs, families, and communities. Although these sources of off-campus support may not have socialized the students to an academic discipline, families and communities played another socializing role for the students that often gave the students a purpose or reason for working hard to persist through their programs.

Naya told us about a group of friends from her past that remained close and supportive of one another. According to Naya, they encouraged one another to remain steadfast in their various pursuits. Anna offered an additional perspective: "It's really hard to be the first one treading that path. So, we rely on each other, you know, to kinda get through. And, even though I went to a school that was five or six hours away from them, it was constant phone calls and support in that manner." Thus, in addition to the support within the department from either faculty or peers, many of the students also relied on their much-needed support from people off-campus. This was particularly important if the students were unable to find supportive peers or faculty on campus.

Family sometimes provided much-needed support as well as a sense of purpose as the doctoral and professional students transitioned into their programs. When asked what their primary sources of support were, many of the participants noted that "family" was integral to their success. Familial support, the students contended, was a source of resilience when the program became challenging. Many of the doctoral students in particular explained that they were first-generation doctoral students, and thus, their degree provided a sense of hope and inspiration to their families. Lisa had a desire to make her family proud, especially her young female relatives. Speaking specifically about her niece, she told us, "If only for her, I'll keep going. I'll graduate from a PhD program just because she's going to follow that example." Likewise, Naya hoped that her family members would consider higher education a possibility after seeing that one of their own successfully completed the program.

Although all of the doctoral students were admitted because of their academic presence and potential, they often attributed their successful transition and progress to God. They also often described God as the reason for earning their degree. Lisa reminded us, "I'm doing it for God, for myself, for my family. I'm not here by myself." Lisa was motivated by her sense of purpose, earning an advanced degree *for* God, her family, and herself. While God and family provided her support, this also offered her a higher purpose for pursuing her degree. Naya offered, "I know that another important thing for me in this program and also in life is my faith. And that is what keeps me going." For Naya, her faith sustained her even when the transition process was difficult. The students, one after another and in separate interviews, consistently asserted that God had a plan for them and would help them to successfully complete the program.

Affinity to community was another source of support and reason for aspiring to complete the doctoral or professional program. Anna remembered growing up in an impoverished community in which outdated materials and insufficient resources hindered her ability to learn. Naya recounted the African American struggle for equality in America. She explained the impact of those experiences, and her desire to uplift her community, on her academic work ethic: "That pushes us to stay up until the wee hours of the morning . . . writing a paper. Knowing where you come from and what your people have gone through." As a result of their historical and personal experiences, these students felt compelled to pursue a professional path that would equip them with the tools necessary for returning to and revitalizing their communities. This was unique to the doctoral students in education, which may indicate that these students self-select into a profession where they can directly impact their communities.

Recommendations

The participants emphasized the way that support structures either facilitated or created barriers to success in advanced-degree programs. The stories shared by our participants added depth to the descriptions of challenges faced by graduate and professional students of color, emphasizing the need for students to find a "sense of belonging" in their advanced-degree programs. Our participants' reflections on their experiences yield a number of recommendations for doctoral students, faculty, departments, universities, and external agencies. Beginning with the practical implications, we offer suggestions toward systemic change and will end by extending, to the scholarly community, a request to continually build upon the experience of this specific group of individuals.

Doctoral Students

There is some onus for socialization that rests on the shoulders of doctoral students. Certainly, students must be willing to take initiative and reach out to faculty and to one another in order to open themselves up to being socialized into the discipline, department, university, and academia more generally. We advocate for students to take initiative in these ways. Yet, the stories shared here indicated that even when students of color were willing to do this, there were roadblocks in the path toward socialization that other students (i.e., White students) may not have faced. At the departmental and university levels, expectations for student initiative should be clear. For example, what are the norms for contacting faculty? What should students generally expect from faculty or from the university? What are the norms or unwritten rules of the department, discipline, or institution? These expectations should be made clear so that doctoral students can then begin to take initiative in ways that will aid in their socialization. That is, *access* must be granted in order for all students to feel as if they can gain entry into the socialization process.

According to these findings, peer support often supplanted a perceived lack of faculty support. Peers served as a type of entry point into the socialization process for many students of color. This relates to other findings regarding racial uplift and the effect of those from marginalized groups coming together to support one another (e.g., Perkins, 1981). Formalized peer mentoring programs, likely facilitated by the department or larger university, would help in socializing and supporting students, according to these findings.

Doctoral students should be encouraged to offer support and encouragement to their peers. An example of this was the research team that led to this chapter. This was a student-initiated team that was guided by a faculty member. As we conducted research, we also informally socialized each other into the discipline and to academia because the team members were at various levels in their programs. We reflect more on this in another paper (Johnson, Winkle-Wagner, Morelon-Quainoo, & Santiague, 2008), but for the purposes of this discussion, the important point is that students can take some responsibility for socializing themselves. However, even this socialization must be in part linked to faculty members. In our research team, we built upon the knowledge gained in coursework and had a faculty advisor who could help answer questions, offer her experiences in academia, and help us to navigate the graduate education "system." While our research team took initiative, it was necessary for this initiative to be supported by a faculty member who served as a socializing bridge-builder to the department, university, and discipline.

Faculty Members

Given that the students of color in this study overwhelmingly described a perception of receiving less support than their White peers, there is a need for greater sensitivity on the part of faculty members regarding the experiences and needs of students of color in advanced-degree programs. Faculty need to become educated on ways that their actions—intentional or unintentional—might be interpreted as exclusionary, unwelcoming, or even hostile by students of color in advanced-degree programs. In addition, faculty need to take it upon themselves to carefully evaluate the possibility that they may be offering opportunities (e.g., the opportunity to teach, conduct research, present findings, publish) to majority (i.e., White) students that they are not affording to students of color.

Ultimately, the department and university must also become involved in encouraging faculty to be more responsive to the needs of students of color. Departments and universities should provide, support, and reward efforts to offer professional development to faculty so that they can become more effective and culturally sensitive advisors and mentors. In an effort to provide faculty the tools they need to serve their students, departments should implement a series of workshops and reward those who take advantage of them. Herzig (2006) asserted that meaningful tasks "support the development and use of effective learning strategies, and give students opportunities to develop responsibility and independence," which lead to student engagement, sustained efforts, and a focus on learning (p. 254). Faculty development should focus on implementing pedagogy that embraces diverse ways of learning and encourage educational ownership by the students.

Departments

Departmental activities and actions need to align with the department's stated mission and goals. Scholars have noted that the advanced-degree population is no longer made up of "traditional" students, but one that often has accumulated years of work experience, brings significant and diverse talents, often has a family, is a full- or part-time worker and has worked some time before leaving employment for graduate school (Herzig, 2006). Departments interested in recruiting talented students and taking credit for the next generation of scholars and policy experts will have to reimagine their program's framework. Since retention is based on a student's ability to negotiate different demands, successful programs will become more intentional about enabling students to create a sense of belonging in a way that complements student needs. Students cannot be the only ones who are expected to change. That is, while socializing students to a department, university, and discipline, faculty and administrators within institutions and departments must also reach out and be willing to change procedures and norms to meet new student needs.

Departments should implement programs to acknowledge and reward faculty who mentor and socialize students well. Programs and faculty members who "haze" students into submission or withdrawal should be sanctioned. Educational institutions and departments must come to terms with faculty or administrators whose agendas support neither the department nor the students' success.

An orientation that immediately immerses students into the culture, norms, and expectations of their field should be offered by departments. In the "Findings" section, a student referenced that she had to learn how to work the "system" (i.e., the procedural aspects related to her department). Student-led portions of an orientation where current students share their knowledge and experiences (e.g., writing support groups, student-led research projects, professional opportunities) could further facilitate the socialization process. While most orientations offer information to help students manage their first year with an eye toward graduation, MacLachlan (2006) also suggested that faculty discuss their projects (on- and off-campus, within and outside the department), associated challenges and outcomes, student involvement, and the placement of recent graduates. Sharing such knowledge early in students' advanced-degree careers can certainly shed light on the triumphs and challenges associated with the discipline.

In addition to orientation sessions that include snippets of reflections on faculty research, it is necessary to provide and support structured and unstructured opportunities for students to interact, learn from, and network with faculty who have complementary interests. Departments should consider a format similar to an undergraduate majors' fair. Ideally, faculty and their students would present their work in a formal setting, allowing newer students to observe the iterative research cycle, speak to advanced students about the process, and ask faculty about possibilities. Publishing opportunities usually happen haphazardly as faculty become familiar with students' quality of work in class. However, departments should implement a series of professional development workshops for students geared toward communicating performance expectations (while also providing examples of good work) as early as possible. In addition, there should be some transparency in terms of how students should go about contacting faculty to ask about research and teaching opportunities. Such interventions are particularly critical for advanced-degree students who have been immersed several years in a professional (rather than academic) environment, have never written scholarly papers, are first-generation graduate/professional students, or simply have no clear understanding of the advanced-degree process. In the aforementioned examples, both cultural and social capital are certainly lacking and could be facilitated by faculty assistance. But, this faculty support must be initiated and supported by departments. The transparency of the "system" has to start at the department and university levels.

Universities

Bluntly put, universities should either "live" the diversity mantra or leave it alone. Throughout our research, students' emphasis on critical mass was pervasive. As our study participants indicated, they are often disillusioned to arrive and find that there is only one or a minimal number of faculty members of color. This disillusionment is compounded by instances where the few faculty of color are spread across many committees while also trying to serve as "representatives" and mentors for all of the students of color in the department. Whether in print or on the web (usually the students' first exposure to the institution), in the classroom, or during formal conversations with faculty or administrators, students are asking about the extent to which an institution actually embodies the diversity message that is communicated.

We suggest a focus on graduate program pipelines that introduce students to the program and university during their undergraduate career (Howard-Hamilton et al., 2009) or during the summer before starting an advanced-degree program. If diversity is an outcome that the institution genuinely wishes to realize, there must be consideration of "bridge" programs that invite and expose students to the campus in ways that encourage them to eventually enroll. This would also be a good time for institutions to ascertain ways to better meet the needs of a diverse student population in advanced-degree programs. Providing students with formal and informal, structured and non-structured opportunities to interact with diverse faculty and administrators is vital. Having a core group of supportive nonminority faculty and professionals is also critical.

In an effort to increase the transparency of the university "system," orientations could also be offered at the university-level regarding the timelines and procedures that students need to understand as they navigate their advanced-degree programs. Often, there is a person within the campus-level graduate studies office who is charged with helping advanced-degree students with paperwork and procedures. This office or this person may be a good person to head up this type of orientation. These orientations should occur at the beginning of students' programs but there should also be sessions offered after students enter candidacy in their doctoral degrees so that they have university-level support in understanding the necessary steps to complete dissertations.

External Agencies

Given the way in which many of the students stated a desire to give back to their families and communities after earning their degrees, external agencies such as community-based organizations could play a role in building a bridge between advanced-degree programs and students' communities. At the under-graduate level, there are a few exemplar programs that provide links between universities and communities. For example, the Cèsar E. Chàvez Institute,[1] part of San Francisco State University's College of Ethnic Studies provides an example of one way that connections between communities and universities can be fostered. Or, the Neighborhood Academic Initiative (NAI), a program to facilitate college enrollment for low-income youth in Los Angeles, offers an example of ways that students could reach out to communities while simultaneously connecting the research within doctoral degrees with the surrounding communities (Tierney & Jun, 2001).

Conclusion

Further research is needed to understand the issues that underrepresented graduate and professional students face in their transition into advanced-degree programs. If the field of higher education is to diversify the professoriate and postsecondary administration (which will affect the recruitment and retention of students of color), it is necessary to explore the potential barriers to the professoriate and to higher education leadership positions (e.g., chancellor and dean). Likewise, if the field of law is to become more diverse, a deeper understanding of the potential barriers of professional school is necessary. This study provides a first step in the process of understanding the factors that influence the socialization of students of color in advanced-degree programs. This examination of terminal degree programs is a necessary step in understanding the larger context of social inequality—if there are barriers to the successful transition and socialization into these programs for students of color, there are potentially negative consequences to their persistence in programs and degree completion.

Note

1. For more information on the Cèsar E. Chàvez Institute, see the following website: http://www.cesarechavezinstitute.org/.

References

Austin, A. E. (2002). Preparing the next generation of faculty: Graduate school as socialization to the academic career. *The Journal of Higher Education, 73*, 94–122.

Bauman, K. J., & Graf, N. L. (2003). *Educational attainment 2000: Census 2000 brief*. Washington, DC: U.S. Census Bureau. Retrieved May 13, 2006, from http://www.census.gov/prod/2003pubs/c2kbr-24.pdf

Beoku-Betts, J. (2004). African women pursuing graduate studies in the sciences: Racism, gender bias, and third world marginality. *NWSA Journal, 16,* 116–135.

Boice, R. (1992). *The new faculty member: Supporting and fostering professional development.* San Francisco: Jossey-Bass.

Cosgrove, T. J. (1986). The effects of participation in a mentoring-transcript program for freshman. *Journal of College Student Personnel, 27,* 119–124.

Cronan-Hillix, T., Gensheimer, L. K., Cronan-Hillix, W. A., & Davidson, W. S. (1986). Students' views of mentors in psychology graduate training. *Teaching of Psychology, 13,* 123–127.

Davidson, N. M., & Foster-Johnson, L. (2001). Mentoring in the preparation of graduate researchers of color. *Review of Educational Research, 71,* 549–574.

Denzin, N., & Lincoln, Y. (2003). *Collecting and interpreting qualitative methods.* Thousand Oaks, CA: Sage.

Fox, M. F. (1984). Women and higher education: Sex differentials in the status of students and scholars. In J. Freeman (Ed.), *Women: A feminist perspective* (pp. 240–247.) Palo Alto, CA: Mayfield.

Gardner, S. K., & Barnes, B. J. (2007). Graduate student involvement: Socialization for the professional role. *Journal of College Student Development, 48,* 369–387.

Gay, G. (2004). Navigating marginality en route to the professoriate: Graduate students of color learning and living in academician. *International Journal of Qualitative Studies in Education, 17,* 265–288.

Glaser, B. G., & Strauss, A. L. (1967). *The discovery of grounded theory.* Chicago: Aldine.

Glazer-Raymo, J. (1999). *Shattering the myths: Women in academe.* Baltimore, MD: The Johns Hopkins University Press.

Hancock, D. R. (2002). Influencing graduate students' classroom achievement, homework habits and motivation to learn with verbal praise. *Educational Research, 44,* 83–95.

Harvey, W. B. (2002). *Nineteenth annual status report on minorities in higher education.* Washington, DC: American Council on Education.

Herzig, A. H. (2006). How can women and students of color come to belong in graduate mathematics? In J. M. Bystydzienski (Ed.), *Removing barriers: Women in academic science, technology, engineering and mathematics.* Bloomington, IN: Indiana University Press.

Hinton, K. G., Grim, V., & Howard-Hamilton, M. F. (2009). Our stories of mentoring and guidance in a higher education and student affairs program. In M. F. Howard-Hamilton, C. Morelon-Quainoo, S. D. Johnson, R. Winkle-Wagner, &

L. Santiague (Eds.), *Standing on the outside looking in: Underrepresented students experiences in advanced-degree programs* (pp. 184–202.) Herndon, VA: Stylus.

Hoffer, T., Selfa, L., Welch, V., Jr., Williams, K., Hess, M., Friedman, J.et al. (2005). *Doctorate recipients from United States universities: Summary report 2003*. Chicago: National Opinion Research Center.

Howard-Hamilton, M. F., Hinton, K. G., & Ingram, T. N. (2009). "God has a purpose and I landed somewhere": Understanding the spiritual journal of racially diverse graduate students. In M. F. Howard-Hamilton, C. Morelon-Quainoo, S. D. Johnson, R. Winkle-Wagner, & L. Santiague (Eds.), *Standing on the outside looking in: Underrepresented students experiences in advanced-degree programs* (pp. 169–183.) Herndon, VA: Stylus.

Howard-Hamilton, M. F., Morelon-Quainoo, C., Johnson, S. D., Winkle-Wagner, R., & Santiague, L. (2009). *Standing on the outside looking in: Underrepresented students experiences in advanced-degree programs*. Herndon, VA: Stylus.

Johnson, S. D., Kuykendall, J. A., & Winkle-Wagner, R. (2009). Financing the dream: The impact of financial aid on graduate education for underrepresented minority students. In M. F. Howard-Hamilton, C. Morelon-Quainoo, S. D. Johnson, R. Winkle-Wagner, & L. Santiague (Eds.), *Standing on the outside looking in: Underrepresented students experiences in advanced-degree programs* (pp. 45–62.) Herndon, VA: Stylus.

Johnson, S., Winkle-Wagner, R., Morelon-Quainoo, C., & Santiague, L. (2008, November). *Doing it for themselves: Examination of an underrepresented minority graduate student research team*. Paper presented at the annual meeting of Association for the Study of Higher Education, Jacksonville, FL.

Lincoln, Y. S., & Guba, E. G. (1985). *Naturalistic inquiry*. Newbury Park, CA: Sage.

Lovitts, B. E. (2004). Research on the structure and process of graduate education: Retaining students. In D. E. Wulff & A. E. Austin (Eds.), *Paths to the professoriate* (pp. 115–136.) San Francisco: Jossey-Bass.

MacLachlan, A. J. (2006). The graduate experience of women in STEM and how it can be improved. In J. M. Bystydzienski & S. R. Bird (Eds.), *Removing barriers: Women in academic science, engineering and technology* (pp. 237–253.) Bloomington, IN: Indiana University Press.

Manning, K. (1992). A rationale for using qualitative research in student affairs. *Journal of College Student Development, 33*, 132–136.

Miles, M. B., & Huberman, A. M. (1994). *Qualitative data analysis: An expanded sourcebook* (2nd ed.). Thousand Oaks, CA: Sage.

National Center for Education Statistics. (2008). *Projections of education statistics to 2016*. Retrieved January 14, 2009, from http://nces.ed.gov/pubsearch/pubsinfo.asp?pubid=2008060

Perkins, L. (1981).   Black women and racial "uplift" prior to emancipation. In F. C.
    Steady (Ed.),   *The Black woman cross-culturally* (pp. 317–334.) Cambridge, MA:
    Schenkman.

Redd, K. E. (2007).   *Data sources: Graduate enrollment by race/ethnicity, 1996
    to 2006: Special analysis from the graduate enrollment and degrees survey re-
    port.* Retrieved January 14, 2009, from http://www.cgsnet.org/portals/o/pdf/
    DataSources_2008_01.pdf

Strauss, A. L., & Corbin, J. (1998). *Basics of qualitative research: Techniques and
    procedures for developing grounded theory* (2nd ed.). Thousand Oaks, CA: Sage.

Tierney, W. G., & Jun, A. (2001). A university helps prepare low-income youths for
    college: Tracking school success. *The Journal of Higher Education, 72,* 205–225.

Turner, J. L., Miller, M., & Mitchell-Kernan, C. (2002). Disciplinary cultures and
    graduate education. *Emergences: Journal for the Study of Media & Composite Cul-
    tures, 12,* 47–70.

PART FIVE

BEYOND SOCIALIZATION

10

DOCTORAL STUDENT DEVELOPMENT

Susan K. Gardner

Eva feels like she comes home from class each week with a headache. Enrolled in a required foundation course that is focusing on issues of diversity, Eva is just beginning to learn about how the educational system has privileged some and disadvantaged others. She is now starting to see how much of what she has encountered in her life has been tainted by racism, sexism, and classism. While she acknowledges that this course has been helpful, she is also really starting to feel resentful in general. Her partner has even suggested that Eva's recent anger has begun to concern her. Eva is both exhilarated and overwhelmed by this class and the feelings it evokes. She wonders how far she will make it before she has a meltdown.

Nate, meanwhile, is busy at work on his advisor's grant research. Nate feels very honored to have been chosen to work one-on-one with his advisor on this project, one commissioned by local industry. He knows not every student was given this opportunity and he also knows the potential this project has to launch his career. One day in the lab, however, he comes across some surprising findings. He runs to his advisor to explain. His advisor, also caught by surprise, literally begins to sweat. He starts mumbling quietly to himself, "They won't be happy," and "This won't do at all." He then abruptly turns on Nate and tells him, "We never had this discussion. This never happened." When Nate asks him to explain, his advisor shuts him down and tells him to start working on a different piece of the project. Nate slowly walks back to the lab feeling very discouraged. He knows that these findings are important, even if they do contradict what the funder had in mind. He doesn't know what to do. His advisor is clearly the authority; he's got the Ph.D. after all, and he is Nate's boss. But he can't deny the reality of what he has found either . . .

Jennifer has been spending a lot of hours in the library, madly working on her dissertation. Needing as much peace and quiet as she can muster, she has started renting a shared carrel space in the library. Her carrel partner, Lisa, is also a doctoral student working on her dissertation in history. The two hit off an easy camaraderie, often taking breaks in their furious writing to commiserate about graduate student life (or the lack thereof). They begin hanging out socially, often going for coffee or dinner after a long day of work. As time passes, Jennifer finds she thinks often about Lisa, even when they're not together. It's been quite a while since she's thought about another woman in this way—she remembers once having similar feelings back in undergrad but never really felt comfortable pursuing it. Jennifer now begins to really think about her sexual orientation. Is she a lesbian? What would that mean? What about Lisa? Jennifer is frustrated by these sudden feelings and anxious about what she should do about them.

While socialization has generally been the predominant lens through which to understand the doctoral student, certain limitations exist in viewing the student solely within a professional context. Indeed, while undergraduate students are viewed as changing and growing cognitively, interpersonally, personally, morally, and professionally (Evans, Forney, & Guido-DiBrito, 1998; Pascarella & Terenzini, 2005), graduate students have generally been seen only through a professional preparation lens. Graduate and doctoral students, however, do change, grow, and develop as a result of their educational experiences (Gardner, 2009a). This chapter focuses on the development of doctoral students, utilizing both empirical findings and the existing literature, culminating with practical suggestions to foster development at the doctoral level.

Defining Development

Student development has been described as "the ways that a student grows, progresses, or increases his or her developmental capabilities as a result of enrollment in an institution of higher education" (Rodgers, 1990, p. 27). To explain the development that students undergo, scholars have posited various theories. Taken together, student development theory has become a leading force in many higher education programs, counseling efforts, and one of the major tenets of the student affairs profession (Evans et al., 1998). When viewed collectively, these theories can be categorized into several main areas that assist us in understanding the totality of the student development experience overall and the doctoral student development experience, in particular. McEwen (2005) described three categories of student development theory:

1. Psychosocial development, or theories concerned with the content of development. In doctoral education, this may include growth or change related to how the student views herself and her abilities, the relationships she has with others in life, and her future direction in life (Chickering & Reisser, 1993). Psychosocial development can also entail development related to adulthood (McEwen, 2005).
2. Social identity development speaks to the ways that students make sense of social identities, including those related to race, gender, ethnicity, and sexual orientation as well as religion, socioeconomic, and ability status.
3. Cognitive-structural development deals with how students think as well as those theories related to moral and faith development. These theories capture the lenses through which students learn to make sense of the world around them.

The remainder of this chapter focuses upon each of these developmental areas and applies it specifically to the doctoral student experience. Within each of the three areas, I will incorporate quotes from my interviews with 177 doctoral students in various research studies (Gardner, 2005, 2008a, 2008b, 2009b, 2010; Gardner & Barnes, 2007; Gardner, Hayes, & Neider, 2007; Gardner & McCoy, 2008; Gardner, Vanek, Fruge, & Neider, 2006) to illustrate these particular developmental turning points and challenges facing the student. While not intended to be an exhaustive discussion (see Gardner, 2009a, for a more thorough treatment), this chapter aims to provide a basis for understanding how to consider doctoral students from a developmental context.

Psychosocial Development

Psychosocial development has been described as the content of development or "the important issues people face as their lives progress, such as how to define themselves, their relationships with others, and what to do with their lives" (Evans et al., 1998, p. 32). Given this definition, doctoral students are certainly still experiencing psychosocial development while in graduate school and, indeed, in the rest of their lives.

Our understandings of psychosocial development originate from the early work of Erikson (1959), who saw stages in the life span beginning at birth and culminating at death. Contemporary views of psychosocial development in higher education, therefore, result from focusing upon one specific stage of Erikson's conceptualization. The work of Chickering (1969, 1993) and his seven vectors of psychosocial development have come to be the predominant view through which higher education professionals and faculty see this stage of development.

Chickering's (1993) seven vectors are as follows:

1. Achieving competence, such as in intellectual areas, physical and manual skills, and interpersonal relationships.
2. Managing emotions, such as learning to control negative emotions in life.
3. Moving through autonomy toward interdependence, or the ability to remove oneself from the need for constant reassurance from authority figures and the movement from being independent to being a part of a larger community.
4. Developing mature interpersonal relationships, or developing awareness of and respect to differences in ideas and people and the development of intimacy between individuals.
5. Establishing identity, such as in relation to gender and sexual orientation, as well as a feeling of self-esteem and stability.
6. Developing purpose, including answering questions such as "Who am I?" and "Who am I going to be?" and intentionality in terms of vocational aspirations.
7. Developing integrity, or clarification and rebalancing of personal values and beliefs.

And, while Chickering's conceptualization of psychosocial development has largely been applied only at the undergraduate level, his work has transcended the traditional 18- to 22-year-old time frame to consider adult development on a larger scale (Chickering & Havighurst, 1981).

Consider the following quotes by students who discussed with me their initial impressions of their doctoral programs:

> Li: "I learned how to write better, connect my ideas, organize my ideas better. I learned how to read, not faster, but I don't know, I can understand things if I read now—I don't have to go back and read it a second time. And then I'm more vocal now."
>
> Brent: "The only thing I had to focus on [in undergrad] was school and now as a Ph.D. student and working full-time and being married, there's other time pressures that I deal with now that I didn't have to deal with then."
>
> James: "When I got to graduate school, [I had] a lack of self-confidence, [I was] very intimidated, very quiet. I think my professors would now be shocked how quiet I was because I didn't say anything. I took extra long writing papers. I was so vulnerable; if they said anything that would impact my confidence or that I was not adequate enough to perform at that level of graduate student, my path would have unraveled."
>
> Donna: "I saw myself moving from feeling like you're just a student; you're just in school, to thinking about it in terms of a career."

Each of these students' comments connect their doctoral experience to their psychosocial development. For example, Li talked about achieving competence in her coursework through the skills needed to be successful in graduate school, such as writing, thinking, and sharing her opinions. Brent, on the other hand, spoke to the ability to balance his personal life and personal relationships within the context of his overall graduate school responsibilities, thereby demonstrating the development of his integrity as well as mature interpersonal relationships. James, however, discussed his movement through autonomy as he transitioned away from needing constant reassurance from his faculty members. Finally, Donna described her development of purpose as she began to see herself in terms of her vocational goals and a professional identity.

As students progress through their doctoral programs, they are also building and sustaining relationships with others; for example, Brent, who is balancing his doctoral program with his personal relationships, or Amy, who is learning to depend on her fellow graduate students to sustain her: "Just knowing that someone's going through this with you at the same time and struggling with the same issues really helps keep you sane." In this sense, psychosocial development is occurring as students work to create mature interpersonal relationships and to move toward interdependence.

At the same time, students are also working to establish relationships with their advisors. Doctoral advisors can be highly influential in the student's program and often in future career success (Bargar & Mayo-Chamberlain, 1983; Zhao, Golde, & McCormick, 2007). Many programs or institutions may distinguish between an advisor, a chair, or a mentor, whereas others may use these terms interchangeably to describe the designated faculty member who guides the doctoral student through the dissertation process. King (2003) pointed out a vital difference between an advisor and a mentor, however: "Rather than being concerned solely with the student's completing the dissertation or developing technical competence, the mentor is concerned with promoting a broader range of psychosocial, intellectual, and professional development" (p. 15). In this sense, the true mentor will assist the student through all portions of his or her psychosocial development, such as this student who shared, "My advisor has always been someone I couldn't imagine being without. She has always helped me through everything."

Social Identity Development

Social identity development is concerned with "*what* students think about their specific social identity and *how* they think about it" (McEwen, 2005, p. 13). Social identity encapsulates identity related to gender, race/ethnicity, sexual orientation, social class, ability and disability, and religion, and how these identities intersect (McEwen, 2005). Much like psychosocial development, social identity development can occur as a result of the student's educational experiences. It is important to note that while we often consider that much of students' identity development will have occurred during the undergraduate years, graduate students may again be faced with developmental challenges that cause them to revisit certain tasks or issues related to their social identities. For example, a woman of color in a science department shared with me:

> I worked really, really hard when I was in industry, and of course I suffered a lot of discrimination. I'm a minority, and I'm a woman, and [there are] tons of ways for me to be discriminated against. I worked really, really hard to get myself into a position where I could just be acknowledged and respected and awarded for my own personal contributions and I come here and I think it's worse.

This student discussed both her gender and her race as the focus of discrimination. As her quote illustrates, she felt she had overcome these issues earlier in life only to be faced once again with similar or worse issues of discrimination in graduate school.

Issues such as these can be common for students whose social identity may be underrepresented or altogether absent in their graduate experiences. Consider the Black student who only has White peers and faculty members, the sole lesbian woman in her department, or the only student with a disability in his institution. One female student in history related, "There is a dynamic afoot in this department that is anti-feminine," while another told me of her experiences as a woman of color and sighed, "I just hope I can make it out of here without too many scars."

In each of these cases, the student may have experienced contexts prior to graduate school that were more diverse or more welcoming of difference and are now in departments or institutions with populations that do not reflect these social identities and may even be hostile toward them (see Sallee, chapter 7, and Winkle-Wagner, Johnson, Morelon-Quainoo, & Santiague, chapter 9, for more discussion). Multiple scholars have examined the underrepresented doctoral student's issues and challenges (Cross, 1996; Ellis, 2001; Gay, 2004; Gonzalez & Marin, 2002), and several national initiatives have been established to address these disparities (Arminio et al., 2000; National Science Foundation, 2004, 2009; The EDGE Program, 2002). Taken together, the challenges and opportunities that students may experience as part of the doctoral program can either be a boon or a hindrance to their development.

One way to understand the development of students' social identity is through the theoretical lens provided by Root (2005). While Root's model is primarily used to understand the identity development of biracial individuals, she also proposed that the model "might be used to understand the process of identity development for persons with different types of 'other' status" (p. 275). In this way, the underrepresented doctoral student in a department or institution holds the "other" status that Root described.

Root (2005) forwarded that to move through developmental stages of her model, students had to be confronted with conflict, generally stemming from political, social, and familial forces. Instead of lock-step stages or phases of development, however, Root describes four resolutions, which are each described as follows:

1. Acceptance of the identity society assigns. Within this resolution, the individual takes for granted the identity group to which he or she has been categorized by the larger community. Root stated, "This strategy reflects the case of a passive resolution that is positive but may stem from an oppressive process" (p. 276). She pointed out that often the taken-for-granted status of the individual is reflective of the region in which he or she lives, and that the conflict may enter in when the individual moves to a different region or place where assumptions may differ.

2. Identification with both groups. At this resolution, students may "simultaneously be aware that they are both similar and different compared to those persons around them. However, they view their otherness as a unique characteristic of self that contributes to a sense of individuality" (p. 276). Root was quick to point out, however, that the strategies individuals utilize in this resolution will not have an effect on other's opinions or behaviors toward them but that the student will need to "have constructive behaviors for coping with social resistance to their comfort with both groups" (p. 276).

3. Identification with a single group. While this resolution may seem similar to the first resolution, it is active rather than passive, as the individual purposefully decides to identify with one group. This strategy may be difficult, however, if others do not perceive the student to be aligned with the group with which he or she identifies. Again, regional differences can play a large role in how this resolution is realized, if at all.

4. Identification with a new group. In this final resolution, the individual will seek out others with whom he or she has identified as similar, neither hiding nor rejecting any part of his or her identity. The student at this resolution may move freely between groups but may feel more comfortable with the newly identified group overall. Despite this alignment, however, the individual may continue to have difficulties with a larger society that still sees identity in a largely binary fashion (Root, 2005).

Again, while Root (2005) did not necessarily intend for her model to be used to describe all students, the concept of "otherness" is salient for underrepresented students. Indeed, Schlossberg (1984) discussed the ideas of marginality and mattering as key influences on student development.

Goodman, Schlossberg, and Anderson (2006) described marginality as a lack of belonging. This sense of marginality can occur particularly with individuals who have transitioned to a new role or a new environment, such as a doctoral student entering a new program or moving to a new area. Individuals want to overcome this marginal status through feeling as if they matter, wherein mattering is "the need to be appreciated, noticed, and acknowledged" (p. 138). Much like the students of color discussed by Winkle-Wagner et al. in chapter 9 experienced, underrepresented doctoral students may not only revisit issues of marginality and mattering but may also revisit identity issues in relation to their new environments.

Even students who can be considered in the "majority," whether from an ethnic, racial, gender, or any sociocultural perspective, may undergo so-cial identity development as part of their doctoral experiences (students may also undergo development in regard to their positionality as researchers and scholars, see Shinew & Moore, chapter 12, for more discussion). For exam-ple, consider this quote from a White doctoral student who discussed her coursework that focused on issues of race and gender: "The emphasis the department places on race and gender I think has changed me a lot in terms of just my perspective in carrying with me a critical perspective on race and gender issues. Being aware of those issues around me in life has changed me a lot." In this way, models such as those related to racial identity develop-ment (Helms, 1993), gender identity development (Downing & Roush, 1985; Josselson, 1973), and sexual orientation identity development (D'Augelli, 1994) may be helpful.

Cognitive-Structural Development

The final theories I discuss in this chapter are those relating to cognitive development. Cognitive development theories "focus on *how* people think, reason, and make meaning of their experiences" (Evans et al., 1998, p. 124). In doctoral education, in particular, students are not just learning how to think about thinking differently (i.e., epistemological development—see Shinew Moore, chapter 12, for more discussion) but they are also learning to see themselves differently in regard to knowledge, learning to be producers of knowledge rather than solely consumers (Council of Graduate Schools, 2005). Accordingly, doctoral students will also begin to develop a changing view of themselves in relation to their faculty members, seeing themselves increasingly as those who can also create and disseminate knowledge.

One theory that assists us in understanding how doctoral students develop in relation to their cognition is that of Perry (1968). Perry's theory consists of nine static positions, generally described as four main areas: (1) duality, (2) multiplicity, (3) relativism, and (4) commitment. Duality or dualism represents a dichotomous worldview, for example, right and wrong, bad or good. Learning typically occurs as a result of the individual gaining information or facts from authority figures, gaining the "right" answers from these figures. The transition from dualism occurs when cognitive dissonance arises, wherein the individual, for example, may find that an authority figure is incorrect. This transition is what Perry described as disequilibrium.

Multiplicity is a status in which the individual is able to consider multiple or diverse views even while not knowing what is necessarily the "right" answer. In this sense, all views are equally valid in the absence of evidence demonstrating otherwise. Individuals often become much more independent thinkers at this position and may become much more analytically inclined in their thinking (Perry, 1968).

Relativism often occurs as a result of the need to substantiate knowledge. At this point, the individual sees knowledge based more upon context and requires evidence to bolster arguments (Perry, 1968).

Commitment results from the integrated knowledge that individuals learn from others as well as their own personal experience and reflection. Part of this commitment is the ability to remain decisive in response to challenges from others (Perry, 1968).

Consider the following quotes of doctoral students in relation to Perry's (1968) scheme:

> Brent: "I guess in my role as a student, to be a little more polished or whatever, I should be able to raise a question that is one that is kind of neutral or at least back it up, either from the literature or from certain research. With undergrad, you're just exploring the world, you don't know too much about the world and you're just exploring as questions come about."
>
> Daniel: "There's not one right answer and everything is up for discussion; everything is up for opinion."
>
> Christopher: "I really learned to critically analyze things. The other thing was to provide evidence to your statements. That was very challenging, but very rewarding, because people like myself are very opinionated

and we can say this and say that, we can write about something, but then to back it up, to provide evidence, it really kind of helped to clarify my own writing and my own thinking."

James: "I think because this is *my* work and *my* research, it's a cultivation of not just subject matter, I have to create subject matter. So it's definitely more of a focus on cultivation of how I've learned rather than what I've learned. Can I now put that into practice?"

To illustrate the stages of cognitive development we can see how Brent, a new doctoral student, talks about his experience as an undergraduate being different from his experience now as a graduate student. However, there are still aspects of Brent's cognitive development through which he sees responses as "correct" or "right" if they come from authorities, or in his case, from "literature" or "certain research." He does not acknowledge his role yet as someone who has the power to be the authority or produce knowledge, instead, still bears signs of dualistic thinking. Daniel, on the other hand, is much more multiplistic in his thinking. He is able to see that multiple viewpoints exist that may or may not be valid, but he is still willing to consider them. Daniel does not mention, however, that these viewpoints should be based upon fact—a sign of relativistic thinking. Christopher, though, is more characteristic of a relativistic thinker, as he expects to find evidence and arguments to support a particular opinion over another. Finally, James sees himself as an individual who can judge arguments and knowledge as well as be a creator of knowledge. In this sense, he is seen at the commitment stage. Of course, we can concede that disciplinary differences may influence how students may be able to view their world cognitively. For example, students in the sciences may not always have opportunities to reflect on different perspectives as those from the social sciences or humanities.

Fostering Student Development at the Doctoral Level: Implications for Stakeholders

Cognitive development, social identity development, and psychosocial development are three main areas in which doctoral students may change and grow over the course of their graduate programs. And, while understanding these developmental areas is important, understanding how to foster this development is the purpose of this final section of the chapter.

Development, at any level, occurs as a result of two conditions: challenge and support (Sanford, 1966). According to Sanford, when individuals are presented with a challenging situation or experience that has not previously been encountered, a new response emerges, thereby resulting in development. However, if too many new situations emerge without the appropriate support to mitigate these challenges, the individual may actually digress in his or her development. Therefore, it is the optimum balance of challenge and support that underlie development.

At the doctoral level, students should receive a balanced amount of challenge and support to facilitate their growth and change in relation to psychosocial, social identity, and cognitive development. I discuss each of the three areas of development with specific suggestion for the doctoral student, the faculty member, the department, the institution, and external stakeholders, as applicable.

Fostering Psychosocial Development

Psychosocial development is concerned with overall development in the individual, particularly in reference to how students learn to integrate their ideas, values, and beliefs along with others' and how they manage these relationships (Pascarella & Terenzini, 2005). Doctoral programs, their faculty, and graduate school administrators can work with students to foster psychosocial development through several approaches. First, facilitating connections with peers early in the students' experience, perhaps through peer mentoring programs, orientation sessions, and social opportunities, can assist them in developing needed supportive relationships. As students progress in their programs, writing support groups and other opportunities for peer interaction, such as through shared office or lounge space or through student organizations, can also be helpful. Furthermore, opportunities for interaction with faculty members in the program should be integrated into students' experiences early on as well as regularly throughout the students' experiences. This can be accomplished through program happy hours, family meet-and-greet sessions, or even departmental colloquia or presentations.

Second, students should be provided with explicit expectations for their performance both inside and outside of the classroom. These explicit expectations will go a long way in facilitating growth and development in students' sense of competence and purpose. For example, although expectations may be clear in regard to coursework assignments, expectations may be less than transparent in regard to examinations (Walker, Golde, Jones, Conklin Bueschel, & Hutchings, 2008) and the dissertation experience (Lovitts, 2007). Furthermore, there are implicit expectations often included in most programs, including publishing and presenting at national conferences, or the networking that is expected at these events. However, without explicit mention of these expectations, some students may not receive the socialization and developmental opportunities that are necessary for success. Structuring purposeful conversations among program faculty to identify these required and desired expectations may not only be helpful for students in this regard but also to the programs as they become more explicitly organized to foster these experiences.

Third, while peer and faculty relationships are important, students may also require additional assistance as they work through emotional issues or other concerns related to or external to their programs. In this way, providing access to counseling services on campus or through their insurance may be quite helpful to students. Furthermore, faculty advisors should be aware that at times they may be required to fill the counselor role, providing empathy and support for students that goes beyond the typical advisor role (King, 2003). Providing educational and professional development opportunities for faculty in this regard may be quite helpful, such as training graduate advisors on how to effectively advise students through difficult times.

Finally, developing purpose and one's professional identity is a key part of the doctoral student's psychosocial development. Providing ongoing professional development opportunities for students will assist them in forming their professional identities. These opportunities can go beyond professional conference attendance but can also include panels of professionals who may discuss myriad career pathways in the student's discipline as well as structured socialization experiences, such as the Preparing Future Faculty program (Council of Graduate Schools, 2003).

Again, it is through purposeful understanding and structuring of the doctoral experience that we may provide students the necessary support and challenge to foster their development in these myriad ways.

Fostering Social Identity Development

Social identity development includes changes or growth in relation to the various sociocultural aspects of the student's identity. This may include development in relation to race or ethnicity, gender, sexual orientation, ability, socioeconomic status, or religion. Program faculty and administrators may also work to create purposeful opportunities for the development of students' social identity in several areas.

First, it is important to consider students who may be from underrepresented sociocultural groups. Providing support mechanisms such as graduate student organizations and peer mentoring programs at the institutional level may assist students in seeking out other students who may not necessarily be in their programs but are nevertheless present at the institution. Since doctoral students' experiences are focused primarily within the department (see Golde, 2005, chapter 4), providing these resources and alerting students to their existence at the institutional level is important. Along the same lines, pointing out faculty and staff who may also represent these students' sociocultural characteristics may provide vital role models. Purposeful hiring can also be beneficial in this regard.

Second, all students, regardless of sociocultural background, should have opportunities to grow in regard to their social identity. Facilitating discussions of issues regarding race, gender, or sexual orientation through coursework, research, and socialization opportunities may be easier accomplished in the social sciences, but nevertheless opportunities to confront these issues abound throughout all of society. Faculty and administrators may consider hosting a colloquium on women in the sciences, for example, or professional development opportunities that speak to sexual orientation issues for students on the job market. While these are only a few examples, being thoughtful and purposeful in attempts to address and support all parts of the student identity will go a long way.

Fostering Cognitive Development

Cognitive development is not concerned with what students think but rather how they think (Evans et al., 1998). In this way, considering opportunities that allow students to push the boundaries of knowledge and that challenge their thinking will facilitate development at this level. As discussed by Shinew and Moore in chapter 12, epistemological development is a piece of cognitive development, as is adult learning, as discussed by Kasworm and Bowles in chapter 11. Fostering cognitive development in graduate education is an integral part of the doctoral experience, as students must go from being those who consume knowledge to those who produce it (Katz, 1976) in their dissertation research.

Baxter-Magolda (1996) highlighted the transition that many graduate students may undergo in their educational experiences, moving from an initial place of discomfort with forming and supporting their own opinions. In her study, the key to students gaining comfort with their ideas was through the encouragement of faculty members. In this way, the role that faculty members play both inside and outside of the classroom can be paramount to students' epistemological development. Baxter-Magolda recommended that faculty move toward roles as facilitators or guides in the classroom, which also would allow for more self-directed learning by students—a key component of adult learning (Merriam & Clark, 2006) and a necessary experience for students in their transition to becoming an independent scholar (Gardner, 2008b).

In addition, coursework and research opportunities allow students to explore cognitive assumptions. For example, facilitating assignments that encourage students to consider alternate viewpoints and to provide support for these viewpoints will assist them in moving beyond a dualistic view of the world, while early research opportunities may allow students to explore more relativistic and multiplistic views of the world. Moreover, experiences that tie together aspects of social identity development with cognitive development (perhaps through discussions of privilege, for example) may go a long way in facilitating students' overall development.

Finally, it is important to remember that taking on the role of knowledge producer may seem particularly daunting for some students. As their previous educational experiences may have provided students only limited experiences to explore their own capabilities in relation to relativistic or committed cognitive roles, the idea that students may be responsible for adding knowledge to their field can prove overwhelming. Again, providing incremental experiences from the beginning of their programs through the dissertation experience can assist students in taking the steps necessary to reach the commitment level of cognition in their programs.

Conclusion

As the authors in previous chapters attest, socialization is a common framework through which to view the doctoral student experience. However, we also know that students are presented with experiences that may influence change and growth in areas other than solely professional socialization. Viewing the doctoral experience through the lens of development allows for a greater understanding of the dynamics of the doctoral student experience and the scope of the changes that may occur as a result of this experience. Faculty and administrators can assist in facilitating growth in areas related to psychosocial, social identity, and cognitive development in doctoral programs through thoughtful and purposeful coursework experiences, social programs, and research opportunities. It is perhaps through this more holistic view of the doctoral student that we can facilitate success.

References

Arminio, J., Mitchell, A. A., Rice, K. L., Noldon, D. F., Scheuermann, C. D., & Stewart, G. M. (2000). *Mirror, mirror on the wall, how can there be empowerment for all?* University of Maryland, Baltimore.

Bargar, R. R., & Mayo-Chamberlain, J. (1983). Advisor and advisee issues in doctoral education. *The Journal of Higher Education, 54*, 407–432.

Baxter-Magolda, M. B. (1996). Epistemological development in graduate and professional education. *The Review of Higher Education, 19*(3), 283–304.

Chickering, A. W., & Havighurst, R. J. (1981). The life cycle. In A. W. Chickering (Ed.), *The modern American college* (pp. 16–50). San Francisco: Jossey-Bass.

Chickering, A. W., McDowell, J., & Campagna, D. (1969). Institutional differences and student development. *Journal of Educational Psychology, 60*(4), 315–326.

Chickering, A. W., & Reisser, L. (1993). *Education and identity* (2nd ed.). San Francisco: Jossey-Bass.

Council of Graduate Schools. (2003). The Preparing Future Faculty Program. Retrieved January 24, 2008, from http://www.preparing-faculty.org

Council of Graduate Schools. (2005). *The doctor of philosophy degree: A policy statement.* Washington, DC: Author.

Cross, W. T. (1996). Pathway to the professoriate: The American Indian faculty pipeline. In C. Turner, M. Garcia, A. Nora, & L. I. Rendon (Eds.), *Racial and ethnic diversity in higher education* (pp. 327–336). Boston, MA: Pearson Custom Publishing.

D'Augelli, A. R. (1994). Identity development and sexual orientation: Toward a model of lesbian, gay, and bisexual development. In E. J. Trickett, R. J. Watts, & D. Birman (Eds.), *Human diversity* (pp. 312–333). San Francisco: Jossey-Bass.

Downing, N. E., & Roush, K. L. (1985). From passive acceptance to active commitment: A model of feminist identity development for women. *The Counseling Psychologist, 13*, 695–709.

Ellis, E. M. (2001). The impact of race and gender on graduate school socialization, satisfaction with doctoral study, and commitment to degree completion. *The Western Journal of Black Studies, 25*, 30–45.

Erikson, E. H. (1959). *Identity and the life cycle.* New York: International Universities Press.

Evans, N. J., Forney, D. S., & Guido-DiBrito, F. (1998). *Student development in college: Theory, research, and practice.* San Francisco: Jossey-Bass.

Gardner, S. K. (2005). *"If it were easy, everyone would have a Ph.D." Doctoral student success: Socialization and disciplinary perspectives.* Unpublished doctoral dissertation, Washington State University, Pullman.

Gardner, S. K. (2008a). Fitting the mold of graduate school. *Innovative Higher Education, 33*, 125–138.

Gardner, S. K. (2008b). "What's too much and what's too little?" The process of becoming an independent researcher in doctoral education. *The Journal of Higher Education, 79*, 326–350.

Gardner, S. K. (2009a). *Doctoral student development: Phases of challenge and support.* San Francisco: Jossey-Bass.

Gardner, S. K. (2009b). *Understanding the experience of the first-generation doctoral student.* Unpublished manuscript.

Gardner, S. K. (2010). Contrasting the socialization experiences of doctoral students in high- and low-completing departments: A qualitative analysis of disciplinary and institutional context. *Journal of Higher Education, 81*, 61–81.

Gardner, S. K., & Barnes, B. J. (2007). Graduate student involvement: Socialization for the professional role. *The Journal of College Student Development, 48*, 369–387.

Gardner, S. K., Hayes, M. T., & Neider, X. (2007). The dispositions and skills of a Ph.D. in education: Perspectives of faculty and graduate students in one college of education. *Innovative Higher Education, 31*(5), 287–299.

Gardner, S. K., & McCoy, D. (2008). *The transition from full-time employment to full-time graduate student.* Paper presented at the annual meeting of the Association for the Study of Higher Education, Jacksonville, FL.

Gardner, S. K., Vanek, G. T., Fruge, C., & Neider, X. (2006). *The Ph.D. as journey: A qualitative exploration of development in doctoral education.* Unpublished manuscript.

Gay, G. (2004). Navigating marginality en route to the professoriate: Graduate students of color learning and living in academia. *International Journal of Qualitative Studies in Education, 17*(2), 265–288.

Golde, C. M. (2005). The role of the department and discipline in doctoral student attrition: Lessons from four departments. *Journal of Higher Education, 76*, 669–700.

Gonzalez, K. P., & Marin, P. (2002). Inside doctoral education in America: Voices of Latinas/os in pursuit of the PhD. *Journal of College Student Development, 43,* 540–557.

Goodman, J., Schlossberg, N. K., & Anderson, M. L. (2006). *Counseling adults in transition: Linking practice with theory* (3rd ed.). New York: Springer.

Helms, J. E. (Ed.). (1993). *Black and white racial identity: Theory, research, and practice.* Westport, CT: Praeger.

Josselson, R. (1973). Psychodynamic aspects of identity formation in college women. *Journal of Youth and Adolescence, 2,* 3–52.

Katz, J. (1976). Development of the mind. In J. Katz & R. T. Hartnett (Eds.), *Scholars in the making: The development of graduate and professional students* (pp. 107–126). Cambridge, MA: Ballinger.

King, M. F. (2003). *On the right track: A manual for research mentors.* Washington, DC: Council of Graduate Schools.

Lovitts, B. E. (2007). *Making the implicit explicit: Creating performance expectations for the dissertation.* Sterling, VA: Stylus.

McEwen, M. K. (2005). The nature and uses of theory. In M. E. Wilson & L. Wolf-Wendel (Eds.), *ASHE reader on college student development theory* (pp. 5–24). Boston, MA: Pearson Custom Publishing.

Merriam, S. B., & Clark, M. C. (2006). Learning and development: The connection in adulthood. In C. Hoare (Ed.), *Handbook of adult development and learning* (pp. 27–51). Oxford: Oxford University Press.

National Science Foundation. (2004). *Alliances for graduate education and the professoriate.* Retrieved February 26, 2006, from http://www.nsf.gov/pubs/2004/nsf04575/nsf04575.htm

National Science Foundation. (2009). IGERT: Integrative graduate education and research traineeship. Retrieved May 9, 2010 from http://www.igert.org

Pascarella, E. T., & Terenzini, P. T. (2005). *How college affects students* (Vol. 2). San Francisco: Jossey-Bass.

Perry, W. G., Jr. (1968). *Forms of intellectual and ethical development in the college years: A scheme.* New York: Holt, Rinehart, & Winston.

Rodgers, R. F. (1990). Recent theories and research underlying student development. In D. Creamer & Associates (Eds.), *College student development: Theory and practice for the 1990s* (pp. 27–79). Alexandria, VA: American College Personnel Association.

Root, M. P. P. (2005). Resolving "other" status: Identity development of biracial individuals. In M. E. Wilson & L. E. Wolf-Wendel (Eds.), *ASHE reader on college student development theory* (pp. 269–279). Boston: Pearson Custom Publishing.

Sanford, N. (1966). *Self and society: Social change and individual development*. New York: Atherton Press.

Schlossberg, N. K. (1984). *Counseling adults in transition: Linking practice with theory*. New York: Springer.

The EDGE Program. (2002). *EDGE: Enhancing diversity in graduate education*. Retrieved March 1, 2006, from http://www.edgeforwomen.org/

Walker, G. E., Golde, C. M., Jones, L., Conklin Bueschel, A., & Hutchings, P. (2008). *The formation of scholars: Rethinking doctoral education for the twenty-first century*. San Francisco: Jossey-Bass.

Zhao, C.-M., Golde, C. M., & McCormick, A. C. (2007). More than a signature: How advisor choice and advisor behaviour affect doctoral student satisfaction. *Journal of Further and Higher Education, 31*, 263–281.

11

DOCTORAL STUDENTS AS ADULT LEARNERS

Carol Kasworm and Tuere Bowles

Given everything, Eva feels she has been very successful in her graduate coursework thus far, being able to manage the demands of graduate work with her full-time professional position and her family. In the course she is in right now, however, her feelings are those of consternation. After working as an educator for 20 years, she feels that she has much to offer her educational administration program. The faculty member leading her teaching effectiveness course, however, does not seem to care what Eva or any other student thinks. Most classes are led through a lecture format, allowing students very little time to discuss their experiences and insights. When Eva has offered her experiences in class to highlight a particular concept, she repeatedly feels "shut down" by the faculty member who does not seem to enjoy sharing the spotlight. Eva is frustrated but doesn't know how to broach this subject with the faculty member. She considers talking to the department chair instead.

Nate, now nearing completion of his research, is preparing for his job interviews for faculty positions. He is excited to finally leave graduate school, but he also feels just plain stuck. He met last week with his advisor who told him that he really needed to begin defining a research agenda and include that in his job talk. Nate admittedly had not considered this before. He just really thought he could continue the work he had done with his advisor. Now faced with the idea of building his own course for research, he feels a bit overwhelmed. He realizes, of course, he soon will no longer be the student with a boss/advisor telling him what to do; rather he will become the boss. This should be easy, right? He wonders why it doesn't feel that way.

I n today's world, doctoral students experience a fractured world of life realities, juggling competing demands to be both the engaged doctoral student while pursuing other key life role commitments. Few doctoral students today are solitary scholars; few live an academic monastic life of the mind focused solely upon intellectual research pursuits. Representing approximately 59,000 students in U.S. institutions (Bell, 2007), today's doctoral students are more diverse and engage in a complex set of life commitments beyond the academy. According to Choy, Geis, and Malizio (2002), doctoral students are on average 34 years of age, with approximately 50% representing women and approximately 43% part-time students. In addition, more than 50% have delayed entry into doctoral studies by at least three years, with more than 35% representing a delay of at least seven years from completion of their undergraduate work. In addition, when asked about their funding support through work, 44% reported that they saw themselves as students working for expenses, while 31% viewed themselves as employees enrolled in school and only about 25% viewed themselves as students who were not working. Almost 40% reported that they worked at least 38 hours a week (Choy et al., 2002). In addition, these students reflect diversity in relation to gender, race, ethnicity, social class, ability, international cultures, family provider commitments, and other specialized backgrounds and lifestyles. As suggested through the vignettes in this book, Ling, Scott, Nate, Eva, and Jennifer are each unique and complex individuals who will engage in both common experiences of doctoral students and also require, seek out, or potentially leave a doctoral program because of their unique worldview and current life circumstances. Thus, faculty, doctoral institutions, and external partners in support of doctoral research are key stakeholders in considering the holistic nature of these complex and diverse students. This chapter will contribute to this broader understanding, offering three key perspectives from the research and literature of adult learning. These three perspectives include the importance of self-directed learning, the impact of forming and re-forming social and personal identities through transformative learning, and the significance of multiple and diverse communities of practice as they influence doctoral student participation. These foundational perspectives undergird effective doctoral preparation for this diverse student population and offer scaffolding supports for the dynamic complexity of doctoral program goals of knowledge creation and professional preparation.

Self-Directed and Critically Reflective Learning in Doctoral Studies

Doctoral studies have historically been viewed as an apprenticeship of immersion experiences that involve observation, collaboration, scaffolding, and assessed demonstration of key doctoral program expectations. These expectations are often viewed by students as risk-taking behaviors and attitudes guided by expert mentoring faculty within a scholarly community. Often, doctoral faculty are not cognizant of doctoral studies as risk-taking behaviors; however, this new world of graduate studies places doctoral students into uncharted territory. Most doctoral students face disjunctures between their sense of self as an adult, their placement as a novice in an expert scholar community, and their development of this new identity as scholar and knowledge creator. In addition, the disciplinary world of doctoral studies is also evolving. As suggested by Austin (2002), Walker, Golde, Jones, Bueschel, and Hutchings (2008), and by other prominent authorities, graduate education is being revisioned with new paradigms, expectations, and possibilities for doctoral preparation. In particular, many programs are rethinking and initiating new approaches to the foundational perspectives of disciplinary paradigms. Several scholars are critiquing the historic perspectives that had often restricted doctoral students' frames of behaviors, of the rigidity of what is considered disciplinary knowledge, and of the tacit resistance to new understandings (Kuhn, 1962). In this climate, one of the key challenges for faculty and doctoral students is to both open the intellectual and social boundaries of community for exploration of new learning and research investigations and to provide support and encouragement for developing confidence and self-efficacy, risk-taking toward innovation, and self-direction.   *goal of phd*

One of the hallmarks of success in these new challenges is doctoral students' abilities and actions to be self-directed learners: being able to pursue learning beyond their mentors, engaging in critically reflective examination of knowledge and disciplinary assumptions, and to become peer scholars to their doctoral mentors. Both institutional statistics and significant anecdotal information suggest that many doctoral students leave their programs at two critical junctures—at the end of the first year and at the end of coursework. Often, this separation comes through dialogue and judgments of the alignment of the individual's goals and strengths with the program and faculty expectations. However, underlying these judgments are many students who drop out of doctoral work because they are unable or unwilling to be independent, self-directed learners and critical thinkers. They are unable to engage in independent investigations; they are unable to engage in detached judgments required of synthesis and critique of the literature. Many doctoral students face significant issues due to their difficulties to craft independent judgment and their lack of key skills in learning how to engage in critically reflective practice (Brookfield, 2000; Smith & Associates 1990).

Although the construct of self-directed learning has significant historic roots explicating the nature of autodidactic learners, current learning theory suggests that the key skills and attitudes of self-directed learning are pivotal for the success of adults in doctoral studies. Grounded in innovative research by Tough (1979), this initial investigation of self-directed learning focused upon doctoral students learning a foreign language for their language competency exam, and how they designed and directed an independent learning effort. Through a number of subsequent major investigations, Tough defined a new perspective of adult learning, self-directed learning, focused upon the forms and processes of learning within the individual's own goals and control and of the individual taking the master planning role of defining and directing the learning experiences in solo or in collaboration with others.

With more than 500 research studies and comprehensive discussions of self-directed learning, this theoretical framework, as well as guiding processes for educators and learners, presents key constructs of self-directed learning representing the planning, execution, and evaluation of the learner's own pursuits (Brockett & Hiemstra, 1991; Candy, 1991; Knowles, 1975; Merriam, Caffarella, & Baumgartner, 2007). This literature suggests a number of models to delineate key elements and interactions in the development and facilitation of self-directed activities. This literature also delineates understandings of individuals as both autodidactics conducting self-directed learning and collaborative and interdependent self-directed learners drawing upon the efforts of a variety of educators, peer mentors, and knowledge resources (e.g., books, computers).

More recent research reflects two new refined perspectives of this phenomenon based in interdisciplinary understandings. The first is represented in Garrison's (1997) meta-cognitive model integrating self-management (contextual control), self-monitoring (cognitive responsibility), and motivation (entering and task) within self-directed learning. Adding to interdisciplinary understandings of self-directed learning is Brown (2002) who considered learning within a social culture as an aligned perspective of self-directed learning efficacy. He suggested, "Learning is a remarkably social process. In truth, it occurs *not* as a response to teaching, but rather as a result of a social framework that fosters learning . . . knowledge is inextricably *situated* in the physical and social context of its acquisition and use" (p. 65).

The development and understanding of both the individual efficacy of learning-how-to-learn strategies and the social cultural environment supporting self-directed learning skills is pivotal for successful doctoral students. One of the more valued applied process models is Grow's (1991) Staged Self-Directed Learning (SSDL) model, outlining a continuum of four distinct stages of development of self-directed learners and related roles of instructors. Each stage in this development model reflects specific understandings and actions of the learner in relation to his or her abilities and skills in self-direction. It also highlights valuable instructor actions to match the stage of the learner's self-directedness to key instructional goals and to also offer moderate challenge enhancements in the development of the learner's SDL knowledge and skills. Although Grow did not focus upon the social context, elaborated understandings of the social culture aligned with each of the stages have been added for additional richness of understandings. This model, as noted later, suggests that learners with lower stages of self-directedness have problematic experiences, if given highly self-directed learning projects or placed in a social culture with similar expectations (Grow, 1991; Merriam et al. 2007). For some doctoral students, a major project requiring high levels of self-directedness can be overwhelming and cause them to fail or to withdraw from this environment. Thus, this model is not only about developing enhanced learning capacity but also about recognizing the significance of successful achievement of learning tasks for doctoral students. This four-stage model includes the following:

> Stage 1—Dependent learners: Learners of low self-direction who need an authority figure (a teacher) to tell them what to do. [Instructors would provide foundational materials, offer lecture and salient points and understandings, and offer relevant and immediate feedback. They

would provide a social environment of specificity, clarity, and structured directions.]

Stage 2—Interested learners: Learners of moderate self-direction who are motivated and confident but largely ignorant of the subject matter to be learners. [Instructors would provide motivation for individual intellectual pursuits through more complex and nuanced materials at the intermediate level through lecture and discussion, including relevant applications. In this social context, key resources would be identified and related skills and understandings would be provided as scaffolding.]

Stage 3—Involved learners: Learners of intermediate self-direction who have both the skill and the basic knowledge and view themselves as being both ready and able to explore a specific subject area with a good guide. [Instructor would engage the learners as co-teacher/learners, including learner engagements in applications, critical analysis, and more individualized learning strategies. When appropriate, the instructor would facilitate learners' engagement in their own projects or related current real-world applications].

Stage 4—Self-directed learners: Learners of high self-direction who are both willing and able to plan, execute, and evaluate their own learning with or without the help of an expert. [Instructors would provide support for independent projects, learner-guided discussions and discovery, with the faculty member acting as consultant and expert monitor. At this stage, the individuals would be expected to be able to identify or to seek select guidance on helpful social cultures of learning engagement to support their pursuits.] (Grow, 1991)

Thus, a faculty member may identify the floundering of entry doctoral students in Stages 1 and 2 because of a lack of individual self-directed abilities. At this stage, faculty may observe these students to have a strong dependency for formal authority figures in teaching–learning roles and have low-level skills and risk-taking abilities to be independent and interdependent of key knowledge figures. These students may lack self-confidence or lack specific academic skills to conduct certain types of self-directed research endeavors or laboratory investigations. This model suggests that doctoral faculty would craft a more structured initial involvement and offer student expectations and related scaffolding experiences to develop stronger and more effective self-directed learning skills. The faculty could mentor students toward developing self-directed learning efficacy and consider the sociocultural supports for engaging in collaborative or individual self-directed learning pursuits, such as through peer student groups or related structured mechanisms of support and challenge (see Gardner, chapter 10).

The third and fourth stages of Grow's (1991) model presume that not only is the focal content of the doctoral program pivotal to the success of the doctoral student, but equally important are the key meta-cognitive skills of identifying key questions, pursuing key learning based upon effectively managing learning episodes, and reflecting upon and evaluating their learning across courses, internships, and research project efforts. Of importance to these later stages of development in the engagement of doctoral students is the additional worth of critical reflection through self-directed learning.

Building upon the generic self-directed learning model of Grow (1991), critical reflective engagement is an essential skill requirement for doctoral students as part of their self-directed learning competence. Doctoral students need to understand and identify the key values, assumptions, and beliefs that shape their possibilities for attention, intention, and action in doctoral scholarship. As scholars pursue research questions, they often identify dilemmas of multiple definitions and understandings, of significant sets of alternative responses, of the ambiguity of conflicting consequences (sometimes without a direct cause and effect relationship), and of the routine uncertainty of the nature of our current world (Bernstein, 1983; Schon, 1983). As is also discussed by Shinew and Moore in chapter 12, a critically reflective stance in these self-directed investigations represents a purposeful, thought-out stance among contested understandings of the epistemology of knowledge and the nature of truth within academic disciplines and knowledge domains (Brookfield, 2000). It suggests that doctoral students should have the capacity and the intellectual space to critique and question both the understandings and theories, but also engage in reframing the key assumptions and perspectives of knowledge and action. Thus, critical reflective agents engage in praxis of action and reflection regarding the validity of knowledge, engaging in research and learning, and acting upon key knowledge and understandings in its varied forms and processes—whether it be books or blogs, mainstream or divergent forms of research, or illuminating the canons of the discipline or challenging those canons through interdisciplinary efforts. In addition, as a self-directed, critically reflective learner, the individual who critiques also requires acknowledging key standards for being a collaborative member of the disciplinary community and a supportive colleague in uncharted intellectual waters. Thus, self-directed learning and critically reflective engagement are pivotal areas of development of doctoral students; these areas will influence their future success and the success of their disciplinary contributions.

Transforming and Forming Social Identities of Adult Doctoral Students

Beyond providing quality classroom engagements and doctoral student supervision, doctoral faculty also need to consider the complex personhood of doctoral students and their ongoing journey with multiple identity and life role commitments. Doctoral faculty often believe that their key tasks are guiding the formation of a doctoral identity, providing compelling intellectual engagement, crafting an environment of socialization into the professoriate and to the profession, and creating knowledge producers and leaders. In addition, faculty need to provide support and sensitivity to other important social identities beyond the role of doctoral student. Most often the key supporting or conflictive social identities represent the key roles of spouse (see Millett & Nettles, chapter 8), family provider, as well as worker. In addition, there may be many other potential interior social identity conflicts based in gender (see Sallee, chapter 7), race (see Winkle-Wagner, Johnson, Morelon-Quainoo, & Santiague, chapter 9), socioeconomic status, and other substantive identity definers. Thus, most doctoral students face interior conflicts in their formation of a doctoral student and disciplinary scholar identity, as well as their key adult life role commitments. To maximize the success of doctoral students, key faculty need to understand the formation and re-formation of these social identities as students negotiate through conflicting values, time commitments, or support systems in their other role identities (see Gardner, chapter 10, for more discussion on identity development).

Transformational learning provides a helpful framework for understanding this difficult process of doctoral student transitions, and forming and re-forming role identities and involvements. It also offers an elegant framework for future research investigations into the complexities of how doctoral student identities engage in these significant psychological transitions. Transformational learning experiences for the adult learner have been theorized and researched through the foundational efforts of Mezirow (1991) and others (Mezirow & Associates, 2000). At the heart of these transformative engagements is the reinterpretation of "an old experience (or a new one) from a new set of expectations, thus giving a new meaning and perspective" (Mezirow, 1991, p. 11). Through the process of transformational learning, "we transform our taken-for-granted frames of reference (meaning perspectives, habits of mind, mindsets) to make them more inclusive, discriminating, open, emotionally capable of change, and reflective so that they may generate beliefs and opinions that will prove more true or justified to guide action" (Mezirow, 2000, pp. 8–9).

However, not all new transition experiences or disjunctures are transformational for the adult. In transformative situations, the adult is both emotionally and cognitively engaged in a disorienting dilemma and through these experiences reexamines past understandings and their frame of reference and seeks new understandings. These new understandings could be based in new ways of acting in the world, or could be through engaging with others in conversations to gain reflective insights of other individuals' sense of understandings, beliefs, and actions. Thus, through this process, adults emotionally and cognitively experience a transformational process modifying their sense of themselves and their meanings within their other identities and worlds, of forming and more often transforming their sense of self and social identities. Although there is no research that has focused upon transformational learning in the doctoral experience, it has been amply demonstrated through a number of studies that adults who enter college may experience perspective transformation and engage in transformational learning by viewing themselves and their social roles and their sense of self in a different way through the educational experience (Mezirow, 1991; Mezirow & Associates, 2000; Mezirow & Marsick, 1978). In both seeking the doctoral experience and the actual engagement in doctoral studies, adults are compelled to rethink who they are, what they desire and value in life, and what they need to commit in their lives in seeking those options. Thus, doctoral students engage in thinking through their life-worlds of past, present, and future. These individuals continually consider their other social identities and roles commitments—of marriage, of spouse and children, of family, of friends and colleagues, of work and profession, of key life values, and sense of religious tradition, of considering their sense of self and being in relation to others, and of their key goals to community, family, and self.

TABLE 11.1
Mezirow's Phases of Meaning in Transformational Learning

1. A disorientating dilemma.
2. Self-examination with feelings of shame, fear, guilt, or anger.
3. A critical assessment of assumptions.
4. Recognition that one's discontent and the process of transformation are shared.
5. Exploration of options for new roles, relationships, and actions.
6. Planning a course of action.
7. Acquiring knowledge and skills for implementing one's plans.
8. Provisional trying on of new roles.
9. Building self-confidence and competence in new roles and relationships.
10. Reintegration into one's life on the basis of conditions dictated by one's new perspective.

Table 11.1 presents Mezirow's (1991) phases of meaning, representing a cognitive approach to transformational learning based in rational, reflective thought and discourse. More recent discussions have broadened this stance and acknowledged the potency of power dynamics and social interactions that have an impact on potential transformational actions within individuals. Studies have also acknowledged the culture–context differentials of this framework, that transformational learning is not just a rational–cognitive approach. In recognition of the impact of transformative learning upon doctoral studies, doctoral faculty may provide support, guidance, and, at times, directed messages to facilitate students as they engage in transformative learning and therefore transform their sense of self and their world.

At the heart of this theory is recognition that most doctoral students will experience a life-altering set of events that influence how they believe and see themselves in the world. The commitment to seeking doctoral work and to participating in a highly stylized, demanding, and competitive environment impacts doctoral students' sense of self and being. They will experience disorienting dilemmas—of challenges to self to become a doctoral student, but also challenges to their other multiple social identities (some of which may conflict intellectually, psychologically, and culturally) with the world of doctoral studies, and some with conflicts in relation to the structural process and demands of this journey. For in-depth implications, Cranton (1994, 1996) provided an informed perspective for applying this theory to adult learners, considering its relationship to the instrumental, communicative, and emancipatory learning domains and the perspectives of psychological, sociolinguistic, and epistemic reflection as well as its relationship to self-directed learning, autonomy, and critical thinking.

In an aligned perspective, many doctoral adult learners entering academic programs initially view themselves with an outsider status. They believe they must prove their worth within an academic environment and seek acceptance and validation. Stewart and Dottolo (2005) conducted research on doctoral socialization into the academy and developing a prominent doctoral student identity. They reported that students, more often with marginalized identities (such as gender, race, working class, older age, ability status), experienced varied direct and indirect messages of needed conformity; subsequently, they often presented modes of resistance aimed at persistence and survival in the academy. In identifying strategies, they noted:

> Most of all, these strategies—though they clearly preserve critical aspects of the self that are threatened by socialization to the academy—are costly in psychic energy used to respond and often result in painful compromise. They make it more difficult for students to answer the questions that Virginia Woolf enjoined them to ask (Woolf, 1938/1966, p. 62): "Do we wish to join that procession or don't we? On what terms shall we join that procession? Above all, where is it leading us . . .?" (Stewart & Dottolo, 2005, p. 185)

The challenge for doctoral faculty is to recognize and aid in the transformation of adults as they face disorienting dilemmas to their personhood and their beliefs. These dilemmas "compete or conflict with the identity under construction. For these students, socialization to the academy carries with it pressures for substantial personal change, and the risk of losses of the self" (Stewart & Dottolo, 2005, p. 168). Doctoral faculty need to structure programs, advisement, and mentorship to acknowledge and aid students in these difficult issues.

Learning in Social Context: Communities of Practice in Doctoral Studies

Studying apprenticeship and how learning occurs in context, Lave and Wenger (Lave & Wenger, 1991; Wenger, 1998) created the term *communities of practice*. Simply defined, communities of practice are "groups of people who share a

defined COPs

concern, a set of problems, or a passion about a topic, and who deepen their knowledge and expertise in this area by interacting on an ongoing basis" (Wenger, McDermontt, & Snyder, 2002, p. 4). The central idea is that outside of formal structures, people come together in groupings to conduct activities where they live, work, go to school, and recreate. Informally created, communities of practice vary in size and scope for the express purpose of developing expertise wherein members share knowledge, solve problems, and support each other. According to Wenger (1998), "Learning is the engine of practice, and practice is the history of that learning" (p. 96). Multiple communities of practice, then, are vital to doctoral student academic success given the wide-ranging roles and identities they may possess (e.g., student, worker, partner, parent, and friend).

The scale and scope of communities of practice can vary. For example, they may emerge within a department, across the university, across various institutions, and within an entire discipline. Moreover, a community of practice could be invisible or highly recognized. Regardless of the types of communities of practice that may form, Wenger (n.d.) identified three structural elements that all must possess: the domain, the community, and the practice. The *domain* of knowledge is the epicenter for communities of practice. It is the areas of interest, topics considered, or prescribed problems that the group considers. The domain sets the parameters for framing questions and organizing the knowledge of the group. As a result, the domain of knowledge provides a strong sense of identity and purpose for the group, thus legitimizing it. The *community* represents the group of people who interact regularly to share ideas and collectively learn together. Within the community, individuals feel a strong sense of belonging, trust, and mutual commitment. Individuals join the community voluntarily; thus, no external mandate or compulsion binds them. Although the community nurtures novices and identifies experts, leadership is shared and distributed. Retention of historical knowledge is especially unique to a community. The *practice* "embodies a certain way of behaving, a perspective on problems and ideas, a thinking style, and even in many cases an ethical stance" along with a shared repertoire of resources such as "cases and stories, theories, rules, frameworks, models, principles, tools, experts, articles, lessons learned, best practices, and heuristics" (Wenger et al., 2002, pp. 38–39). In short, practice is a way of doing things within a particular knowledge domain. To successfully work together in practice, there is an assumed baseline of common knowledge that all members should know with an expected commitment to problem solving and new knowledge creation around advances in the field. Communities of practice differ sharply from interest groups, networks, or project teams. Unlike an interest group or network that may only need to share information and build relationships or a project team that focuses only on a specific task, a community of practice aims to create and exchange knowledge and develop individual expertise.

In doctoral preparation, students encounter a wide variety of communities of practice in their departments, universities, disciplines, and so on. As newcomers, exactly how do they join and negotiate their role and identity? Lave and Wenger (1991) and Wenger (1998) proposed that *legitimate peripheral participation* explains the trajectory of how newcomers are immersed into the community, engage in practice, learn through participation, and potentially obtain full membership. Inextricably linked is one's evolving participation and identity development. Therefore, newcomers learn not from an abstract curriculum but from adapted forms of participation. To prepare newcomers, Wenger (1998) argued, "Peripherality provides an approximation of full participation that gives exposure to actual practice" and can be accomplished by "lessened intensity, lessened risk, special assistance, lessened cost of error, close supervision, or lessened production pressures" (p. 100). That is to say, within actual practice, novices can engage in modified participation to learn how the community operates. Wenger cautioned, "Note that the curriculum is then the community of practice itself. Teachers, masters, and specific role models can be important, but it is by virtue of their membership in community as a whole that they can play their roles" (p. 100).

Just as peripherality is important in explaining how newcomers join communities of practice, legitimacy matters equally. To be considered a potential member of the community, newcomers must obtain legitimacy (e.g., sponsorship) from old-timers who are experts. Providing examples of legitimacy, Wenger (1998) illustrated the concept of legitimacy by providing an apropos example in doctoral studies: "Today, doctoral students have professors who give them entry into academic communities" (p. 101). In the process of learning, however, it is highly probable that newcomers could make errors and falter along the way. Thus, legitimacy provides a covering for the newcomer during the learning process so that they do not run the risk of neglect or elimination from the community. Doctoral students as newcomers to a community are potentially legitimate peripheral participants who may initially engage in basic knowledge creation, knowledge sharing, skill development, and tasks that further the goals of the community. Doctoral students learn the profession not in isolation or as passive consumers of knowledge but by being actively engaged in the practice. Old-timers introduce newcomers to the practices of the group. As newcomers increase their active engagement within the culture and gain valuable experiences, they potentially move from the periphery to the center of the community. Through sustained participation, ultimately newcomers become old-timers.

Within every aspect of doctoral students' lives, there are potential groups of people with whom they interact, seek advice, share their aspirations, and deepen knowledge and expertise. Such communities of practice may be invisible or visible; members may participate fully or infrequently. Nonetheless, these groups learn together; that is to say, learning is quintessentially enmeshed in practice.

Conclusions and Implications for Doctoral Students as Adult Learners

Three major premises underlie the discussion presented in this chapter. First, doctoral students are unique learners with varied experiences and backgrounds. Doctoral students bring to bear years of accumulated prior learning and rich experiences into their studies. Invariably, no generic doctoral adult learner exists. Doctoral students possess varied motivations, learning styles, and cognitive abilities, and all come from diverse sociocultural contexts. Second, the approach to learning for many doctoral students occurs on a continuum from autonomous to relational. The autonomous learner prefers to learn alone and values independence, whereas the relational learner finds solace in connectedness to others and interdependent action. Finally, given the uniqueness of doctoral students, there is no one theory or model that captures how all learn and construct knowledge. The context of doctoral preparation with the aim of developing scholars for the academy, business or industry, government, nonprofits, or as public intellectuals help to identify the most salient perspectives.

Scholarly formation, by definition, entails learning. It is the "central business, the core task" and "the learning in question is often of a very special kind because it breaks new ground and builds new knowledge" (Walker et al., 2008, p. 11). To facilitate a shift in how adult learning is conceptualized and fostered in doctoral studies, three perspectives were reviewed (see Table 11.2): self-directed and critically reflective learning; the formation and transformation

TABLE 11.2

Comparison of Salient Perspectives to Doctoral Students as Adult Learners

	Self-Directed /Critically Reflective Learning	*Transformative Learning Theory*	*Situated Learning: Communities of Practice*
Goals	To enhance the ability of students to be self-directed in their learning; to foster critically reflective learning	To facilitate awareness of distorted and limiting views; to recognize alternative perspectives; to make meaning out of our lives	To build community where newcomers/novices can encounter the profession by creating and sharing knowledge and developing expertise
View of the Learner	Student with developmental and personal needs and interests	Student coping with change, disjuncture or disorienting dilemmas	Student moving from peripheral to active to the center of engagement; student developing scholarly identity
View of the Educator	A resource among many	Facilitator of personal and social transformation	Expert who guides and legitimates novices
Settings for Learning	Primarily formal educational settings; yet, learner determines additional settings	Learner's total life	Physical or virtual settings where members of the community interact around core issues, interests, and needs
Curriculum	Students structure learning needs and goals within the confines of doctoral studies requirements as a master planner	Students reflects and dialogues about their views, perspectives, and experiences to decide on personal and societal action	Students seek opportunities within the community to engage in practice and share and produce knowledge
Key Concepts	Autonomy	Experience; critical reflection; development	Legitimate peripheral participation
Contributions	Serious attention to the needs of the individual	Emphasis placed on student critical reflection and engagement (praxis)	Increased awareness of the value in community and interdependent ways of learning and knowing
Problems	Concern that student may not be at a developmental stage to make proper judgments; the extent to which the context affects learner autonomy	Overreliance on rationality in perspective transformation; focuses too much on individual transformation at the expense of social change	Difficulty in assessing learning and new knowledge creation; apparent assumption that a community is supportive and nurturing

of social and personal identities through the lens of transformative learning; and learning in context highlighting communities of practice. Based on the perspectives examined, what strategies and recommendations should various stakeholders consider? We offer several implications for doctoral students, faculty members, university administrators, and external agencies.

Creating a Path Toward Self-Directed Learning

Doctoral students who are self-directed take the initiative with no or limited help from others to identify their needs, establish goals, ferret-out resources, employ learning strategies, and evaluate the success of their efforts. It helps when self-directed doctoral learners choose intellectually challenging projects and complex problems to solve. To what extent doctoral students can truly be self-directed, especially during the early stages of their doctoral process, is a contentious issue; yet, there is extreme wisdom in them valuing an interdependent pathway. Thus, doctoral students should not only learn in isolation but also welcome interpersonal ways with experts and peers in the classroom and at disciplinary meetings and conferences. Self-directed doctoral students should view their academic journey as an opportunity to learn and grow both personally and professionally. Doing so requires self-knowledge and immersion into the culture of the program and discipline.

Valuing the scholarly success of doctoral students, faculty should encourage a learning environment of trust and mutual respect wherein self-directed learners can create their own pathways. For example, faculty can include opportunities for doctoral students to negotiate independent learning contracts for courses and plan independent research opportunities. Self-directed learners really need access to information of all formal program and course requirements in order to design and plan their own learning. University faculty best support self-directed learners through transparency of these explicit and tacit requirements and expectations. In addition, university administrators should consider flexibility in the curriculum and innovative assessment measures to value the creativity and uniqueness of doctoral adult learners.

Forming and Transforming Social Identities

Through critical reflection and guided action, transformative learning is when students question previously held beliefs, values, and assumptions to establish new understandings and identities. Thus, doctoral students should interrogate their disciplinary understandings through an interdisciplinary lens to foster critical, multicultural, and global perspectives. Given that we live in a global world with multifaceted problems, faculty members should intentionally create space in the curriculum for service-learning and participatory action research projects for doctoral students to engage in praxis. Furthermore, university administrators could champion interdisciplinary doctoral degrees. External entities (e.g., trade and disciplinary associations) could be supportive by providing funding for applied projects addressing emerging societal issues.

Recognizing that doctoral students are likely to experience life's expected and unexpected events such as the birth of a child, personal/family illness, and death, departments and universities need to identify mechanisms that support doctoral students, especially in crisis. In addition, university administrators should consider creating understandings of alternative graduate pathways that reflect multiple social roles and commitments (e.g., parent, worker, and student). The full support of external agencies, such as accrediting bodies, in assessing and promoting alternative graduate pathways would be ideal.

Nurturing the Power of Communities of Practice

Recognizing the inherent value in learning from context, doctoral students should engage in multiple communities of practice that align with their passions and knowledge interests. Communities of practice in the form of writing groups, mentoring groups, research laboratories, participatory action research initiatives, and so on provide tacit and explicit knowledge sharing opportunities. Engaging in the practices of communities facilitate collaborative interactions and new learning opportunities for students with old-timers/experts.

Although time and effort invested in communities of practice by faculty members may not neatly align with the reward structure of academe, this participation is invaluable for new knowledge creation and sustaining doctoral students' intellectual curiosity. Communities of practice foster a strong sense of student belonging, identity development, and networking opportunities that directly support student retention and completion. Departments, universities, and external agencies are potentially prime investors in nurturing the exponential power of communities of practice by providing material resources, facilities, and equipment toward the generation and dissemination of new knowledge.

Conclusion

This chapter presented the significance of three salient perspectives of doctoral students as adult learners. The future impact and effectiveness of doctoral faculty and programs will reside in responding to this changing clientele and their engagements as adult learners, as well as in being responsive to their complex adult roles and commitments and their multilayered learning expectations oriented to both self and communities of practice.

References

Austin, A. (2002). Preparing the next generation of faculty. *Journal of Higher Education, 73*, 94–122.

Bell, N. (2007). *Graduate enrollment and degrees: 1997 to 2007* (Revised November 2008). Retrieved April 27, 2009, from http://www.cgsnet.org/portals/o/pdf/R_ED2007.pdf

Bernstein, R. (1983). *Beyond objectivism and relativism: Science, hermeneutics, and praxis*. Philadelphia, PA: University of Pennsylvania.

Brockett, R., & Hiemstra, R. (1991). *Self-direction in adult learning: Perspectives on theory, research, and practice*. New York: Routledge.

Brookfield, S. (2000). The concept of critically reflective practice. In A. Wilson & E. Hayes (Eds.), *Handbook of adult education and continuing education* (pp. 33–50). San Francisco: Jossey-Bass.

Brown, J. (2002). *Learning in a digital age*. Retrieved May 10, 2009, from http://net.educause.edu/ir/library/pdf/ffpiuo15.pdf

Candy, P. (1991). *Self-direction for lifelong learning*. San Francisco: Jossey-Bass.

Choy, S., Geis, S., & Malizio, A. (2002). *Student financing of graduate and first-professional education, 1999–2000: Profiles of students in selected degree programs and their use of assistantships*. Retrieved April 27, 2009, from http://nces.ed.gov/pubs2002/2002166.pdf

Cranton, P. (1994). *Understanding and promoting transformative learning: A guide for educators of adults*. San Francisco: Jossey-Bass.

Cranton, P. (1996). *Professional development as transformative learning: New perspectives for teachers of adults*. San Francisco: Jossey-Bass.

Garrison, D. (1997). Self-directed learning: Toward a comprehensive model. *Adult Education Quarterly, 48*, 18–33.

Grow, G. (1991). Teaching learners to be self-directed: A stage approach. *Adult Education Quarterly, 41*, 125–149.

Knowles, M. (1975). *Self-directed learning: A guide for learners and teachers*. New York: Association Press.

DOCTORAL STUDENTS AS ADULT LEARNERS   *241*

Kuhn, T. (1962). *The structure of scientific revolutions*. Chicago, IL: University of Chicago Press.

Lave, J., & Wenger, E. (1991). *Situated learning: Legitimate peripheral participation*. New York: Cambridge University Press.

Merriam, S., Caffarella, R., & Baumgartner, L. (2007). *Learning in adulthood: A comprehensive guide* (3rd ed.). San Francisco: Jossey-Bass.

Mezirow, J. (1991). *Transformative dimensions of adult learning*. San Francisco: Jossey-Bass.

Mezirow, J., & Associates. (Eds.). (2000). *Learning as transformation: Critical perspectives on a theory in progress*. San Francisco: Jossey-Bass.

Mezirow, J., & Marsick, V. (1978). *Education for perspective transformation. Women's re-entry programs in community colleges.* New York, NY: Center for Adult Education, Columbia University. (ERIC Reproduction Document No. ED 166367)

Schon, D. (1983). *The reflective practitioner: How practitioners think in action*. New York: Basic Books.

Smith, R. M., & Associates (1990). *Learning to learn across the life span*. San Francisco: Jossey-Bass.

Stewart, A., & Dottolo, A. (2005). Socialization to the academy: Coping with competing social identities. In G. Downey, J. Eccles, & C. Chatman (Eds.), *Navigating the future: Social identity, coping, and life tasks* (pp. 167–187). New York: Russell Sage Foundation.

Tough, A. (1979). *The adult's learning projects: A fresh approach to theory and practice in adult learning* (2nd ed.). Toronto, Canada: Ontario Institute for Studies in Education.

Walker, G., Golde, C., Jones, L., Bueschel, A. B., & Hutchings, P. (2008). *The formation of scholars: Rethinking doctoral education for the twenty-first century*. San Francisco: Jossey-Bass.

Wenger, E. (n.d.). *Communities of practice: A brief introduction*. Retrieved April 24, 2008, from http://www.ewenger.com/theory/index.htm

Wenger, E. (1998). *Communities of practice: Learning, meaning, and identity*. New York: Cambridge University Press.

Wenger, E., McDermontt, R., & Snyder, W. M. (2002). *Cultivating communities of practice: A guide to managing knowledge*. Boston, MA: Harvard Business School Press.

Woolf, V. (1938/1966). *Three guineas*. San Diego, CA: Harcourt Brace Jovanovich.

12

EXPLORING EPISTEMOLOGICAL DIVERSITY IN A DOCTORAL SEMINAR

Dawn Shinew and Tami Moore

Jennifer, still laboring away on her dissertation, decides she needs a respite from the drudgery. She and her partner Lisa decide it would be fun to audit a class together. They look around and find one in women's studies on feminist theory that looks compelling. Jennifer, once in the course, finds herself blown away by the content. While she always considered herself a feminist, she now realizes that the way she viewed the world before was still one based on very different assumptions. Learning everything that she is now, she feels motivated to do something important. She toys with the idea of changing her dissertation to utilize a feminist lens. She has a feeling, however, that her advisor will be nonplussed, to say the least.

Eva is still plugging away at her program in educational leadership. She is now in the midst of taking methodological coursework, allowing her to consider different approaches for her dissertation research. In her educational research course, however, she is astounded to find that the faculty member simply skims over the discussion about paradigmatic assumptions. After her experience in the diversity course last year, Eva feels a strong connection to the postmodernist views of the world. As the course progresses, she begins seeing the strongly positivist stance that the instructor takes in the course and even in his language. She wonders how her paper proposal on critical race theory will be received by her professor and worries a little bit as well.

M any in the education research community have debated what it means to do "good" research (Berliner, 2002; Feuer, Towne, & Shavelson, 2002a,b; Hoestetler, 2005; Pellegrino & Goldman, 2002). Such questions take on new relevance with increased pressures to respond more effectively to the seemingly overwhelming needs of schools, universities, and communities. Indeed, the future of education may rest on our abilities to conduct thoughtful, informative research in, with, and across, a wide variety of contexts in order to address these pressing societal needs. These needs raise numerous questions regarding how to prepare future educational researchers to meet these challenges (Eisenhart & DeHaan, 2005). While some scholars dismiss the relevance of multiple epistemologies (e.g., Siegel, 2006), Washington State University's College of Education has made such understandings the cornerstone of a recently revised doctoral research core.

This case study focuses on students' experiences in a course titled "Education, Research, and Epistemology" and the ways in which they mobilize these understandings throughout their academic careers. Discussions, even debates, about the importance of epistemology are not new to education. Scheurich and Young's (1997) call for researchers to "color" our epistemologies generated heated interactions among many scholars, regardless of race or ethnicity. As Tyson (1997) pointed out a decade ago, scholars of color (i.e., Hill-Collins, 1990) had been promoting more diverse epistemologies in research even before Scheurich and Young's call was published. More recently, scholars such as Rolon-Dow (2005) and Milner (2007) have continued to emphasize epistemology as fundamental to the ways in which we conceptualize, conduct, analyze, and present research. These scholars, and many others, have asserted that race, gender, ethnicity, sexual orientation, and other issues of identity shape the way in which individuals see the world, and how knowledge is constructed, in fundamental ways.

However, not all academics agree. Siegel (2006) asked whether we are making "much ado about nothing much?" in this focus on epistemology. Siegel argued that terms such as *epistemologies* and *epistemological diversities* are meaningless, unless more clearly defined. While his call for more precise language is useful, Siegel concluded that "the call for epistemological diversity is not, where justified, as radical or significant as it is often taken to be; and that, where it is radical or significant, it is not justified" (p. 3). His position is valid, however, only if one accepts his premise that those who advocate for epistemological diversities are unwilling to subject these beliefs to any type of critical review. The case study presented in this chapter focuses on students' perspectives on a doctoral seminar designed to prepare future scholars to engage in just such a deep, deliberate analysis of epistemological diversity in educational research.

The Case: A Seminar in Epistemology, Inquiry, and Representation

In 2003, Washington State University's College of Education was invited to participate in the Carnegie Initiative on the Doctorate (CID). Our goal, like that of the other 83 programs across 6 fields who participated in the project, was systemic and meaningful change to our Ph.D. program. The CID project provided faculty and administrators with the necessary push to engage in an ongoing conversation about what it means to be a "steward of the discipline" (Golde & Walker, 2006) in education. One issue that virtually everyone agreed upon in the college was the importance of reconsidering our students' preparation in the area of research. Throughout the discussions, there was general consensus that graduates of our doctoral programs should be prepared to be consumers and producers of research, and that doing so required that they also be proficient in both quantitative and qualitative methods. In addition, many faculty members felt it was important that students understand not just the technical applications of research but also the ways in which one's assumptions about knowledge and the world shape one's decisions in research.

Consistent with Pallas's (2001) recommendations regarding the need to prepare education doctoral students for epistemological diversity, our college initiated a doctoral seminar focused on epistemology and inquiry. Virtually all doctoral students are required to take this course during the first semester of their doctoral program. The course serves as a prerequisite for five subsequent research classes: one "fundamentals" of research class, two qualitative research courses, and two quantitative research courses, as well as a one-credit seminar in which various faculty members share their research that students are required to take twice. The goal is for all students to emerge from our doctoral programs with a deep, thorough understanding of the philosophies that guide research, as well as the methodologies available to them. As Paul and Marfo (2001) emphasized, "One must have some philosophical as well as technical knowledge about the genres to understand and interpret the language and the research" (p. 532). Students are required to demonstrate competency in both qualitative and quantitative methods in order to ensure that they are prepared to be producers and consumers of multiple forms of research.

The faculty members who designed and teach the course on epistemology and research assert that there are, indeed, multiple epistemologies that drive scholarly work and that understanding these underlying assumptions helps beginning researchers think more critically and analytically not only about their own research but also about the research they consume. The seminar is designed to help doctoral students negotiate what has often been referred to as the "contested" or "shifting" terrain of educational research (Langemann, 1997; Labaree, 2003; Popkewitz, 1997). How do novice researchers, who sometimes identify themselves as "feminists" or "critical race theorists," explain how such theoretical frameworks shape their understandings of knowledge, the knower, and the known? How do such beliefs impact other dimensions of their academic lives? How do doctoral students reconcile competing epistemologies within the academy? How do they explain their work in the context of their epistemologies? The answers to these questions reflect Neumann's (2006) conclusions that boundaries between personal beliefs and scholarly work are blurred and warrant more deliberate exploration if future faculty members are to work, and live, with passion. Achieving this needs to become an important goal of doctoral education in all fields given Golde and Dore (2001) and Austin's (2002) findings, which suggest that many Ph.D. students are turning away from academic or scholarly careers because of their perception that academia is no longer a path to pursuing individual passions.

While the course is not "owned" by any particular faculty member, the same professor has taught the course six of the seven times it has been offered. As different faculty members eventually rotate into the course, the intent is for the objectives of the course to remain consistent regardless of the instructors. However, specific readings and assignments for the course will vary by instructor. Consequently, this case study focuses on the experiences of the six cohorts of students taught by the first author of this chapter (Shinew). This chapter's second author (Moore) was a student in the class during the first semester it was offered. The course has undergone minor revisions each semester but the general structure, assignments, and many of the readings have remained consistent.

Throughout the semester, doctoral students in the "Epistemology, Research, and Education" course read and discuss pieces from numerous theoretical orientations, including postpositivism, feminist theory, critical race theory, postcolonial theory, place-based education, poststructuralism, and queer theory. The bulk of the course engages students in deep readings and discussions of the assigned articles and chapters. In virtually every case, the collection of readings includes several pieces that could be considered "foundational" in establishing the philosophy in contemporary educational research, as well as one or two more recently published examples that demonstrate more current trends. Each student assumes responsibility for facilitating the discussion of one set of readings, a responsibility that includes meeting with the instructor in advance to discuss ideas and possibilities.

In addition, students conduct an interview with an established scholar. Questions for the semi-structured interviews are developed collaboratively (with guidance from the faculty coordinator) to ensure consistency across the interviews. These interviews focus on the scholars' definitions of research, what they consider "quality" research, how they believe research should be represented, and more general issues of their academic life. Students record and transcribe the interviews, as well as read at least one example of the scholar's work. Students then develop an "epistemological case study" about the scholar that they share with the rest of the class. These projects serve as concrete illustrations of the ways in which scholars' work is informed and shaped by epistemologies, theories, and methodologies, as well as their personal passions and convictions. At the end of the semester, students are asked to compose a personal "position statement" in which they align themselves with one or more theoretical orientations and explain their position in light of class readings and discussions. This culminating project is considered a "work in progress" as it is assumed that students' understandings and interests will continue to evolve.

Methods and Data Sources

As stated earlier, the researchers for this project include the faculty coordinator for the course and her former doctoral student who was a member of the first cohort to complete the newly revised doctoral research core. In many ways, the case study could be considered an action research project. Using the guidelines established by Herr and Anderson (2005), the researchers developed a participatory model with the goal of understanding and improving students' experiences in the research seminar, as well as exploring ways to improve the course. The instructor, and co-researcher, identified questions based on her experiences with the course (i.e., How do students make sense of the readings after the class? How did the exposure to these ideas influence their thinking about research?). The data collected were then used to inform future revisions in the course.

Data for the study came from open-ended surveys from students who have completed the course and are at various stages of their doctoral studies or professional careers; follow up, semi-structured interviews with 10 of these participants; students' reflective journals; artifacts from the class (course evaluations, syllabi, and assignments); and participant observation notes (from the faculty coordinator). In addition, we have included feedback from faculty members teaching subsequent core research courses to illustrate how the course functions in the newly revised research core. The purpose and outcomes of the action research project were shared with all participants. Data (with confidentiality ensured) were also shared for member checking. Bullough and Pinnegar's (2001) suggested guidelines for self-study research inform the criteria for quality developed for this study. The conclusions of this study have informed revisions in the course and assignments.

Findings

Several important insights emerged from the data, collectively providing insights not only into these students' experiences with this particular course but also into the ways in which the structure, content, and teacher of this course shaped students' identities as scholars. While certainly not true for all students who completed the class, a significant number of students—particularly those considering faculty careers—describe their experiences as "life-changing" and "pivotal" in their development as researchers. Themes emerged in the data, reflecting the key elements of students' experiences that overlap with each other and also bridge from this class to their socialization as scholars. As part of establishing their identity in the academy, they (a) find their voice, (b) embrace a community of scholarship, and (c) seek intellectual mentorship for the transition into this new, and sometimes unfamiliar role.

"Walking the Walk and Talking the Talk": Finding Voice in the Academic Discourse

One of the most pervasive findings marked students' perception regarding the power of interacting with "high theory" (as one student described the types of philosophical frameworks addressed in the course) early in one's doctoral studies. In presenting his case that doctoral students in education be introduced to epistemological diversity, Pallas (2001) suggested that "educational researchers will need to engage with multiple epistemological perspectives to the point that members of different communities of educational research practice can understand one another, despite, or perhaps through, their differences" (p. 7). Consistently, most students shared that while they found such ideas intimidating and "overwhelming" early in the semester, they felt a high degree of satisfaction and accomplishment in being able to read and analyze theoretically rich and complex pieces. While clearly exposure to the philosophical foundations of research was one of the primary goals of the course, the degree to which students referenced this increased familiarity (and comfort) with academic discourse as an essential part of their experience surprised us somewhat. One student explained: "Most important was my growth in understanding where knowledge comes from and what our society believes is 'True' forms of research and ways of knowing."

Each week, students came to class having read a set of six to eight articles or chapters focused around a particular theme. From the first class, the instructor communicated an expectation that students not only read the articles carefully before class but be prepared to "pull them apart," line by line if necessary, in order to better understand each article independently, as well as the connections and contradictions across the readings. For many students, this was their first encounter with the type of "deep reading" that often characterizes the life of a scholar. One student described being

> challenged intellectually in a way that was very hard at times but very rewarding. I experienced challenges in a different way than I ever had before. [The experience also challenged my self-image as a student by being in a class where I was asked to] do something different with the reading, rather than just read and apply ... I had to learn how to read, pull apart the ideas, and apply them ... [It was] learning how to get into a zone, understanding things in that zone, and then applying what you learned in the zone.

Other participants expressed the same sentiment numerous times in the surveys, interviews, and in artifacts from the course. For many, being pushed to read intellectually challenging materials, though not easy, "fed a hunger" (as one anonymous student explained in a course evaluation) that "I didn't even know I had."

Not all students appreciated being pushed into "the zone," however. One participant in the study emphasized that

> [The course] was very confusing and difficult. I do not think it socialized you much into graduate school. If anything it proved how difficult the program would be, and without professors' patience, guidance, and mentoring that you would not make it. As far as research it did provide some interesting theories but I think it was very overwhelming.

For most students, however, their growing ability to "talk the talk of academics" increased their confidence in other classes as well. All of the participants in this study, even those who found the readings somewhat inaccessible, indicated that they had used the readings and ideas in discussions and assignments in other courses, as well as in preliminary exams, dissertations, and conference presentations:

> This [course] has enabled me to speak up more in my other classes without hesitating with the assumption that my answer must be perfect and correct . . . . rather, I learned that the struggle, the wrestling with and making sense of . . . is as much a part of the learning process as is the outcome.

Several students also indicated that they returned to their "position statements" from the class when writing their preliminary exams, dissertation proposals, and/or research projects in which they were asked to position themselves in their research. While each of them noted ways in which their positions had changed and evolved, the seeds of these understandings and beliefs were cultivated in the seminar on epistemology and research. In some cases, though not coordinated by the instructors, students encountered a few of the same readings, though usually presented with a different purpose or lens.

This synergy among the readings and students' program is not entirely serendipitous since each reading is selected quite purposefully and effort is made to ensure that, collectively, the readings feel inclusive to students who come from different program areas within the college. In addition, the readings frequently include series from *Educational Researcher* that present a feature article, as well as numerous responses to the piece, and then a rejoinder. Consequently, many of the authors build on one another's work, so students frequently see references to pieces they have read. One student described the experience: "It's like there's this ongoing conversation and we get dropped into it. It takes a while to figure out who's talking and what they're saying but, by the end of the semester, I feel like I can follow along—and maybe even participate." In this sense, the course serves as "a model of professional socialization, which sees doctoral students coming to learn appropriate skills and values as they move through a set of developmental stages" (Pallas, 2001, p. 7, citing Simpson, 1979). Another student summarized her experience by saying, "I think on some level, I started to take myself a little more seriously as a doctoral student ... [through this experience, I learned] that I was capable, even though intimidated, to find my own voice and stand by it through our exchanges and through the readings that we discussed at length."

The impact of considering the assumptions that undergird various frame-works has been notable even to other faculty members. The statistics instructor of a course that follows the epistemology course in the research sequence made a point of mentioning the "difference in students' thinking" after the work in epistemology. "They ask different questions," she observed, "and tend to see the bigger connections" than students who, for various reasons, had not yet taken the epistemology course. Another instructor who regularly teaches the doctoral-level qualitative research methods course made similar observations. An important component in developing students' voice was being in an environment that supported their growth and development.

"Creating a Safe Space": Establishing and Maintaining "Intellectual Communities"

One of the keys to students' comfort and willingness to take risks in sharing their understandings of the material was the small size of the class (limited to no more than 15 students). The course was organized so that each week a different member of the class took the lead in facilitating the discussion of the readings. Several students mentioned the pressure to participate in class discussions to "help" a peer, knowing that his or her "turn was coming" as discussion leader. While the instructor clearly communicated her expectation that students come to class prepared and ready to engage, for many students, it was their peers' behavior and attitudes that influenced them most significantly:

> The most challenging I would have to say . . . It wasn't so much to do with the course itself. It had to do with the cohorts of students. I was blessed to have a really good set of students for my entire program . . . For me, as a new student, my earliest challenge was from . . . my colleagues. They challenged me to come to class every time and ready to be on top of things.

In addition, when designing the Ph.D. programs in the college, faculty members were intentional about including experiences, such as the course in epistemology, in which students from various programs came together. This deliberate attempt to bring emerging scholars from different fields together is very much in keeping with what Tate (2008) describes as the "metalevel theme" for CID, "Create as many opportunities for community-centered reflection as possible" (p. 51). One student explained the outcome of such reflection:

> [Having students from different programs in the class] was a huge advantage and enabled us to peel apart the content from a variety of lenses. I also gained an appreciation for the different ways that my peers were approaching their research as well as their disciplines. I saw us as a diverse, capable, invested group that brought many perspectives and insights to the table, which forced us to think about our topics in different ways. They influenced me and challenged me in good ways to also challenge myself and my thinking.

The benefits of such an experience, according to several participants, "cannot be measured." "It is imperative," one argues, "to expose PhD students to various viewpoints."

Pallas (2001) discussed the impact of narrowly defined "communities of practice" that socialize new educational researchers into a particular philosophy and research methodology. His point is that common conversations and understandings about research often do not yield opportunities to question the underlying assumptions of one's position. In encouraging a more comprehensive preparation of doctoral students, Pallas argued that we must move beyond our "communities of practice" and into what Walker, Golde, Jones, Bueschel, and Hutchings (2007) referred to as "intellectual communities."

Almost all of the participants in the study, as well as comments from course evaluations and discussions, support the importance of doctoral students developing, and sustaining, this intellectual community:

> The course played a huge role in socializing me to grad school in terms of developing collegial academic relationships with a number of people outside of my own program . . . this impact was most profound due to the fact that it was one of my first courses on the campus. However, now that I have taken more classes, I recognize a unique character to my epistemology course in terms of establishing a sense of familiarity and comfort with my colleagues, regardless of whether their views matched mine.

Another student explained that "growing into a debating, discussing community with my classmates impacted me most profoundly and shifted my expectations of myself as an isolated researcher to one who benefits from discussion with my peers." The lasting impact of the type of community established in the course is evident in the extent to which members of the class continue to meet after the course ends. One group of students continued to have regular gatherings over coffee several semesters after the course ended; students (and Shinew) attended as they were able but there was a determined effort to sustain the community.

"Hanging on Her Every Word": Seeking a Guide to the (Epistemological) Universe

To some extent, we expected to hear much about the (positive) impact of being introduced to challenging theoretical debates and the importance of doing so in a supportive, peer-driven environment. The passion and commitment students expressed around these concepts did, however, surprise us. We did not anticipate the final theme that emerged from the data: the pivotal role of the instructor to students' experience in the course. For the faculty member (Shinew), this was somewhat unexpected. While students' evaluations have always been high for the course, Shinew often explained her pedagogical approach as having the "good sense to get things moving and then get out of the way" as students engaged with the ideas and one another. However, in responses to surveys and interview questions for this action research project, students frequently mentioned the impact she had on their experience of the course. One student offered this typical analysis of the role that the instructor played in the student experience:

> The method she used to allow each person to agree or disagree with various epistemologies, while challenging their constructed knowledge made the class the highlight of my educational career (which has been long!). Dr. Shinew was the most inclusive of all viewpoints and never revealed her epistemological stance, which allowed each student to feel free to express themselves.

The goal of the course was for students to know and understand the debates surrounding these issues and begin the process of identifying themselves, and their work, within this contested terrain. This student's comment reflected Shinew's approach to achieving this goal: Throughout the course, she made a conscious effort to critique (and advocate for) all of the frameworks under consideration as equally as possible. One student explained that the instructor "interjected when it was necessary, always asking the critical question that got us to see things in a new light or to get us back on track." And, in fact, the instructor attempted to hold her comments and let the discussions unfold. While she assumed this resulted in her taking up "less space" in the conversation, this project has helped her understand that her influence may have taken on a different significance than initially expected.

A couple of students referred to the class's tendencies to "hang on (the instructor's) every word" and desire for Shinew to "reveal" her epistemological stance at the end of the course. Coincidentally or not, many of the students who expressed these feelings were in the first semester of their doctoral program. The transition from undergraduate experiences, and even many master's programs, to a doctoral program—from following others' directions for learning to taking ownership for the process—may not have been complete for these participants (see more discussion about cognitive development in Gardner, chapter 10). At least part of the students' emphasis on the role of the instructor may be a lack of awareness of the extent to which they are now taking responsibility for their own learning and growth.

This chapter's second author (Moore) represents something of a stereotypical student in this class. She drank in her experience in this course with

enthusiasm from the first meeting, credits Shinew with many critical socialization experiences, and prepared diligently through her doctoral program for
her current position, as a tenure-track faculty member at a research university now teaching epistemology to her own students. From her perspective,
students' comments about the importance of the instructor summarized here
stand as proxies for experiences that students may not have the language or
self-awareness for early in their careers. Reflecting on the experience of studying and now teaching epistemological diversity, five years after completing
the course, Moore sees three key elements of Shinew's practice as instructor
reflected in students' comments: a very carefully designed syllabus provok-
ing increasingly deeper engagement; an implicitly communicated confidence
in students' ability to rise to the challenges of articulating emerging understandings; and explicitly communicated expectations that her students meet
those challenges. Such an environment fostered the intellectual communities
and individual achievements highlighted here in the summary of our findings. Studies of cognitive development in doctoral students (Baxter-Magolda,
1998) further highlight the value of this kind of experience as a foundation of
training in research.

Obviously, these results are limited by the focus on one course. However, the findings in this case study certainly warrant further investigation, with the possibility of collaborating with faculty who teach similar
courses at other institutions to determine if outcomes on the students'
thinking and behavior are consistent. For the authors, this study has allowed us to think about our own work with doctoral students, as well as
the role of faculty in fostering students' efforts to build communities of
practice. Based on the results of this case study, several recommendations
emerge regarding the organization, instruction, and expectations of doctoral
programs.

Recommendations for Supporting Socialization

This case study highlights the continued salience of two long-running debates: the role of epistemological diversity in educational research and the
preparation of doctoral students in education. While scholars have debated
the importance of addressing the epistemological foundations of educational
research (Milner, 2007; Rolon-Dow, 2005; Scheurich & Young, 1997; Siegel,
2006; Tyson, 1997; Willower, 2001), the emphasis that students in this course

placed on the critical role such exposure had on their thinking clearly supports including such considerations early in one's scholarly development. In addition, this study has implications for the ongoing conversations about the most effective strategies for preparing doctoral students (Eisenhart & DeHaan, 2005; Golde & Walker, 2006; Labaree, 2005; Pallas, 2001). Consistently, students referenced the importance of participating in a community that supported and encouraged their intellectual growth. Reviewing the findings of this case study in light of the larger discussion of these issues highlights possibilities for other doctoral programs.

These two sets of opportunity emerge from the data as particularly important to graduate student socialization. One of the most consistent findings from this case study is the importance students place on being exposed to multiple perspectives/epistemologies early in their academic careers. While Milner (2007) reminded us of the "dangers seen, unseen, and unforeseen" in the process of engaging diverse epistemological frameworks and positionalities, most students from the course seem able to work through these "dangers" and create possibilities for themselves and their research. Perhaps, as one participant told us,

> It would be a lot easier to only learn one or two stances but if there is a true commitment to my learning then I need and want to play with options, see their application, be expansive in what I'm learning and then practice the application ... let me wrestle with how they work or don't when it comes to my research interest or my lived experience. I cannot think of any disadvantages to being introduced to diverse epistemologies.

The result is a process of "find[ing] my voice," "trying on" diverse epistemologies, and "stretch[ing] big time." Students also told us that surrounding themselves with a strong intellectual community provided support for their intellectual development at a critical time. As one of the few places in which all of the programs come together, the research core demonstrates its strong capacity to promote collaborative relationships outside of individual programs. As the first course in the core, the seminar on epistemology and research has unique potential to encourage these connections. Students, faculty members, departments, universities, and external agencies can all play important roles in introducing beginning researchers to epistemological diversity, and to create intellectual community for their students.

Recommendations for Students

Introducing Epistemological Diversity

- Embrace formal course assignments as opportunities to explore diverse epistemologies. Whether the program offers formal coursework in this area or not, one can use reading and writing assignments in courses on social, cultural, or philosophical foundations or the history of the discipline to look into diverse understandings of knowledge and research. By understanding the broad range of ideas on these topics, students are opening a range of options for research design and further study.
- "Try on" ideas, and "stretch" one's skills by taking up unfamiliar stances and applying them to familiar topics or research findings. What would a critical race interpretation of received knowledge in an area bring to light, for example?

Creating Intellectual Community

- See peers as professional colleagues, and begin building relationships, which will develop and enhance one's academic work. Students should find or create opportunities to engage in close reading of texts and grapple with difficult ideas together. These experiences are excellent training for the academic profession, and they are also the way to build and sustain communities based on ideas and shared passion for the work.
- Use the epistemology seminar, or some other common experience or core course, as the springboard for other reading/writing groups and activities throughout one's degree program. Through the discussions early in a student's career, one can find colleagues interested in similar ideas, theories, or methodological approaches, and draw on conversations with one other to inform different ways of thinking about familiar topics.

Recommendations for Faculty/Mentors

Introducing Epistemological Diversity

- Be deliberate in selecting course materials to ensure that readings include a variety of theoretical and methodological approaches. In analyzing these pieces, faculty should encourage students to look for authors' assumptions about knowledge, research, and the role of the researcher.

- Encourage students to think and write about their own positionalities and how these affect what and how they "know." Such reflections might serve as the basis for an in-class exchange of ideas, or they may be appropriate for formal written assignments.

Creating Intellectual Community

- "Have enough sense to get out of the way." This case study demonstrates the importance of supportive mentoring; but a subtext of students finding their way to intellectual independence is the real key when one thinks specifically about the socialization of students in doctoral programs. Faculty members play key roles in crafting learning experiences that compel students to find their own voices and try on new ideas.
- Provide opportunities for students to view themselves and one another as sources of knowledge and insight. For example, students in this research seminar were given the option of writing weekly reflections on the readings or participating in peer discussion groups. While some students chose the written reflections (which required a deep reading of the materials), many opted to meet weekly outside of class with small groups of their peers. These "peer exchange groups" were often referenced during class discussions and students' other class projects.

Recommendations for Departments

Introducing Epistemological Diversity

- Create opportunities for students to take up diverse epistemological stances early in their coursework. These opportunities may be the result of new courses developed for this purpose, or the systematic redesign of learning objectives for existing courses to include relevant topics and experiences.
- Encourage faculty members to talk about their research not only in terms of the final outcomes but also in terms of the processes and beliefs that shaped their research. Again, such discussions could occur through a series of "brown bag" lunches or more intentionally integrated into existing coursework.

Creating Intellectual Community

- Be intentional about developing seminars either for credit or as a part of a new culture in the program/department/college with embedded opportunities for building intellectual community. As Walker et al. (2007) asserted, "One strategy for creating intellectual community is to create research seminars that bridge sub-specialties; such connections are especially important as disciplinary boundaries blur" (p. B7). The power of such intellectual communities is almost palpable in the data from this study.

Recommendations for Universities

Introducing Epistemological Diversity

- Foster interaction between students across disciplines, in both traditional and nontraditional groupings. For example, the seminar on epistemology and research has, in recent years, included students from outside the College of Education, including doctoral students in mathematics, engineering, and communication. The epistemological diversity even among the students allows for a rich environment for thinking about how differences in understanding knowledge play out in the research enterprise.

Creating Intellectual Community

- The seminars described above at the departmental level can be implemented at a campus level as well. Many campuses encourage interdisciplinary collaboration and research initiatives; Lattuca (2002) has explored how faculty learn interdisciplinarity, highlighting an important "prior step" required for faculty to "take advantage of policies or programs that encourage interdisciplinarity" (p. 711). As Holley suggests in chapter 5 of this book, initiatives that encourage interaction across and among disciplines better prepare future faculty to engage in creative work that transcends traditional disciplinary and epistemological landscapes.

Recommendations for External Agencies

Introducing Epistemological Diversity

- Golde's discussion in chapter 4 highlights the significant impact of discipline on the socialization of doctoral students. Disciplinary associations and funding agencies have excellent opportunities for encouraging emerging scholars to explore epistemological diversity, as it exists within particular disciplines. For instance, the National Science Foundation's (2008) Innovations in Engineering Education, Curriculum, and Infrastructure Program (NSF 08-610) called for proposals in four areas, one of which included "Engineering epistemologies: Research on what constitutes engineering thinking and knowledge with current and future social and economic contexts" (p. 4). By acknowledging the presence of different conceptions of knowledge and what it means to know something, and providing funding and presentation/publication venues to study and report on these, external agencies become active partners in introducing the value of epistemological diversity.

Creating Intellectual Community

- The course highlighted in this chapter was developed as part of Washington State University's participation in the Carnegie Foundation for the Advancement of Teaching's Initiative on the Doctorate, a program aimed at providing funding and technical support to improve the quality of doctoral education at U.S. research universities. This program is fundamentally focused on the creation of intellectual community. Other initiatives, such as the Emerging Scholars workshops hosted by organizations such as the American Educational Research Association, Division J: Post-Secondary Education, and the National Outreach Scholarship Conference, move beyond institutional boundaries to create intellectual community at the disciplinary level.

Conclusion

In an era in which education research is scrutinized in light of "evidence-based" and "scientifically-based inquiry," it is essential to remind ourselves and novice researchers that *all* scholarship emerges from a set of assumptions about the nature of the world, reality, and our (as researchers and persons) relationship to what is "known" or constructed. Such assumptions influence the ways in which research is conceptualized, operationalized, and evaluated—though these beliefs are often left unexplored and unspoken. In responding to the many challenges facing education, researchers are encouraged to expand "civic capacity." Consistent with calls from other scholars in education (see Anderson & Herr, 1999; Bernal, 1998; Gage, 1989; Harding, 1991; Hill-Collins, 1990; Ladson-Billings, 2005; Rolon-Dow, 2005; Scheurich & Young, 1997), students in this seminar were introduced to a myriad of epistemological orientations that collectively echoed the need for multiple and diverse ways of understanding our world(s).

Growing an environment that supports experiences such as these suggested here requires thoughtful and intentional contributions from multiple constituents, including the administrators who oversee programs, the faculty who teach and mentor in them, and the students who make these programs their academic homes. The recommendations listed earlier encourage and support doctoral students' exploration of epistemological diversity and emphasize the importance of developing a community of scholarship. These recommendations reflect the findings from our study; they also demonstrate that there are many constituencies who have an interest in the outcomes of doctoral student socialization and who can also contribute directly to the introduction of epistemological diversity, and more importantly to creating intellectual community. For most students, it was within (and because of) this community that they were willing to take risks and open themselves to new possibilities. Students repeatedly referred to the importance of working through readings and ideas together, of sharing ideas in a supportive environment, and of feeling more secure in the knowledge that their peers also struggled with some of the concepts and language in the readings.

The deliberate analysis of how future researchers make sense of these epistemologies, as well as the ways in which they are able to use these understandings in their own research, provide important insights for other research institutions responsible for preparing "stewards of the discipline" (Golde & Walker, 2006). The importance of this experience is summarized by a student from the course: "Epistemology is Research Boot Camp with a wise, kind, gentle but firm mentor and it is an experience that everyone should have as soon as possible in their programs."

References

Anderson, G., & Herr, K. (1999). The new paradigm wars: Is there room for rigorous practitioner knowledge in schools and universities? *Educational Researcher, 28,* 12–21, 40.

Austin, A. E. (2002). Preparing the next generation of faculty: Graduate school as socialization to the academic career. *The Journal of Higher Education, 73,* 94–121.

Baxter-Magolda, M. B. (1998). Developing self-authorship in graduate school. In M. S. Anderson (Ed.), *The experience of being in graduate school: An exploration* (pp. 41–54). San Francisco: Jossey-Bass.

Berliner, D. (2002). Educational research: The hardest science of all. *Educational Researcher, 31,* 18–20.

Bernal, D. D. (1998). Using a Chicana feminist epistemology in educational research. *Harvard Educational Review, 68,* 555–582.

Bullough, R. V., & Pinnegar, S. (2001). Guidelines for quality in autobiographical forms of self-study research. *Educational Researcher, 30,* 13–22.

Eisenhart, M., & DeHaan, R. (2005). Doctoral preparation of scientifically based education researchers. *Educational Researcher, 34,* 3–13.

Feuer, M., Towne, L., & Shavelson, R. (2002a). Scientific culture and educational research. *Educational Researcher, 31,* 4–14.

Feuer, M., Towne, L., & Shavelson, R. (2002b). Reply. *Educational Researcher, 31,* 28–29.

Gage, N. L. (1989) The paradigm wars and their aftermath: A "historical" sketch of research on teaching since 1989. *Teachers College Record, 91,* 135–150.

Golde, C. M., & Dore, T. M. (2001). *At cross purposes: What the experiences of doctoral students reveal about doctoral education.* Philadelphia, PA: A report prepared for The Pew Charitable Trusts. Retrieved January 24, 2008, from http://www.phd-survey.org

Golde, C. M., & Walker, G. E. (Eds.). (2006). *Envisioning the future of doctoral education: Preparing stewards of the discipline. Carnegie essays on the doctorate.* San Francisco: Jossey-Bass.

Herr, K., & Anderson, G. L. (2005). *The action research dissertation: A guide for students and faculty.* Thousand Oaks, CA: Sage.

Harding, S. (1991). *Whose science whose knowledge.* Ithaca, NY: Cornell University Press.

Hill-Collins, P. (1990). *Black feminist thought: Knowledge consciousness and the politics of empowerment.* New York: Routledge.

Hoestetler, K. (2005). What is "good" education research? *Educational Researcher, 34,* 16–21.

Labaree, D. (2003). The peculiar problems of preparing educational researchers. *Educational Researcher, 32*(4), 13–22.

Ladson-Billings, G. (2005). Racialized discourse and ethnic epistemologies. In N. Denzin & Y. Lincoln (Eds.), *Sage handbook of qualitative research* (pp. 257–278). Thousand Oaks, CA: Sage.

Langemann, E. (1997). Contested terrain: A history of education research in the United States, 1890–1990. *Educational Researcher, 12*, 5–17.

Lattuca, L. R. (2002). Learning interdisciplinarity: Sociocultural perspectives on academic work. *Journal of Higher Education, 73*, 711–739.

Milner, H. R. (2007). Race, culture, and researcher positionality: Working through dangers seen, unseen, and unforeseen. *Educational Researcher, 36*, 388–400.

National Science Foundation. (2008). *Innovations in engineering education, curriculum, and infrastructure (IEECI) program announcements*. Retrieved February 15, 2008, from http://www.nsf.gov/funding/pgm_summ.jsp?pims_id=13374

Neumann, A. (2006). Professing passion: Emotion in the scholarship of professors at research institutions. *American Educational Research Journal, 43*, 381–424.

Pallas, A. (2001). Preparing education doctoral students for epistemological diversity. *Educational Researcher, 6*, 1–6.

Paul, J., & Marfo, K. (2001). Preparation of educational researchers in philosophical foundations of inquiry. *Review of Educational Research, 71*, 525–547.

Pellegrino, J., & Goldman, S. (2002). Be careful what you wish for—you may get it: Educational research in the spotlight. *Educational Researcher, 31*, 15–17.

Popkewitz, T. (1997). A changing terrain of knowledge and power: A social epistemology of educational research. *Educational Researcher, 12*, 18–29.

Rolon-Dow, R. (2005). Critical care: A color(full) analysis of care narratives in the schooling experience of Puerto Rican girls. *American Educational Research Journal, 42*, 77–111.

Scheurich, J., & Young, M. (1997). Coloring epistemologies: Are our research epistemologies racially biased? *Educational Researcher, 26*, 4–16.

Siegel, H. (2006). Epistemological diversity and education research: Much ado about nothing much? *Educational Researcher, 3*, 3–12.

Tate, W. (2008). From the desk of the president: Building a stimulating and sustainable research enterprise. *Educational Researcher, 37*, 51–52.

Tyson, C. (1997). A response to "coloring epistemologies: Are our research epistemologies racially biased?" *Educational Researcher, 26*, 21–22.

Walker, G. E., Golde, C. M., Jones, L., Bueschel, A. C., & Hutchings, P. (2007, December 14). Nurturing ideas. *Chronicle Review*, B6–B8.

Willower, D. (2001). Epistemology, science, and moral practice. *Interchange, 32*, 1–16.

CONCLUSION

Susan K. Gardner and Pilar Mendoza

Our five students, Eva, Jennifer, Ling, Nate, and Scott, are now approaching the end of their doctoral journeys. Each has encountered unique challenges and issues that have tested their mettle as doctoral students and as individuals. We conclude the book with a look at each student's experience and how, given what we have learned about doctoral student socialization and development in each of the preceding chapters, these students could have been assisted along the way. The intention here is to demonstrate the theoretical and practical implications of the nuanced doctoral student experience as we work toward forming future scholars.

Eva

Eva is now close to completing her dissertation and is proud to have made it thus far in her program, particularly in light of the many challenges she faced throughout. Having to balance full-time work with her family and her program has been difficult. Moreover, being older than most of her peers often makes her feel awkward and this uneasiness sometimes even extends to her faculty members. Eva has also been challenged by her coursework. In some cases, she really feels she gained a lot, while at other times she has felt like her knowledge and professional background has been unacknowledged and unvalued. Reflecting back over it now, she wonders how things might have been different.

- Part-time doctoral students and students managing families may have more difficulties being socialized to the research culture of their programs (Weidman, chapter 2) and may need more assistance connecting with peers and faculty to assist them through these difficulties.

- Older adults who return to graduate school may find difficulties in the classroom and expect more inclusion in their coursework and more applicability to their professional goals (Kasworm & Bowles, chapter 11), and faculty members should be cognizant of adult learning theory and its principles when designing their coursework.

- Students may also experience challenges in their identity and epistemological development as a result of their programs and coursework (Gardner, chapter 10, and Shinew & Moore, chapter 12) or as a result of being underrepresented in their programs or institutions (Winkle-Wagner, Johnson, Morelon-Quainoo, & Santiague, chapter 9). Therefore, assistance and support should be offered through peer groups, counseling services, and support offered by trained faculty members.

Jennifer

Jennifer is ready to go on the job market for a teaching position in English. She knows she faces stiff competition for one of these positions, but she is also confident that her extensive TA experience as well as her extra preparation and professional development will make her stand out. On top of this, she thinks that her dissertation with a feminist post-structural lens will make her a bit more competitive for a few of the shared positions between women's studies and English she has seen advertised. Wherever she ends up, however, Jennifer is happy her partner Lisa will be coming with her. As Jennifer prepares for interviews, she thinks back over the journey she has made in graduate school.

- Doctoral students who desire to pursue faculty careers need more socialization and professional development related to teaching and pedagogy (McDaniels, chapter 1), a more comprehensive view of the faculty role (Ward, chapter 3), as well as instruction in adult learning theories (Kasworm and Bowles, chapter 11); however, one-size-fits-all approaches to these opportunities should be reconsidered in relation to the disciplinary cultures in which the students are situated (Golde, chapter 4).

- Students will continue exploring their identity while in graduate school (Gardner, chapter 10) and supportive services should be offered for these purposes.

Ling

Ling is completing her interdisciplinary program with an award-winning disser-
tation. Although she plans to return to her country after graduation, she realizes
she will miss the friends she made here. She is even more thankful for these friends
as they were a long time in coming and difficult to meet. Ling is also thankful
for the unique research experience she had in the United States. She feels she has
learned a lot about research connections with industry and is excited to share these
insights when she returns to China. Packing her suitcases with papers, book, and
mementos of her time here, Ling reflects upon the difficult but rewarding journey
she has taken.

- Students transitioning to the expectations of doctoral education may often struggle with the independence required to complete research (Weidman, chapter 2), and these challenges may be amplified in interdisciplinary fields (Holley, chapter 5). Programs and program faculty can assist students through these changing expectations through providing clear structures, guidelines, and supportive services.
- Burgeoning research relationships with industrial partners can also create challenges in the socialization of doctoral students (Mendoza, chapter 6), and universities and their faculty should be purposeful but cautious in modeling behaviors and forming agreements with these entities.
- Although Asian students are not considered underrepresented in regard to race in most doctoral programs, they will still experience myriad challenges in relation to their status. Stereotyping and a lack of supportive peers and faculty can be debilitating for students of color (Winkle-Wagner et al., chapter 9), and women are still considered underrepresented in many science and engineering fields, making it difficult for them to make connections with peers and find mentors among faculty members (Sallee, chapter 7). Programs can assist students through educational and support structures, such as peer mentoring programs, as well as professional development for faculty.

Nate

Nate has just landed a research position at a prestigious university. He feels his new
position will serve him well and is confident that his interdisciplinary experience

is what made him most marketable. He has been informed he will start working immediately with another interdisciplinary group that has just been funded by a local chemical company. Nate feels ready to take on these tasks given his experience. Setting up his new office, he unpacks some of his old papers and reminisces about the difficulties he encountered while he was in graduate school.

- Interdisciplinary programs can be lonely for students, and program faculty and universities should be cognizant of providing support structures that assist students in finding the intellectual communities that may be lacking (Holley, chapter 5).
- Doctoral students will continue their development in graduate school, including their ethical and moral development (Gardner, chapter 10), their epistemological development (Shinew and Moore, chapter 12), and the way they see themselves in the teaching–learning relationship (Kasworm and Bowles, chapter 11). Students may require support as they struggle with issues that arise in coursework or during their research.

Scott

Scott is overjoyed to have just been offered a position teaching child psychology in Boston. He looks forward to being in a more diverse area and in a department that has several other faculty members of color, including several men. He has already bonded with the search chair, his soon-to-be colleague, and Scott feels this faculty member will be an excellent mentor for him as he begins his academic career; he believes this mentoring will be especially important as he learns more about teaching. Even better, Scott is ecstatic that the university was able to find a suitable position for his wife on campus. Thinking back over his graduate experience, it was both bitter and sweet. He is happy to have been offered the opportunity to advance his education but wonders how the struggles he faced have changed him.

- Students of color, particularly in underrepresented fields, may face many challenges (Winkle-Wagner et al., chapter 9), as may students who are different from their peers in regard to gender (Sallee, chapter 7).

Peer networks, faculty mentors, and campus-wide support groups can be beneficial to students who struggle.

- Students who are married and partnered face both challenges and opportunities in graduate school (Millett & Nettles, chapter 8), but programs should be aware of the disconnect it may create with the students' peers, an important support mechanism in graduate school.

- Teaching and service opportunities are important for students who seek faculty positions upon graduation (McDaniels, chapter 1; Ward, chapter 3). Socialization to the entire faculty role is important for future career success.

Concluding Thoughts and Future Directions

The preceding chapters represent a rich resource for faculty, administrators, institutions, external constituents, and even students. As McDaniels, Weidman, and Ward demonstrated, preparing future faculty through socialization to teaching, research, and service roles is vital. Furthermore, we learned from Golde, Holley, and Mendoza that understanding how socialization varies by discipline and by research emphasis will assist faculty and universities in designing support structures and professional development opportunities. Students' experiences will also differ on the basis of demographic differences, such as gender, race, and marital status, much like Sallee, Millett and Nettles, and Winkle-Wagner et al. shared. Finally, Gardner, Kasworm and Bowles, and Shinew and Moore demonstrated how students will also change and grow as a result of their graduate experiences and how programs and coursework experiences can assist students through these developmental challenges.

But more must yet be explored in relation to the doctoral student experience. Future researchers should consider how many of the variables described in preceding chapters interact and influence other parts of the doctoral experience. For example, how is race played out in interdisciplinary programs, how is gender experienced in relation to teaching and learning at the doctoral level, how do part-time students engage with research, and how is epistemological development encouraged in various disciplines? We must also continue to explore and understand demographic populations, including subpopulations, ethnic minorities, and international students. In addition, while Golde and Holley shared with us the tremendous influence that disciplinary culture exerts upon the doctoral experience, we have only begun to explore the impact of institutional culture upon the doctoral experience. In essence, while we have learned much about the doctoral experience there is still much more to learn. Perhaps through continued exploration we will finally begin to apply the lessons learned in graduate education and best assist our doctoral students in becoming scholars of the future.

CONTRIBUTORS

Tuere Bowles is Assistant Professor in the Department of Adult and Higher Education at North Carolina State University. She teaches graduate courses in adult learning theory and qualitative research methods. Complex analyses of social justice and equity issues in education (race, ethnicity, gender, and social class) unify Dr. Bowles' research agenda. Theoretically, she employs critical, feminist, and ecological frameworks to ground her interdisciplinary endeavors and employs mixed methods in both research and evaluation studies. Two specific themes persist in her scholarship. In the first theme, she explores the socialization and educational experiences of people of color across the lifespan in both formal (i.e., secondary and postsecondary) and nonformal (e.g., community, religious, social movement) settings. With the second recurring theme in her scholarship, gender and diversity in the environmental sciences and engineering, she identifies the underrepresentation of minority women in science, technology, engineering, and mathematics (STEM) disciplines and careers as a social justice issue.

Susan K. Gardner is Associate Professor of higher education at the University of Maine in Orono, Maine. Her research surrounds the two interwoven areas of organizational theory and development. Specifically, she is interested in how different institutional and cultural contexts influence the success of students and faculty, particularly those from underrepresented areas. She has written and presented widely on issues related to doctoral student success and development, including a recent monograph by Jossey-Bass, *The Development of Doctoral Students: Phases of Challenge and Support*. Gardner's work can be seen in *The Review of Higher Education, Journal of Higher Education, Journal of College Student Development*, and *Higher Education*, among others. Before coming to Maine, she spent two years at Louisiana State University, after receiving her Ph.D. in higher education from Washington State University.

Chris Golde is the Associate Vice Provost for Graduate Education at Stanford University. Prior to her work at Stanford, Dr. Golde was a Senior Scholar for The Carnegie Foundation for the Advancement of Teaching, playing a leadership role in the Carnegie Initiative on the Doctorate (CID). Her scholarly interests include doctoral student attrition, the doctoral student experience, the influence of disciplinary differences in graduate education, and improving graduate programs. Her publications include the influential report *At Cross Purposes: What the Experiences of Today's Doctoral Students Reveal About Doctoral Education*, with Timothy Dore. Her CID work included two books. She coedited volume of essays, *Envisioning the Future of Doctoral Education: Preparing Stewards of the Discipline*, and coauthored *The Formation of Scholars: Rethinking Doctoral Education for the 21st Century*. In her administrative role at Stanford, she has the opportunity to put research findings into practice by developing programs, shaping policy, and consulting with students and faculty. She holds a Ph.D. in education and a master's degree in sociology, both from Stanford University.

Karri Holley is Assistant Professor of higher education at the University of Alabama. Her research interests include interdisciplinarity, graduate and professional education, organizational change in higher education, and qualitative inquiry. She received her M.Ed. and Ph.D. from the University of Southern California and her B.A. from the University of Alabama. She is currently working on two research projects: first, a study of first-generation doctoral students (with Susan Gardner); and second, an analysis of emerging interdisciplinary collaborations related to educational neuroscience. Her monograph, *Understanding Interdisciplinary Challenges and Opportunities in Higher Education*, was recently published by Jossey-Bass. Her research has appeared in *Higher Education*, *Studies in Higher Education*, and *Educational Researcher*.

Susan D. Johnson is Program Officer at Lumina Foundation for Education. Prior to joining Lumina, she served as a research analyst for the Office of University Planning, Institutional Research, and Accountability at Indiana University, where she focused primarily on diversity and equity issues.

Throughout her career in higher education, she acquired intimate knowledge of the policies and practices affecting student success with research interests in ethnic- and gender-identity development, student engagement, and institutional research as it relates to strategic planning at colleges and universities. She has held professional positions in student affairs at Louisiana State University and the University of North Dakota and currently serves on the governing board of the American College Personnel Association (ACPA) as Director of Equity and Inclusion. Johnson earned her B.S., M.S., and M.Ed. degrees from the University of Florida and her Ph.D. in higher education and Student Affairs at Indiana University. In 2008, she was the recipient of the NASPA Hardee Dissertation of the Year Award.

Carol Kasworm is Professor of adult education and department head of the Department of Adult and Higher Education at North Carolina State University. Her research interests have focused upon the nature of learning engagement and participation patterns of adult students in higher education, the nature of adult learning within varied higher education contexts, and of the role of adult higher education in a lifelong learning society. Dr. Kasworm's scholarship includes five books, 28 book chapters, 75 refereed and non-refereed journal articles, as well as numerous conference proceedings, monographs, and conference presentations. She is currently the coeditor of the 2010 *Handbook of Adult and Continuing Education* and a Fulbright Senior Specialist in Finland. Select honors include induction into the International Adult and Continuing Education Hall of Fame; Distinguished Professional Achievement Alumni Award from the College Of Education, University of Georgia; and the Imogene Okes Research Award, American Association for Adult and Continuing Education. She has previously served as Associate Dean for Research and Technology at University of Tennessee-Knoxville, as Interim Provost and Associate Provost for Faculty and Program Development at University of Houston-Clear Lake, and as Program Director for Adult and Higher Education at University of Texas at Austin.

Melissa McDaniels is Project Director of Michigan State University's National Science Foundation ADVANCE program. She has written and presented widely (domestically and internationally) on topics related to the professional development of doctoral students and faculty members. She holds a Ph.D. in higher, adult, and lifelong education from Michigan State University and is active in professional associations encouraging dialogue on policy and research related to maximizing the quality and diversity of the faculty workforce. Her current scholarship explores intergenerational dynamics in the faculty workplace, with a particular focus on how doctoral students and early career faculty can be effective mentees.

Pilar Mendoza holds a bachelor's degree in physics from the Universidad de los Andes, Colombia, and a master's in the discipline from the University of Massachusetts Amherst. She taught undergraduate physics and mathematics at both universities before seeking her Ed.D. in Education Policy and Leadership from the University of Massachusetts Amherst. Dr. Mendoza is currently Assistant Professor in higher education at the University of Florida. Previously, she served as Assistant Professor in the Department of Educational Leadership at Oklahoma State University. Dr. Mendoza's research agenda focuses on the impact of academic capitalism on the public good of higher education. In particular, she is interested in how market forces coupled with federal and state policies affect the academic profession, graduate education, as well as issues of equity, access, and affordability in higher education.

Catherine M. Millett is Senior Research Scientist at the Policy Evaluation and Research Center at the Educational Testing Service in Princeton, NJ. Her research focuses on access, persistence, and achievement for students from various population groups at the postsecondary level. One area of her current research is on the doctoral student experience. Millett chairs the Doctoral Education Across the Disciplines special interest group for the American Educational Research Association. She serves on the Technical Review Panel for the Educational Longitudinal Study 2002 as well as the Beginning Postsecondary Study 2004–06 both sponsored by the National Center for Education Statistics. She is also a member of the Science & Engineering Human Resources Expert Panel, Division of Science Resource Statistics, National Science Foundation and the Advisory Board, Harvard Medical School Center for the Study of Diversity in Science. Millett has been a visiting lecturer at the Woodrow Wilson School of Public and International Affairs at Princeton University. Dr. Millett received a Ph.D. in education from the University of Michigan. She is also a graduate of Trinity College (B.A. in economics), the Harvard Graduate

School of Education (Ed.M. in Administration, Planning and Social Policy), and the Radcliffe Seminars Program (Graduate Certificate in management).

Tami Moore is Assistant Professor of higher education in the Educational Leadership Program at Oklahoma State University Tulsa. Her research agenda focuses broadly on the role of higher education institutions in the communities they serve, employing social and critical theory in the reading of community engagement. Her current projects explore issues related to faculty work and community-engaged scholarship, and the relationship between geographic place and community engagement in the United States, the United Kingdom, and Australia. She is founding cochair of the Emerging Engagement Scholars Workshop at the National Outreach Scholarship Conference, and recipient of the AERA-J Dissertation of the Year Award in 2009. Moore and Shinew, along with doctoral student and faculty colleagues at Oklahoma State and Washington State, are also pursuing a research project exploring the impact of faculty epistemologies, and epistemological diversity, on the socialization of graduate students in engineering disciplines.

Carla Morelon-Quainoo currently serves as the Director for Undergraduate Studies/Honors Program at Dillard University in New Orleans, LA. Her major areas of interest encompass issues of access, retention, and postbaccalaureate aspirations for underrepresented students. Over the course of almost 20 years in higher education, she has championed student success both within and outside the academy, mentoring students and facilitating college workshops in her Arkansas hometown while enrolled in graduate school. She received her B.A. from Grambling State University, a master's in higher education administration from Vanderbilt University and a Ph.D. in higher education administration from Indiana University – Bloomington.

Michael T. Nettles is Senior Vice President and the Edmund W. Gordon Chair for Policy Evaluation and Research at the Educational Testing Service in Princeton, NJ. He has a national reputation as a policy researcher on educational assessment, student performance and achievement, educational equity, and higher education finance policy. Nettles' publications reflect his broad interest in public policy, student and faculty access, opportunity, achievement, and assessment at both the K-12 and postsecondary levels. His current professional activities include serving on two National Research Council boards:

the Board on Testing and Assessment (BOTA) and the Board on Higher Education and the Workforce (BHEW). Nettles is a member of the Bank Street College of Education Board of Trustees. He also serves on the Board of the NSF sponsored Center on Research on Teaching and Learning (CRTL); the Board of the Center for Enrollment Research, Policy, and Practice (CERPP) at the University of Southern California; and the Harvard University Medical School Advisory Committee on Diversity. A native of Nashville, Tennessee, Michael earned his bachelor's degree in political science at the University of Tennessee, master's degrees in political science and in higher education, and a Ph.D. in education, at Iowa State University.

Margaret W. Sallee is Assistant Professor of higher education in the Department of Educational Leadership and Policy Studies at The University of Tennessee. Her research interests focus on two broad areas: academic work and the student experience. With academic work, she explores the nature of faculty work and the steps that institutions take to create and sustain diverse faculties. As part of that work, she also focuses on issues of work–family balance within higher education. With student experience, she brings a gender lens to the experiences of graduate students. Her most recent study investigated the experiences of male graduate students in two disciplines, considering the relationship between socialization, discipline, and masculinities. Prior to joining the faculty at the University of Tennessee, she earned her Ph.D. in urban education with an emphasis on higher education from the University of Southern California.

Lilia Santiague graduated from Indiana University's department of Educational Leadership and Policy Studies Department with a concentration in Higher Education and Student Affairs. Currently, Dr. Santiague is an adjunct professor at Nova Southeastern University. She teaches classes in diversity through the Instructional Design and Diversity Education Department. Her dissertation is on the college experience of Haitian and Haitian American Students. Her research interests are on access and retention of minority and Caribbean students. She earned a master's degree in student personnel in higher education at the University of Florida. While at the University of Florida, she served as coordinator and adviser for the Decision & Information Sciences Department in the College of Business.

Dawn Shinew is Associate Professor and Berry Family Fellow in the Department of Teaching and Learning at Washington State University. Shinew received her Ph.D. from Ohio State University in 1998. She teaches courses in social studies education, epistemology and inquiry, and qualitative research. In 2008, she received the Washington State Excellence in Teacher Preparation Award. Her research interests include the role of epistemology and conceptual change in educational practices and research. Shinew recently coauthored a book entitled, *Redefining Normalcy: A Queer Reconstruction of the Family* (VDM Publishing), with former doctoral student Dr. Deborah Thomas-Jones. In addition, Shinew has published in journals such as *Action in Teacher Education* and *Theory and Research in Social Education*. Most recently, Shinew has collaborated with colleagues in the fields of engineering and mathematics to explore the relationships between epistemological assumptions and the socialization of women and underrepresented populations in those fields.

Kelly Ward is Professor of higher education at Washington State University in Pullman, Washington. Her research addresses issues related to faculty development and socialization. In particular, she examines how work and family shape faculty decisions about their career and also how involvement in community engagement fits with other aspects of the faculty career. Ward is the author of *Faculty Service Roles and the Scholarship of Engagement* (Jossey-Bass), and coauthor of *Putting Students First* (Anker) and *Developing New Faculty as Teachers and Scholars* (Anker) as well as many articles and chapters on related topics.

Rachelle Winkle-Wagner is Assistant Professor of higher education at the University of Nebraska. Her research focuses on the sociological aspects of race and gender in higher education and she considers such issues as: the experiences of underrepresented students in undergraduate and advanced-degree programs, critical qualitative research methodology, and the influence of college on the identity of underrepresented students. She is also the author of *The Unchosen Me: Race, Gender, and Identity among Black Women in College* (Johns Hopkins University Press, 2009), the lead editor on *Bridging the Gap Between Theory and Practice in Educational Research: Methods at the Margins* (Palgrave MacMillan, 2009, with Cheryl A. Hunter and Debora H. Ortloff), and an editor on *Standing on the Outside Looking In: The Experiences of Underrepresented Students in Advanced-Degree Programs* (Stylus Publishing, 2009, with Susan D. Johnson, Carla Morelon-Quainoo, Lilia Santiague, and Mary Howard-Hamilton). She earned her Ph.D. in education policy studies from Indiana University and her master's degree in higher education administration and bachelor's degree from the University of Nebraska.

Also available from Stylus

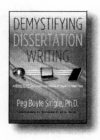

Demystifying Dissertation Writing
A Streamlined Process from Choice of Topic to Final Text
Peg Boyle Single, Ph.D.
Foreword by Richard M. Reis, Ph.D.

"I highly recommend this book to all directors of doctoral programs. *Demystifying Dissertation Writing* provides a blueprint for facilitating a dissertation-writing seminar. Our students and their advisers rave about Peg's seminar and her book." —*Susan Hasazi, Stafford Distinguished Professor of Education Leadership & Special Education and Director of the Doctoral Program in Educational Leadership & Policy Studies, University of Vermont*

Teaching Your First College Class
A Practical Guide for New Faculty and Graduate Student Instructors
Carolyn Lieberg

"I highly recommend it as an essential textbook for a course on college teaching." —*Laurie Bellows, Director of Graduate Student Development and of the McNair Scholars Program, University of Nebraska-Lincoln*

"It will be particularly useful for those who are unfamiliar with the scholarship of teaching and interested in a comprehensive, practical guide to the mechanics and details of their craft." *Teaching Theology & Religion*

What They Didn't Teach You in Graduate School
199 Helpful Hints for Success in Your Academic Career
Paul Gray and David E. Drew
Illustrated by Matthew Henry Hall
Foreword by Laurie Richlin, Steadman Upham

"In just under 150 pages the authors, of course, do not get deeply into any subject, but they hit the mark so many times and in such an entertaining and succinct way that readers will feel well informed when they finish. This book will be a welcome and valuable addition to the bookshelves of all graduate students and new faculty. We plan to buy one of these for each of our incoming faculty and doctoral students. Take a look. It's a wonderful read, a fast one, and available at a discount for bulk purchases."—*Dennis E. Gregory, The Review of Higher Education*

22883 Quicksilver Drive
Sterling, VA 20166-2102

Subscribe to our e-mail alerts: www.Styluspub.com